*Joyce, Milton, and
the Theory of Influence*

The Florida James Joyce Series

The Florida James Joyce Series
Edited by Zack Bowen

The Autobiographical Novel of Co-Consciousness: Goncharov, Woolf, and Joyce, by Galya Diment (1994)

Shaw and Joyce: "The Last Word in Stolentelling," by Martha Fodaski Black (1995)

Bloom's Old Sweet Song: Essays on Joyce and Music, by Zack Bowen (1995)

Reauthorizing Joyce, by Vicki Mahaffey (1995)

Joyce's Iritis and the Irritated Text: The Dis-lexic Ulysses, by Roy Gottfried (1995)

Joyce, Milton, and the Theory of Influence, by Patrick Colm Hogan (1995)

Joyce, Milton, and the Theory of Influence

Patrick Colm Hogan

University Press of Florida

Gainesville / Tallahassee / Tampa / Boca Raton
Pensacola / Orlando / Miami / Jacksonville

Copyright 1995 by the Board of Regents of the State of Florida
Printed in the United States of America on acid-free paper
All rights reserved

00 99 98 97 96 95   6 5 4 3 2 1

Library of Congress Cataloging-in-Publication Data

Hogan, Patrick Colm.
Joyce, Milton, and the theory of influence / Patrick Colm Hogan.
p. cm.—(The Florida James Joyce series)
Includes bibliographical references and index
ISBN 0-8130-1405-0 (alk. paper)
1. Joyce, James, 1882–1941—Knowledge—Literature. 2. Milton, John, 1608–1674—Influence. 3. Influence (Literary, artistic, etc.)
I. Title. II. Series
PR6019.O9Z587 1995
823'.912—dc2095-14549

Portions of chapter 4, "*Ulysses:* Remorse and the Epic," were originally published in *James Joyce Quarterly* 24, no. 1 (Fall 1986): 55–72.

The University Press of Florida is the scholarly publishing agency for the State University System of Florida, comprised of Florida A&M University, Florida Atlantic University, Florida International University, Florida State University, University of Central Florida, University of Florida, University of North Florida, University of South Florida, and University of West Florida.

University Press of Florida
15 Northwest 15th Street
Gainesville, FL 32611

Lalitae Uxori

Contents

Foreword by Bernard Benstock   ix

Preface   xi

Abbreviations   xv

1. The Economy of Innovation and the Grammar of Influence   1

2. Joyce Agonistes: Reading Milton in Contexts   48

3. A Romantic Milton Masked with Dante Alighieri's Face: Joyce and Milton before *Ulysses*   93

4. *Ulysses*: Remorse and the Epic   113

5. Dreaming of Eden: The Paladays Last of *Finnegans Wake*   154

Appendix: Joyce's Milton   205

Bibliography   213

Index   225

Foreword
———————

The relationship between John Milton and James Joyce has hitherto been carefully ignored, except for the predictable statement of the obvious: that a few remarkable similarities were quickly offset by enormous differences. Blind geniuses who have written works of epic proportions, Milton and Joyce were separated by more than just three centuries—most important, by their nationalities and religion, and perhaps most of all by their vastly divergent creative temperaments. Joyce can easily be viewed as playing the cavalier to Milton's roundhead.

In *Joyce, Milton, and the Theory of Influence,* Patrick Hogan has looked far beyond these superficies and has isolated conjunctive factors that reopen many significant issues in *Ulysses* and *Finnegans Wake,* through the nature of a potent Miltonic influence—and beyond it. His fresh approach to the often tenuous aspects of literary influence provides him with a tool with which to view both Milton and Joyce anew, and in the process offers literary critics a theoretical method that can be extended to other authors as well. Yet, just as Milton is employed as a method for reading and reevaluating the Joyce texts, he also emerges newly explicated in the process. Joyce and Milton share the stage in their own rights, the theoretical materials elucidating the works of both geniuses.

Bernard Benstock

Preface

The purpose of this book is twofold: to set out and illustrate a theory of influence and to explore the ill-understood relationship between James Joyce and John Milton, not merely as an exercise in literary history and the psychology of creation but as a way of understanding Joyce's literary works, especially his most difficult and rewarding works, *Ulysses* and *Finnegans Wake*. I undertook the former task as previous theories of influence appeared to me lacking in one of two ways. Some have sought deep explanations of influence, but have failed to make clear arguments, or even very clear generalizations; others have limited themselves to description, which has made their analyses clearer but often has rendered them superficial. In addition, writers on this topic have tended to focus on social aspects of influence to the exclusion of psychological aspects, or vice versa. In the opening chapter, I undertake to present a clear descriptive and explanatory account of influence, including both social and psychological factors. Moreover, in connection with the latter, I seek to articulate an understanding of influence that is coherent with recent developments in cognitive science as well as psychoanalysis.

Following some general remarks on Joyce's relation to precursors, the second chapter takes up Joyce's troubled relation to Milton, isolating some of the important political, psychological, and literary factors that entered into this complex influence, and emphasizing the ways in which the influence of one precursor is bound up with the influences of other precursors, events in the author's life, and so on. The third chapter concerns the less

Miltonic of Joyce's major works: *Dubliners*, *A Portrait of the Artist as a Young Man*, and *Exiles*. The fourth and fifth chapters are devoted to *Ulysses* and *Finnegans Wake*, respectively, two works that are, I argue, deeply Miltonic in structure. These chapters also reinterpret aspects of *Ulysses* and *Finnegans Wake*—for example, the nature of Stephen's mourning and the thematic function of wakean cycles—that are important to our understanding of those works independent of their relation to Miltonic precedents. (The appendix gives a brief description of the editions of Milton that Joyce is known to have owned and used.)

Influence is like a thread woven through the affections and cognitions of an author; it both enters and redefines patterns of transference and understanding at once literary, social, and biographical. It is the product of an author's relation not only to a precursor's works but also to that precursor him- or herself, to the works and judgments and values of yet other authors through or against which the precursor and his or her works may be understood, to the larger social and political histories in which these occur, and so on. Moreover, any elements drawn from a precursor are necessarily warped by the pressures of the work at hand, its structures and sentiments, even its literary aims and market.

Indeed, in this way, influence is not one thread but many, entering in many different patterns. Because of these multiple ramifications, because of the tight interweaving of different threads, no single influence is ever pure or univocal—except in works that we would refer to as derivative. Milton's influence on Joyce is definite and isolable, at points fully explicit. But what is most important in this literary filiation is discernible primarily in implication, in nuance. Although based upon a number of unequivocal connections, the pattern as a whole is a pattern of suggestion—what Sanskrit aestheticians such as Anandavardhana referred to as *dhvani* and saw as the crucial element in literary art and in our aesthetic experience of that art. The study of influence, then, is not tidy, reducible to a list of references and straightforward borrowings—though these are certainly important. To examine the influence of one writer on another is, rather, to seek the vague presence of a precursor in the complex dhvani of a work, to seek a pattern in one text through which the shaded patterns of other texts are still visible.

In the following pages, therefore, the discussions of Joyce's relation to Milton will lead inevitably to Joyce's relations with other authors and, more significantly, to broader themes, larger patterns in Joyce's writings. A study of influence does not, most important, yield unequivocal derivations, but looser connections that, ideally, add breadth to our understanding of an author's writings and further resonance to our response to those writings. The theoretical purpose of this study is to provide the beginnings of a clear, descriptively adequate, and explanatorily plausible account of literary influence. The critical purpose, however, is more intimate: to explore the suggestions of a Miltonic presence in order to enrich our associative and aesthetic experience of Joyce's works.

Some sections of chapter 4 appeared in an earlier version in the *James Joyce Quarterly* (vol. 24, no. 1 [fall 1986], 55–72). The University of Connecticut Research Foundation generously supported the library work required to complete this study. I am grateful to my father, Patrick Hogan, for helping with the Irish in *Finnegans Wake* (and for first reading with me the early pages of the *Wake*, seventeen years ago). I am indebted to Guy Davenport and John Shawcross for reading some of my early efforts on Joyce and Milton, for commenting, and for encouraging. Thanks are also due to the students in my seminar on Joyce and influence; their responses to my ideas about influence and their own research on the topic were stimulating and informative. I am grateful to Walda Metcalf for her initial interest in the project and for the care with which she saw it through the first stages of publication. Shelly Brivic, Joe Cary, Lalita Pandit, and Brandy Kershner read the entire work, providing valuable criticisms and suggestions. My interest in and understanding of Milton may be traced in large measure to a seminar I took with Northrop Frye in 1977. Finally, like many Joyceans I owe a particular debt of gratitude to Bernard Benstock for his encouragement, practical help, and painstaking criticism. Berni was a fine literary critic and a kind man.

Abbreviations

Joyce: CW *Critical Writings*

FW *Finnegans Wake*

SH *Stephen Hero*

SL *Selected Letters*

U *Ulysses*

Milton: PL *Paradise Lost*

Information on particular editions may be found in the bibliography.

Chapter 1

The Economy of Innovation and the Grammar of Influence

It is commonplace to observe that modernist writers sought to refashion literature in both form and subject. Novelists such as D. H. Lawrence worked to extend the domain of literary matter to the taboo; poets such as Stephen Spender broadened the scope of the aesthetic to include the "ugly." In a complementary movement, authors such as Virginia Woolf undertook the creation and elaboration of novel stylistic devices. James Joyce did all of this.

For some, these innovations were part of a struggle for realism. Like artists engaged in the (Popperian) development of representational painting described by E. H. Gombrich in *Art and Illusion*, a development through conjecture and refutation, some modernists saw themselves as overcoming the errors of past representation. In a well-known letter to Stanislaus, Joyce criticized George Moore in the following terms: "Damned stupid. . . . A lady who has been living for three years on the line between Bray and Dublin is told by her husband that there is a meeting in Dublin at which he must be present. She looks up the table to see the hours of the trains. This on DW and WR where the trains go regularly: this after three years. Isn't it rather stupid of Moore" (*SL* 44). In his 1900 essay "Drama and Life," Joyce insisted that drama functions "to portray truth" (*CW* 41). "Art is true to itself when it deals with truth," he asserted (43–44). In his first essay on James Clarence Mangan, Joyce called beauty "the splendour of truth," and though in the "Pola" notebook he separated the two, there is more than ample evidence that he never retreated from his commitment to achieving greater representational accuracy. Even in the 1920s Joyce was insisting to Arthur Power that "an author must not write for the arty. There must be a sound basis of fact in his work" (Power 73), and he described *Ulysses* as the harbinger of "the new realism" (53), pointing out that "in *Ulysses* I tried to keep close to fact" (98; see also 33–36, 57–58).

For Joyce, however, realism was never a matter of mere facts, mere "reportage" in Georg Lukacs's term. It always involved what Lukacs called "portrayal," locating facts in the context of a larger pattern that made sense of them. As Joyce put it in "Drama and Life," drama, the highest form of literary art, concerns itself with "the underlying laws" of life, while lesser literature addresses "whimsicalities and circumstances," accidents (*CW* 40). Indeed, Joyce's notion of the epiphany as the proper moment of art was based on his abiding concern for realism, along with his deep belief that realism and aesthetic symbolism are not irreconcilable—for a Joycean epiphany is nothing other than the realization of the symbolic, the universal, in the most mundane reality. "[A] sudden spiritual manifestation," he has Stephen call it (*SH* 211). But it is a sudden spiritual manifestation discovered in vulgarity. It is like the banal reality of a day, transfigured by death. As Joyce wrote to Stanislaus, when a man dies unexpectedly, all the trivial events of his last day become significant—what he said when leaving home, how he entered the tram, whether he turned this way or that; art turns to the quotidian this same plenary attention, raising it from obscurity to meaning. Like Stephen, Joyce "felt that the spirit of beauty had folded him round like a mantle and that in revery at least he had been acquainted with nobility." But unlike Stephen, he did not distinguish this aesthetic rapture from the rapture to be found "in the midst of common lives . . . amid the squalor and noise and sloth of the city" (*A Portrait* 177).

No doubt politically oriented writers such as Auden and Spender saw their revisionary project likewise in terms of veracity. And there were others also. For example, Virginia Woolf's feminism—which was, of course, deeply bound up with her view of what exactly was true about men and women in life and art—entered into at least certain of her innovations. Indeed, if we seek diligently enough, we can find an avowed search for realism in rather unlikely modernist quarters. Thus as Jaako Hintikka has argued, certain of Picasso's cubist innovations, and most particularly his simultaneous representation of profile and full face, are motivated by a sort of constructivist attempt at achieving the Kantian noumenon. Specifically, Hintikka argues, Picasso's self-conscious destruction of perspective was not antirealist, but realist in the extreme. By multiplying perspectives and presenting them simultaneously, Picasso sought to paint things not as they appear, but as they are.

But there is undoubtedly more to the need for novelty than such an upstanding concern with verisimilitude. What is most striking, perhaps, in all the cases mentioned, is the degree to which these innovations serve to devalue the work of competitors—in most cases, artists of the preceding generation (broadly defined, though usually with greater emphasis on near contemporaries). Spender scrutinized the unnatural, and he valorized this scrutiny by appeals to both realism and politics (see, for example, Spender 279–80), which is to say objective factors independent of the individual poet. This functioned to devalue the poetry of simple country pleasures so common among the immediately preceding Georgians (see Weatherhead 83–84), while more broadly undermining the romantic celebration of nature and the aestheticist focus on the beautiful, as well as romantic and Victorian expressivism and the resultant concentration on the psychology of the individual poet. Picasso's destruction of perspective was aimed directly at the impressionist refinement of perspective that he had earlier sought to imitate. His innovations can be seen as a search for realism, but they can more easily be seen as an attack on impressionism. Woolf's feminism, insofar as it entered into her literary project, operated similarly in diminishing the status of male writers, especially relative to the female writers invoked in Woolf's argument and to Woolf herself. The relatively small number of women in the literary canon of Woolf's time, along with more general sexist attitudes, added sex to generation as a crucial literary opposition.

In a sense, then, Spender, Picasso, and Woolf may be understood as trying to eliminate the competition. Each found him- or herself in an artistic society in which the rules, as determined already, offered little scope for artistic success. Spender would never have become known as a romantic, and Picasso would have been merely a minor impressionist. Woolf's problem was politically very different, but involved many of the same relations nonetheless. Clearly, Woolf was not concerned with being a male writer, significant or insignificant. However, she needed to be accepted as an artist and not rejected simply because she was a woman. She too had to eliminate the competition, even if the competition was in her case a result of patriarchal bias as much as past achievement.

Needless to say, Joyce was no exception to this general rule. His call to realism was, explicitly, an attack on the Irish literary revival, especially William Butler Yeats. In "Drama and Life," Joyce wrote "Life we must accept as we see it before our eyes, men and women as we meet them in the real world, not as we apprehend them in the world of faery" (*CW* 45). The target of his realism could not be clearer. Likewise, his repeated invocation of Aristotle and St. Thomas was in part a response to the Platonism and eastern mysticism of Yeats and others in the movement that was quite clearly defining the aesthetic culture of Dublin in Joyce's early years. In later life, Joyce told a friend that, of the two, Yeats was the greater writer (Ellmann *Joyce* 660n). Had Joyce followed Yeats's principles, tendencies, interests, he would not have become the greatest prose fiction writer of the twentieth century. He would have been a minor scribbling Hibernian.

This is not to say that writers such as Spender and Joyce did not in fact advance in realism, at least in certain respects. They did. (I remain less convinced about Picasso.) Nor is it to say that Woolf did not sincerely, importantly, justly, and effectively, address genuine feminist concerns. She did. It is only to say that, as artists, they addressed these concerns with their eye on the competition. Indeed, they had no choice in the matter.

Walter Jackson Bate begins *The Burden of the Past and the English Poet*—perhaps the most insightful study of influence available (along with Goran Hermeren's *Influence in Art and Literature*)—by pointing out that the question every artist must face when looking at a canvas or a sheet of paper is, What is there left to do? He then quotes a touching epigram from an Egyptian scribe, written four thousand years ago: "Would I had phrases that are not known, utterances that are strange, in new language that has not been used, free from repetition, not an utterance which has grown stale, which men of old have spoken" (Bate 4–5). It is commonly believed that concern for artistic originality is a peculiarly modern and European phenomenon; Bate argues briefly but forcefully that this belief is mistaken (39n). The scribe's epigram well illustrates Bate's point. He might have cited any number of other ancient and non-Western examples as well, including the third-century Chinese *Wen-Fu,* in which Lu Chi speaks of his poem "Glowing like many-colored broidery, mournful as multiple chords." Yet, "I must renounce the piece," he laments, for "it coincides with earlier masterpieces. . . . True, the arrow struck my heart; what a pity, then, that others were struck before me" (15). Even more germane is the fourth book of the ninth-century Sanskrit treatise on poetics, the *Dhvanyāloka,* where Ānandavardhana gives advice to writers on ways in which they might successfully innovate; one powerful strategy, he explains, is minute realism (708)—a strategy well known to Joyceans, for the composition of *Ulysses* proceeded to a great extent by the grand accumulation of otherwise banal minutiae.

Bate also delimits possible solutions to the dilemma of what Harold Bloom calls the artist's "belatedness" (see Bloom, chapter 4 of *A Map*): "the opening up of new subject matters" and, echoing Ānandavardhana, the development of a "new particularity even in the treatment of traditional or familiar subjects" (Bate 116, 117). It is important to add to Bate's list another common strategy for revising traditional material, a strategy we might call "change of register." High modernist innovation is not infrequently based on the secularization and ironizing of culturally important myths. Thus, for example, in *The Trial*, Kafka transforms the myth of Satanic rebellion into a vaudevillian struggle against an all-knowing bureaucracy. Joyce extensively employed these modernist devices as well.

Complementary to such strategies, Bate outlines a number of characteristics common in artists' explicit stance toward influence, several of which we have seen amongst the writers discussed already. For example, Bate emphasizes the importance of the rebellion against the preceding or "parental" generation of artists and the invocation of an earlier or "grandparental" authority—as when Joyce rejected the Celtic revivalists and invoked Aristotle as authority over their Neoplatonism. Beyond this, an artist might champion a different tradition rather than a grandparental generation. We can see this in the invocation of past Irish writers by Yeats and other figures in the Celtic revival, in Picasso's celebration of African art, and in Woolf's isolation of a female literary tradition. Along similar lines, George Bornstein has noted that "poets who wrote in a different language can liberate later poets from the intimidations of their own immediate predecessors in their own language" (8). And Anna Balakian has stressed that the struggle against immediate or "parental" precursors is most often internal to a national literature; thus a given author might readily accept and even celebrate work by foreign writers of that parental generation (quoted in Hermeren 43)—a principle well illustrated in Joyce's quite different relations to Yeats and Ibsen.

These possibilities derive from the different positions of various precursors in determining environmentally relevant aesthetic standards, the standards most in evidence in the younger artist's directly relevant milieu. In an Ireland virtually ignorant of Ibsen, where the aesthetic standards of the most artistically active group were, in effect, Yeatsean, Ibsen was no threat; Yeats, however, was—and quite a threat. (Later on, in Paris, the threat of

Yeats faded, as did Joyce's criticism, which surged rather against nearer competitors.) The same point could be made for Yeats and the ancient Irish bards, Picasso and the anonymous Africans, even Woolf and the various women novelists she cites (one might contrast her more critical relation to such contemporary competitors as Katherine Mansfield).

But still the nature of the innovative urge is unclear. As I understand him, Bate emphasizes the importance of an artist's concern to create art that is worthwhile. No doubt Bate is right to see the artist as a man or woman who seeks aesthetic achievement. But this is hardly adequate. (Of course, Bate never claims it is. This is not his concern.) For example, as Bate points out, one danger facing the artist who seeks to cope with the "perfection of the past" is the temptation to random innovation, "novelty for its own sake" (82), and thus novelty *not* for the sake of art—rather, decadent novelty. But it seems very unlikely that an artist would replace aesthetic intention with aesthetically unmotivated innovation if aesthetic concerns were the driving force behind the innovation in the first place. Indeed, it is not even clear that purely aesthetic concerns should lead to innovation (compare the passage from Lu Chi quoted above).

Harold Bloom has argued that innovation is to a considerable degree a response to anxiety. As Bloom puts it "[w]hen a poet experiences incarnation *qua* poet, he experiences anxiety necessarily towards any danger that might *end him* as a poet"; specifically, a poet experiences "[t]he anxiety of influence" (*Anxiety* 58). In Bloom's well-known model, a writer enters into a sort of literary transference relation with a precursor, struggling with that precursor as a young child struggles with the parent of the same sex in an Oedipal triangle (see, for example, *Anxiety* 11, 91). As a defense against the influential threat of the precursor, the new writer misreads him or her, represses his or her themes and style. As Bloom states his "argument's central principle": "Poetic Influence—when it involves two strong, authentic poets—always proceeds by a misreading of the prior poet, an act of creative correction that is actually and necessarily a misinterpretation" (*Anxiety* 30).

Presumably, Bloom means that the poet represents to him- or herself a distorted or transformed image of the precursor's work, while being unconsciously cognizant of the poet's actual work. Bloom certainly indicates that this is the case in the relation between Pascal and Montaigne or between Arnold and Keats. As Bloom puts it, "Pascal huffed: 'It is not in Montaigne, but in myself, that I find all that I see in him,' an assertion that becomes funny when we consult a good edition of Pascal, and study the immense lists of 'parallel passages' that demonstrate an indebtedness so pervasive as to be a scandal. Pascal attempting to refute Montaigne while wearing his precursor's coat is rather like Matthew Arnold sneering at Keats while writing *The Scholar Gipsy* and *Thyrsis* in a diction, tone, and sensuous rhythm wholly (and unconsciously) stolen from the Great Odes" (*Anxiety* 56). Perhaps Bloom considers Pascal and Arnold weak poets, and thus beyond the scope of the "central principle." But then, it becomes unclear in precisely what sense strong poets are influenced at all. In other words, if strong poets do not do what Arnold did, that presumably means that both consciously and *unconsciously* they believe their distorted representations of the precursor and his or her work. In effect they have no unconscious relation to the precursor—and thus should have no anxiety. Though I do not find Bloom entirely clear on this issue, I take him to be claiming that even strong poets repress, that even strong poets have a repressed, unconscious understanding of their precursors' works, an understanding against which the conscious misunderstanding, or misprision, is a defense.

But like all repressions, the repressions of the new writer are only partially successful. Symptoms appear in the cracks, the points where repression is weakest. Thus the new writer's works can be read almost as symptoms, signs bearing traces of the repressed precursor. As Bloom puts it—in a statement that grossly oversimplifies the multiplicity and complexity of writers' relations to various precursors and their various works—"Every poem is a misinterpretation of a parent poem" (*Anxiety* 94). Moreover, for Bloom, every poem is a misinterpretation functioning through the distortions of "revisionary ratios," literary defenses directly assimilable to the classical defense mechanisms (see the table of equivalences, or parallels, in *A Map* 84). For Bloom, then, the great poet is "strong," psychologically powerful enough to keep the precursors in check. The "weak" poet, however, is unsuccessful, and merely derivative.

Although it seems clear that writers do suffer from an "anxiety of influence" and may indeed enter into transferential relations with precursor poets, and although Bloom is to be credited with emphasizing these important points, a great deal of Bloom's analysis appears clearly mistaken. First of all, Bloom provides virtually no evidence for his claims. Indeed, many of his claims are so vague or metaphorical that it is difficult if not impossible to tell what could possibly count as evidence for or against them. For example, it is very hard to say precisely what Bloom means when he speaks of "the Primal Scene for a poet *as poet*" and explains that this is "his Poetic Father's coitus with the Muse" (*Anxiety* 36–37; emphasis in original). The notion that "the poetic father has been absorbed into the id" is equally obscure (80). (Of course, the precursor's work is presumably the work that gives the writer aesthetic pleasure, but how that can be understood as incorporation into the id is opaque.) And when Bloom claims that "[s]ource study is wholly irrelevant" to the study of influence because "we are dealing with primal words, but antithetical meanings, and an ephebe's best misinterpretations may well be of poems he has never read" (70), he appears to combine obscurity (in his incomprehensible reference to Freud's essay on primal words) with self-contradiction and a sort of new age mysticism (in claiming that writers misread poems they do not read at all). As Goran Hermeren points out, in order to evaluate Bloom's claims "one must know more precisely which thesis he is arguing for and how this thesis should be understood; and in order to know this, further clarification of [Bloom's] key concepts . . . is needed" (311–12).

As to the more evidently comprehensible claims of Bloom, it is certainly the case that we distinguish derivative writers from "original" writers. But it is far from clear that Bloom's distinction between weak and strong writers goes beyond this in any useful or theoretically rigorous way, despite Bloom's addition of Oedipal struggle and a baffling array of "revisionary ratios." Specifically, it is not clear that Bloom can supply criteria for poetic strength that are ultimately independent of notions of or intuitions about derivativeness. Indeed, it is not even clear quite how Bloom's psychoanalytic apparatus might explain the intuitive distinction. Similarly, it is not obvious that writers always suffer from anxiety of influence rather than, say, anxiety of failure, or of strangulation by the rules that define and value the precursor's work. No doubt writers are sometimes engaged in a struggle for identity—finding a voice, as it is called—but equally often their conflict with precursors is a matter of evaluation rather than identity.

This brings us to a more general point about Bloom's theory. Bloom takes psychoanalytic ideas and applies them to literary relations *removed from* the more general relations of psychosexual development. The psychoanalysis of literature is an uncertain undertaking at best. But its removal from the basic principles of psychoanalysis—for example, the grounding of transference in infantile psychosexual development as understood through both child observation and clinical analysis—seems to undermine any possible validity of psychoanalytic literary interpretation. Even if, as Bloom insists, artists rebel "more strongly against the consciousness of death's necessity than all other men and women do" (*Anxiety* 10), and even if there are other differences along these lines, a purely literary Oedipal struggle makes little sense. Again, it is no doubt true that some writers do enter into a sort of transferential relation with precursors. And perhaps such transferences have some special characteristics, just as transferences to teachers or employers may have special characteristics. However, it would seem that they have to be transferences in the ordinary sense—roughly, transferals of repressed infantile, usually Oedipal, fantasies onto nonparental figures. (For a historical and conceptual overview of the concept of transference, see the entry in Laplanche and Pontalis and citations.) According to standard psychoanalytic theory and practice—from Freud to Lacan, from Hartmann to Schafer—insofar as Joyce had a transferential relation with, say, Yeats, this was an ordinary transference, of the sort he might have had with anyone else (Roberto Prezioso, for example); it was not a special literary transference—a notion that makes little or no sense in standard psychoanalytic theory.

If Bloom wishes to argue for a special literary transference, he must explain what such a thing is and how it is possible. If, on the other hand, he does not wish to maintain that literary transference is distinct from ordinary transference—and he does evidently maintain this—he has to explain why he believes this ordinary transference to be an invariant occurrence in literary creation, at least during certain periods; why it invariably leads to misreading in particular, seeing that misinterpretation of the same sort might ordinarily be considered a somewhat unexpected outcome of transference; and how this could ever result in great art—that is, how the product of a transference, however like a symptom, could escape actually being a symptom, and thus being, presumably, aesthetically ineffective. Again, transferential relations may be part of any given author's relations to precursors—they are certainly part of Joyce's relations to precursors. But, in the first place, these seem to be ordinary relations of transference, and, second, they do not appear in any way to define the specifically aesthetic characteristics of the new work—especially in a one-to-one transformative relation, sometimes with an unread precursor poem, as Bloom maintains.

The Economics of Innovation: A Context for Influence

No doubt the urge to novelty has many sources. Different artists feel the urge with greater or less urgency and this presumably relates in part to their own idiosyncratic psychological dispositions. Thus psychology and psychoanalysis are by no means irrelevant to the study of literary innovation. I would argue, however, that the most crucial factors in determining the importance of such innovation are economic. The need for novelty is, in my view, less determined by an author's psyche than by an author's public, less by his or her relations to parents than by relations to patrons and publishers. The conditions for valuing innovation lie less in an Oedipal scenario than in concrete economic conditions. Of course, to some degree all writers acknowledge this. Thus Bloom notes the increasing "belatedness" of writers after the sixteenth century (see, for example, *Anxiety* 11, 122). And Bate refers more lucidly to the same period, explaining that, "the means of preserving and distributing the literature (and more recently the other arts) of the past have immeasurably increased, and to such a point that we now have confronting the artist—or have *in potentia*—a vast array of varied achievement, existing and constantly multiplying in an 'eternal present'" (4).

Bloom and Bate are certainly right to indicate that the valorization of novelty has increased in recent centuries. Indeed, this fact is crucial to the development of a social and economic, rather than psychological, account of innovation. But it is important to emphasize that innovation had not by any means steadily increased in value over the preceding two millennia, as their accounts may be taken to imply. Rather, as Arnold Hauser has shown in his classic *Social History of Art,* the value of novelty has wavered. And as innovation most often has meant innovation in increasing realism (recall Ānandavardhana's advice), this has meant that there has been an alternation of realism and mannerism both historically and geographically, an alternation, Hauser argues, based on economy. Specifically, there is a fairly straightforward correlation between the degree of realism in a society's art and the degree to which the society is economically free. Conversely, there is a fairly straightforward correlation between the degree of stylization or mannerism in a society's art and the degree to which the society is economically rigid or feudal. The requirement of innovation in art varies more or less directly with the requirement of innovation in the economy at large. As Hauser puts it, "dynamic and antitraditionalistic tendencies [are] usually associated with trade and communications and with an urban money economy" (130).

In a free market, producers must continually compete with other producers for markets. They can achieve economic success only by innovation, only by providing new products to old markets or by cultivating new markets. The former may be achieved either by creating new demands, obsolescing the objects of earlier demands, or (what is really a special case of the second) by supplying products, such as food, for which there is a guaranteed recurrence of demand. Certainly, not all free markets are the same. There are always certain sorts of ideological constraint that limit the freedom of production, distribution, and so on, and there is always political constraint as well. (The division between feudal and bourgeois is not absolute.) There are differences in degree of competition, accessibility of markets, technological possibilities for both production and distribution. There are differences in relations of ownership. Perhaps most relevantly for our purposes, and in part due to factors already mentioned, there are differences in the proportion of the economy focused on any given aspect of market innovation. Thus in "primitive" economies, the supply of recurrent demands may be most important; in imperialist economies, such as nineteenth-century England, the opening of new markets; in product-saturated consumer economies, such as the United States today, the obsolescence of earlier products and the creation of new demands. But whatever sort of innovation may be most important at any given time and place, all three are present in varying degrees.

There are two ways in which the broader economic importance, indeed necessity, of innovation might affect artistic production. The first is straightforward. As Mikel Dufrenne explains, in a capitalist economy "art is essentially a . . . business, subject to the laws of competition. Its commercialization involves the works themselves, their sale, their execution, their performance, or their distribution" (11). In short, books, paintings, musical compositions, are commodities. Even the briefest glance at a history of publishing—with discussions of printing costs, booksellers's pricing, bookseller and publisher profit per book, print run decisions, pricing agreements, "wars" over pricing, (see, for example, Mumby and Norrie)—makes one aware of the degree to which a book is necessarily a commodity. At the simplest level, for books to be read, they must sell; and in order to sell, they must innovate within the context of the current market. The degree of requisite innovation will thus in large part depend on the economics—demand, distribution networks, and so on—of the specific product type (books, in this case). However, it will also depend in part on the more general pressures toward innovation in the society as a whole. In other words, the book market affects the need for innovation in books, but so too does the general economy; if the economy as a whole values innovation, that will have an impact on book production whatever the dictates of the narrower market in books. In imperialist and late capitalist societies, the more general urge to innovate is particularly strong.

Unfortunately, however, literature is not simply literature, nor art art. Since the eighteenth century there has been an increasing split between popular and elite art (see, for example, Bate 99–100). There are a number of reasons for this. First, focusing only on literature, the past three centuries have seen an enormous growth in literacy. Thus in some ways the development of a division between elite and popular literature prior to the eighteenth century was almost impossible. There simply was no common reader prior to this time, no mass readership that might define a position for an elite readership. (The situation was slightly different for arts such as drama, which did not require literacy. But in these cases the relevant division is elite/folk, which is rather different.) Correlatively, the means of communication, preservation, and transportation of literature grew immensely in the same period. In the 1630s, John Milton could take out six years in order to read and master everything significant ever written in Europe. Milton's notion was grandiose, but not absurd. A century later, this would have been a laughable idea. As the realm of "great literature" grew wildly beyond the scope of casual reading or basic education and came to require specialization for serious understanding, a split developed between popular literature, which presupposed little familiarity with classic texts, and elite literature.

This is certainly an intellectual and aesthetic division. However, it is an intellectual and aesthetic division that is founded on target populations, on markets, and not on absolute aesthetic values. Thus, works of elite literature presuppose what Sanskrit literary theorists have called the *sahṛdaya*, defined by Edward Dimock as "'the man of sensibility': meaning sensibility to a particular chain of associations which the poet could arouse in the minds of people from his own tradition" (xvii). And elite works presuppose the sahṛdaya, not merely as an ideal reader, but as a consumer, a purchaser. Of course, works of popular literature are not aesthetically presuppositionless. Like works of elite literature, they presuppose knowledge of historical, scientific, and other principles; they presuppose familiarity with certain storytelling techniques; and so on. Moreover, they may presuppose a certain degree of understanding of popular literature—though only current popular literature, and only some of that.

These distinctions are, of course, a matter of degree. An author can aim at an audience with minimal knowledge of elite literature, intimate knowledge of elite literature, something in between (for example, they know *Hamlet* and *Pride and Prejudice,* but not *Ulysses*), or some combination (as in cartoons that work perfectly well for preschool children and highly educated adults, but no one else). Similarly, the readership for popular literature is far from uniform. (See, for example, Thomas J. Roberts's typology of readers and reading strategies; though not framed in terms of the economics of consumption, Roberts's anatomy clearly maps out distinct readership markets, based in part on breadth and depth of literary expertise.) But such variation does not affect the crucial point that the field of literature is structured by markets and that these markets define the context—including the literary context—in which individual works are produced and consumed.

The situation in literature, as it has gradually developed since the eighteenth century, is the following. There is a range of literary works, clustering at the extremes of elite and popular. The elite works are aimed at highly educated people and, increasingly, at schools and universities, where they are intensively and repeatedly studied in the context of a lengthy history of elite literary works. The popular works are aimed at ordinary people (some of whom are highly educated) who read them once only and do so in the very limited literary context of other recent popular fiction, television, and so on. Popular literature, then, is aimed at satisfying a sort of recurrent demand. It requires minimal novelty, for this reason. Enough novelty is required to establish basic difference in plot and character across contemporaneously popular works, but that is all (for a discussion of this point, see Nash). Obviously, nonliterary factors enter and guide various changing tendencies in popular literature—for example, a political focus on terrorism generates an interest in popular novels concerning terrorism. However, it does not seem appropriate to refer to this as innovation in the sense just discussed.

The situation with elite literature, however, is quite different. Here we are dealing with a limited market that is already highly saturated. While the very nature of elite literature (that is, its reference to a tradition) limits the possibility of actually obsolescing earlier works, the economic situation drives writers of elite literature to increasingly rapid innovation. Or rather it drives publishers and consumers of elite literature increasingly to value innovation (or what they perceive as innovation). To see innovation in elite literature as economically based is not necessarily to claim either that writers of elite literature are motivated by purely economic concerns or that all writers of elite literature feel compelled to innovate. Rather, it is to claim that writers make it into the canon of elite literature for economic reasons and that radical innovation has become increasingly important for admission into the canon of elite literature due precisely to market considerations.

As some readers will no doubt be disturbed by my references to the canon, I should emphasize that this is not a valorization of elite literature per se. Clearly, literary discernment can derive from and encourage greater aesthetic sensitivity, but it can also reflect and serve unjust forms of social hierarchization. Although I certainly have high esteem and deep love for many of the figures in the standard Western literary canon, I have argued elsewhere that the racism, sexism, and ethnocentrism of our canon demand its extensive reconstruction—possibly through drastic means (see Hogan "Mo' Better" and *Politics* 211–12).

The difference between popular and elite literature, as I am using the terms, is not, first of all, a matter of authorial intent but of different sorts of market success. Authors may seek to write elite literature due to the desire for immortality, as Bloom stresses. Aware of the longevity of elite works and the ephemeral character of popular works, they may choose the lesser monetary gains of the former for a gain in fame—or they may try for both. Whatever their interest in making for themselves monuments more lasting than bronze, and whatever their other motives, they most often share a desire to create art that is aesthetically effective, works that are beautiful or sublime. Both popular and elite readers seek pleasure in literary works—static and kinetic, aesthetic and pornographic, to allude to Stephen Dedalus's distinction (see *A Portrait* 205). However, in the case of elite literature, there is a huge body of aesthetically effective literature that is not only available but also in some sense demands understanding as a whole, each work having as its context all preceding elite works (as T. S. Eliot has most famously emphasized, in a noneconomic context). The primary means for a new work to find its way into this canon is through innovation. Moreover this innovation is often not aesthetic at all, but rather productive, innovation that bears less on elite readers' experience of beauty than on their need to use literary works, both pedagogically and professionally, their need to generate classwork and publishable essays.

Cutting across this popular/elite spectrum, are other market segments based on various sorts of affiliation—nationality, class, sex, and so on. It is well known that the rise of the novel was related to the historical development of a class of women literate in the vernacular, but not in the classical languages (see, for example, Watt 151–52, 298–99; see also McKeon 51–52). (The earliest division of elite and popular was closely related to this division in linguistic competence; the decline in classical learning, however, and the development of vernacular canons subsequently shifted the entire scale.) The Irish Renaissance is to a degree the product of the development of a large body of Irish men and women literate in English—the result of a swift rise in literacy throughout the nineteenth century, combined with the decline of the Irish language (see Lee 13). These market divisions may operate in various combinations. Literary works may be aimed at English or Irish or both, men or women or both, elite or popular or both, and so on. Most writing of the Irish Renaissance—Yeats being one obvious exception—was for local consumption. It reached only the Irish market, with minimal overflow to extranational consumers. Indeed, even Yeats was not successful in the continental market (see Ellmann *Eminent Domain* 52). By contrast, from the outset Joyce aimed his work at an international elite, unconfined by region or sex or any other division. The tardiness of Joyce's success, relative to such other Irish writers as Colum or Stephens, was due primarily to this. He was aiming at a different and potentially more rewarding market—but also a more competitive market, already glutted with innovation, and, indeed, a market in which it was if anything a disadvantage to be Irish.

None of this means that aesthetic considerations of authors or readers do not enter into canonization. It means only that, when they do, they are subordinated to economic conditions. Indeed, when I speak of works of elite literature presupposing a canon, I am implicitly making reference to the aesthetical intent of the author and the aesthetical experience of the reader. Literature is written and read with many different intents. There are propagandistic intents, unconscious and symptomatic intents, referential intents, and so on. But insofar as a given work of literature is produced or read as an aesthetic object, as an object of beauty or sublimity, it is thereby produced or read with "aesthetical intent." When authors write a work of literature, they approach that work, as they produce it, in the aesthetical attitude; they view it as an object of aesthetical pleasure—just as a reader does on approaching the work as a work of literature (rather than as a source of historical information, the starting point for a publishable essay, kindling material, or whatever). In the aesthetical attitude, we broaden our concern with a text. We do not narrowly focus on referential intent or inferential relations, as we might when approaching a piece of discursive prose. In reading a work in the aesthetical attitude, we listen to the sounds and rhythms of the language, visualize and reconstrue the images, fuse and diffuse the metaphors, and allow our minds to play about our associations—especially, in elite literature, those that are available through the canon.

The classical Sanskrit aestheticians referred to the aesthetic quality of a literary work as a *rasa*, a sentiment or flavor, and assimilated the aesthetic experience of a literary work to the savoring of a flavor. As the tenth-century theorist Abhinavagupta put it: "Aesthetical experience takes place, as everyone can notice, by virtue, as it were, of the squeezing out of the poetical word. Persons aesthetically sensitive, indeed, read and taste many times over the same poem. In contradiction to practical means of perception, that, their task being accomplished, are no more of any use and must be abandoned" (*Aesthetic Experience* xxxii).

Part of the "savoring" of the aesthetical attitude, whether in the aesthetical intent of the author or the aesthetical reception of the reader, involves allowing one's mind to play about the literary associations of the work. In this way, an elite work is always much larger than itself. It is, as poststructuralists like to say, not so much text as "intertext"—although, contrary to poststructuralist and other idealist views, it is intertext only through the minds of authors and readers. An elite literary work is (most often) produced in a literary context and, when read in the aesthetical attitude and as an elite literary work, it is read in a literary context as well. It is that context, that intertextuality to which I refer when I say that a work of elite literature presupposes a historical body of elite literature. Popular literature can be produced and received in the aesthetical attitude as well. Popular literature can be equally intertextual. But the contexts of its intertextuality are limited in time and number. And the works themselves are not intended—or marketed—to be savored, but rather, continuing the metaphor, to be devoured. Thus, insofar as I refer to either as having literary presuppositions, I imply as the "location" of these presuppositions a productive aesthetic intent on the part of the author and a receptive aesthetic attitude on the part of the reader.

Returning to the more narrowly economic conditions, at one level Joyce was well aware of the economic basis of elite canonization. I believe that Joyce set out to create and succeeded in creating some of the most exquisitely beautiful literature in the English language. However, I also believe, and imagine Joyce believed, that his radical product innovations and, related to these, the remarkable resources his works provide for pedagogic and professional production, their openness to economic exploitation—as evidenced once more in the present volume—satisfy a necessary condition for the achievement of a high canonical position. Had they been as beautiful but less economically productive their canonical stature would have been correspondingly diminished. As Joyce himself commented wryly on *Ulysses:* "it will keep the professors busy for centuries" (quoted in Ellmann *James Joyce* 521).

Thus the urge for innovation is, it would seem, fundamentally an economic, not a psychological principle—in the production of art as in the production of any other commodity. For this reason its force and nature vary with economic conditions, historically and geographically. However, the specifics of a given author's relations to influence are not so generally economic. Economic principles form the basis for reception and canonization. Thus the general valorization or lack of valorization of literary or other innovation is, principally, a function of economy. But the manner in which a given author responds to precursor figures, the specific ways in which he or she innovates are primarily a function of individual psychology. Thus, the following discussion of Joyce's relation to influence in general and to the influence of John Milton in particular, while presupposing a broad economic context of market conditions and relations, will focus not on the features of economy common to a broad range of modernist writers, but on the particular features of Joyce's own psychology of influence.

Learning How to Write: Influence and Cognition

Before beginning a discussion of Joyce, however, we must gain an understanding of the more general psychology of influence. First, we must distinguish cognitive and affective components. In part, the relation of one author to a precursor is a matter of feeling, of fantasy, of repression and desire. In part, it falls within the province of psychoanalysis. This is the aspect of influence that has been most important to Bloom. However, there is also a cognitive aspect to influence. In part, the relation of one author to a precursor is a matter of thought, perception, recollection, and generalization, and falls, therefore, within the province of cognitive psychology.

While the cognitive aspect of influence has been less intensively examined than the affective aspect, it has not gone unnoticed. For example, in his excellent study of Joyce and Ibsen, Bjorn Tysdahl points out that

> there is, in the life of a writer and in the genesis of a work, a preparatory stage at which a *Weltanschauung* and basic principles about literary art are sought for and adopted. At this stage there is no conflict between the use of earlier writers and the inner "laws" of a finished work, for this is the time when these "laws" are being conceived. There may also be intermediate stages in the development of a work of art at which new finds in earlier writers can be incorporated without any damage to the coherence and unity of the finished prod-

uct. But the strict demands of what is there already will grow; and when the work is actually being written, there will in most cases be very few opportunities for such inclusions. (Tysdahl 220)

Here Tysdahl develops a plausible scheme of artistic composition in relation to influence. Even in this short description, he clearly indicates the different cognitive elements—from broader conceptions to more particular details—that enter into influenced poieisis.

Elsewhere, Tysdahl is more specific. In discussing the ways in which even clearly autobiographical works can be powerfully influenced, he indicates the importance of precursors in defining what we might call *selection principles*. An author's life is not a story, but a manifold of events, perceptions, feelings, and fantasies. When that author writes of his or her life, he or she necessarily selects certain aspects for presentation and leaves aside others. One cognitive function of the influence of a precursor is in providing principles for such selection. As Tysdahl puts it, Ibsen's "early plays offered an interpretation of Joyce's personal history, and they could suggest what sort of incidents he could use in his fiction" (82). Hugh Kenner noted this phenomenon as well when he argued that Joyce did not impose Homer on Dublin but rather found Homeric patterns in Dublin (*Dublin's Joyce* 180).

Joyce himself makes a similar point in *A Portrait* when he writes of Stephen's literary associations with the ordinary objects he passes on his way to the university (176):

> The rainladen trees of the avenue evoked in him, as always, memories of the girls and women in the plays of Gerhart Hauptmann; and the memory of their pale sorrows and the fragrance falling from the wet branches mingled in a mood of quiet joy. His morning walk across the city had begun, and he foreknew that as he passed the sloblands of Fairview he would think of the cloistral silverveined prose of Newman, that as he walked along the North Strand Road, glancing idly at the windows of the provision shops, he would recall the dark humour of Guido Cavalcanti and smile, that as he went by Baird's stonecutting works in Talbot Place the spirit of Ibsen would blow through him like a keen wind, a spirit of wayward boyish beauty, and that passing a grimy marinedealer's shop beyond the Liffey he would repeat the song by Ben Jonson which begins:
> *I was not wearier where I lay*

Here as elsewhere, Stephen's experience of the world is completely aestheticized—which is to say that he approaches all his experiences in the aesthetical attitude. Although this passage is not without irony at the expense of Stephen, it nonetheless clearly illustrates the way in which precursors provide artists with selection principles for isolating aspects of their life, when that life is approached or recollected in the aesthetical attitude—as it always is when artistic ends are in question.

The process to which Tysdahl, Kenner, and Joyce refer is in part an instance of a more general cognitive activity, termed *encoding*. To encode a perception or experience is, first of all, to categorize it. A great deal of learning is a matter of encoding properties and relations that we previously failed to encode. For example, learning a language involves encoding new phonological differences. Ordinarily, English speakers do not encode the difference between a *t* pronounced with the tongue forward on the alveolar ridge (the ridge just behind one's front teeth) and a *t* pronounced with the tongue at the back of the alveolar ridge. In other words, they do not hear the difference. However, in learning Hindi, they must come to discriminate between these sounds—just as Hindi speakers must come to discriminate *v* from *w*. (For a discussion of encoding, see John Holland et al. 55–56.) To provide selection principles is, in part, to encode either properties or relations in an author's experience—thus rendering them salient and opening them up to cognitive reconfiguration or transformation.

Selection principles also link such newly salient properties and relations to complexes of associated principles. This too is an ordinary cognitive process—given, in this context, an aesthetic inflection. Consider again the passage from *A Portrait*. Joyce presents us with a series of images drawn, one assumes, from his own experience. Of the infinitely many properties and relations he could recount, the works of his precursors render salient only a handful. Thus Hauptmann's work selects for him one aspect of the avenue—its trees—and renders salient one property of these trees—their wet fragrance. In connection with this, a cognitive link is established between that fragrance and a set of literary "memories" drawn from Hauptmann. Note that this is not simply an abstract idea of a connection. It is, rather, a cognitive fact. The scent of those trees causes the artist's mind subconsciously to access information, images, and feelings, experienced in reading Hauptmann's plays and stored in long-term memory. (Here and below I use *subconscious* to refer to nonconscious cognitive processes; in order to avoid a confusing ambiguity, I use *unconscious* in the psychoanalytic sense of ideas, etc., that are repressed.) In sum, selection principles help define a cognitive content, through rendering salient certain objects and relations, and help to locate that content in a larger cognitive framework—thereby making it available for literary or aesthetic use.

More exactly, cognitive activity, whether literary or not, relies on a system of organizing structures—most important, schemas, prototypes, exempla, and models. These terms are used somewhat inconsistently in the cognitive science literature. I shall be using them in the following way: A *schema* is a cluster of abstract rules that define the general features of a certain set of events or objects. These are arranged in what is called a "default hierarchy," such that the standard features are on top, with common exceptions listed below. Thus our schema of a bird would include the property "able to fly" as the default value, with various exceptions ("newborn," "injured," "penguin") listed as alternatives. A standard example of an event schema is that of going to a restaurant: we enter (exception: dining in a piazza), sit down (exceptions: go to counter, drive through), read a menu, and so on.

An *exemplum* is a single instance of a type—an individual object, event, or whatever. James Joyce is an exemplum of a writer, of a man, of an exile, and so on. Note that exempla too are defined by clusters of rules. My understanding of a friend is not merely a matter of, say, perceptual memories. Rather, it involves a wide range of inferences and patterned expectations. If I say, "Joe would never do that!" or "That's just like Arvind!" I am implicitly judging some recent behavior by reference to a principle that I have previously, and tacitly, formed concerning his attitudes, ideas, and actions.

A *prototype* is between a schema and an exemplum. It is a sort of prime case of a type, and is usually constructed out of exempla. For instance, our prototype of a bird is, roughly speaking, a robin—not a penguin or an ostrich or a hen, and not a particular robin, but a sort of robin in general. A prototype is, in effect, a schema fully specified for all default values (compare Bordwell 137).

A *model*, as I am using the term, is any cognitive construction—exemplum, prototype, or schema—that is employed outside of its standard domain of application. If I do not understand Biff very well and notice a certain similarity between Biff and Blinkie, I may try to use my knowledge of Blinkie to understand Biff. If so, I am using Blinkie, an exemplum, as a model for understanding Biff. But I may also try to understand the atom by drawing on my schema of a solar system, or I may investigate literary influence by drawing on my schema of language. In these cases, a schema is being employed as a model. (I should warn the reader that this use of *model* is somewhat idiosyncratic, though I think it captures much of what cognitive scientists wish to get at by means of the notion of a model—for example, its dynamism [see Holland et al. 12–14]. As I am using the term, *model* is more closely related to what Holland et al. term "analogical mapping" [292–96] and to the broad conception of metaphor in Lakoff and Johnson, or Kittay.)

Note that all these terms are, to a degree, contextual. Schema, prototype, and exemplum mark out a spectrum of abstraction. In other words, their values are relative, not absolute. I may have a schema of birds, with the robin as a prototype. But I may equally have a schema of robins. My friend Biff may be an exemplum of a human, but I may have a schema of Biff's way of writing an essay or dressing or speaking, with corresponding exempla of each. These terms indicate relations among mental entities, not properties of those entities considered in isolation.

It is also important to stress that all these terms refer to elements in a cognitive system that exists purely at the level of individual psychology. The clusters of rules that define schemas, prototypes, and exempla are, to use the model of linguistics, *idiolectal*. However much they may overlap from person to person, such rules must not be considered in any way autonomous or supraindividual. Some notion of a nonidiolectal language is unquestioningly assumed in most current literary theory. And when I discuss schemas with literary theorists, they invariably identify these with the meanings of some supraindividual language. However, in contemporary linguistic theory, the notion of a supraindividual language is widely rejected as at best redundant, at worst nonsensical (see, for example, Chomsky 25–31). As much recent work indicates, we have every reason to believe that there are only idiolects and that there is no such thing as "language" in the (vague) sense widely presupposed in literary study. These linguistic conclusions apply to literature *pari passu*—for the autonomous existence of a literary work is nothing other than the autonomous existence of language; no autonomous language means no autonomous linguistic objects (for example, words or sentences), and this means no autonomous literature. In the creation and reception of literature we find a range of structures at various levels of abstraction or generality. But all these structures are human and mental. They are not in the literature (indeed, I would argue that such a notion makes no sense). Rather, they are in the minds of authors and readers.

Turning to the nature and operation of these structures, we find that the broadest cognitive schemas employed in poieisis apply to all or most literary works (or types of literary work), cross-culturally and transhistorically. Others apply only within a culture, or period, or movement, or within the work of a single author. In other words, we may distinguish between the invariant features of plot, character, and so on, and the variable features, much as linguists distinguish the invariant features of syntax and morphology, and the variable features. The invariant features would be the object of a universal poetics, of the sort adumbrated in, for example, the work of Kiparsky (see, for example, "Roman Jakobson," "The Role of Linguistics"). The latter would be the object of sociological or psychological study, including studies of influence.

We may think of individual writers as having at their disposal a range of structures, of varying degrees of idiosyncrasy, but organized into an invariant structure according to universal principles. More exactly, we may conceive of literary conceptual structures as organized along the lines of an internal or mental lexicon. The mental lexicon is, roughly, a sort of dictionary plus encyclopedia stored in the mind as it might be stored in a computer. (For a clear, nontechnical introduction to the mental lexicon, see Aitchison. There is some controversy about precisely how lexical material is stored—see, for example, Garman 244; Schreuder and d'Arcais 409–10. Fortunately, none of this is crucial for our purposes.) Schemas, prototypes, and exempla are listed under appropriate categories with some sort of cross-indexing that leads from one entry to other relevant entries—from "Tuesday" to "Wednesday," for instance (see Garman 269). One can think of this cross-indexing as comparable to *see also* instructions in a dictionary. The set of items delimited by this cross-indexing is sometimes referred to as a "semantic field." The days of the week would form such a semantic field; hence the lexical entry for each day of the week would be cross-indexed to all the others, in this case probably by reference to the larger structure (for example, the entry for "Tuesday" might include something like: "Unit in series: days of the week [*see* 'days of the week']"). (For an excellent discussion of the various organizations of semantic fields, see Kittay 230–44.)

To take a more literary example, our entry for "character" is likely to include a series of types: hero, villain, and so on. These would be cross-indexed with separate entries for each item, and would form several semantic fields (a large one for character, smaller ones perhaps for "tragic character," "comic character," and so on). In other words, under "character," following some general properties, we would have the equivalent of "*see also* 'hero,' 'villain.'" Moreover, each of these cross-indexed entries would itself include a list of relations and properties (that is, heroic properties for the hero, villainous ones for the villain) as well as subcategories (for example, "romantic hero" and "romantic villain"). Moreover, they too would be cross-indexed for various relations, including: Opposition—for example, "romantic hero" would be cross-indexed with "romantic villain" ("Opposite of: romantic villain [*see* 'romantic villain']"). Identity or similarity—for example, "romantic villain" might be cross-indexed with "rival" ("Commonly equivalent to: rival [*see* 'rival']"). And various common plot links—for example, "romantic villain" might be cross-indexed with "beloved" in this way ("Action: romantically pursues hero's beloved [*see* 'beloved']").

In addition to the properties and relations that define such schemas, the cognition of literary character—whether productive (on the part of an author) or receptive (on the part of a reader)—involves prototypes and exempla as well. The exempla need not be biographical in origin; they may equally be historical or literary. And prototypes may combine features of all three. These often serve the most important modeling functions in both creation and understanding. To take a simple illustration, writers may define a fictional beloved in general terms through the use of one or more schemas, but they may go on to specify the particular attitudes or behaviors of that beloved by tacitly referring to their own nonfictional spouse as a model; similarly, they may rely implicitly on the exemplum of a historical figure or a character from another literary work. Ultimately, such biographical, literary, and historical exempla, along with related prototypes, contribute to the constitution of a set of principles specific to the character now being created, so that this character is defined not merely by a list of properties and relations, and not merely by analogies with preexisting models, but by a distinct generative structure. This is what makes a character well-formed, or autonomous. It is what allows authors or readers to judge what a character might do in new situations. In this case, the new character, too, becomes an exemplum.

Note that in the vast majority of cases all of this is subconscious. Certainly authors may plan to invoke a particular schema or to employ prototypes to specify a character or situation. But for the most part, and necessarily, they cannot be self-conscious about any but a fraction of their mental processes. Writing is like any other activity in this regard. If one wishes to do something as simple as catch a ball, one can hardly be thinking: "Now I must lift my left leg, pushing forward at the knee, and straightening my right foot, as I press with the ball of my right foot against the ground," and so on. Understanding and imagining are necessarily as highly automatic as jumping and running.

Note also that encoding too is a function of these mental structures. In the most ordinary cognition, we subconsciously invoke schemas, prototypes, and exempla to organize and interpret experience. Indeed, it is these schemas, prototypes, and exempla that function to delineate properties and relations in that experience. Take, for example, our ordinary understanding of other people. When we meet or even when we are told about someone, we are presented with a range of information. But only some of that information assumes saliency in our interpretation of that person's character. We may take into account certain aspects of their dress, their accent, their vocabulary, their specific opinions or references. Some of this we consider self-consciously. Most, we do not. These aspects are rendered salient by the schemas, prototypes, and exempla that we are implicitly using to understand our new acquaintance. Thus I may go away distrusting a new acquaintance, later realizing that he or she "reminded me" of the thoroughly untrustworthy John Doe. In other words, I was, subconsciously, employing John Doe as a model for understanding my new acquaintance.

As I come to know a person better, however, I rely decreasingly on other exempla and prototypes. I have, instead, subconsciously constructed a cluster of principles specific to that individual. This cluster too serves to encode certain properties and relations. For instance, it renders salient certain idiosyncratic signals of mood, so that I may know a good friend is angry or sad or happy through small and normally insignificant behaviors ("He always clears his throat like that when he's angry"). On the other hand, the earlier exempla do not become entirely irrelevant. Elements from these and from relevant prototypes and schemas (that is, principles drawn from individuals and from types) may be incorporated into the new structure. Moreover, the older constructs may be invoked at any time (as when, having been friends with someone, I revert to an initial, negative opinion: "I knew he was as untrustworthy as Doe right from the beginning" or, drawing on a schema rather than an exemplum, "How could I have let myself trust a self-proclaimed poststructuralist?").

This cognitive process is virtually identical to that found in the reading of literature. When interpreting a literary work, I tacitly invoke schemas, prototypes, and exempla—literary, as well as historical and personal. These mental structures function to encode information about, for example, characters, just as they might about real people; they also allow me to fill in unstated information, infer implicit motives and actions, and so on. Eventually, however, I come to construct the new character as a distinct exemplum, defined by clusters of rules, and these—rather than other exempla used as models—function to define the character in her or his particularity. In other words, as I am reading *A Portrait of the Artist*, I come to understand Stephen much as I might come to understand Jane Doe (a real person whom I meet) or James Joyce (a real person about whom I read).

More important for our purposes, a writer does the same thing when producing a work, as Tysdahl's nontechnical description of literary creation indicates. Whether beginning with personal experience (as did Joyce) or drawing on literary or other sources (as did Milton), authors use prior schemas, prototypes, and exempla as models for organizing and thinking through their material—until that material comes to be defined by its own distinct set of generative rules. Thus Joyce understood himself and those around him through such models, prominently including models drawn from literature. But as he began to write about Stephen or Cranly or Simon Dedalus, he began to form these characters themselves into exempla.

In all cases, the new exempla continue to be related in important ways to the models from which they were generated. Most obviously, they fit into larger schemas (for example, Stephen fits into the schema of the poet). And they maintain many properties of relevant prototypes. Conversely, they contribute to the redefinition of such schemas and prototypes. In constructing Stephen, Joyce slightly shifted his, and our, conception of the poet; by defining a new exemplum, he reconfigured the semantic field that determines the schema and, even more, the prototype. Finally, other exempla, as well as prototypes and schemas, may be invoked by the author or reader to explain, define, predict aspects of the new exemplum not yet determined by cognitive rules. (Again, these distinctions are relative, not absolute.)

Joyce's concept of the betrayer, one of his standard character schemas, illustrates these points and is illuminated by them. First, it involves universal elements. For instance, the emotional force of betrayal—as opposed to more general treachery—derives in part from the universal intensification of emotion through unexpectedness (see, for example, Ortony, Clore, and Collins 64–65). More idiosyncratic properties are in Joyce's schema as well: for example, a recurring connection of male, homosocial love with deceit, deceit related to a conflict over principle—for what stands between Joyce and his betrayers is Joyce's absolute commitment to principle, specifically aesthetic principle, the cursed Jesuit strain injected the wrong way. Beyond this, Joyce draws on various exempla: larger cultural exempla, such as the betrayal of Jesus by Judas (contributory to the more specific prototype for personal betrayal), or the betrayal of Parnell by Irish Catholics (contributory to the prototype for political betrayal), as well as exempla from personal life—especially Cosgrave and Gogarty.

Like any relational term, "betrayer" must be linked with another schema—in this case, the victim of betrayal. For Joyce, this victimized figure was specifically the rebel, or nonconformist, and the betrayal is linked to this nonconformism. This schema too has more general and more specific properties, associated prototypes, and so on. It incorporates the definitional elements of disestablishmentarian thought, as well as romantic elements of spiritual isolation, poetic elevation, and ill health. It cross-indexes a number of Christian martyrs as exempla, as well as a series of literary versions of Satan, beginning with Milton and extending through Defoe, Blake, Shelley, Byron, Marie Corelli, and others. These versions of Satan coalesce to form a prototype of Satan, or rather of the Satanic poet-rebel. Predictably, Joyce incorporated into this schema—and into the Satanic prototype—many elements of his own personality, physical condition, and so on.

In the preceding examples, I have focused on character, primarily because Milton's influence on Joyce is to a great extent manifest in terms of character. However, the same mental constructions operate in the same way at all levels of literary composition, from word choice to sentence formation to plot structure. Consider word choice. In some cases, a precursor poet can have a very strong influence on a writer's lexical preferences. Joyce alludes to this when he has J. J. O'Molloy mock the writers surrounding AE as the "opal hush poets" (7.783–84), the idea being that these writers have a striking preference for certain words, including *opal* and *hush*. This sort of lexical influence seems to operate in the following way. Our internal lexicon is not rigidly structured, like the list of words in a dictionary—"aardvark" always first, "zygote" last. Rather, it is akin to a word list in a computer, open to various sorts of reordering. Roughly speaking, the order of this lexicon represents the order in which we access items, and it is determined by context. Put crudely (and somewhat inaccurately), different words will be on top depending whether we are talking about the Gulf War or Wordsworth's prosody. Writing poetry provides a context comparable to any other, and thus it too engages a reordering of the lexicon. When a precursor influences a writer's diction, to a great extent this means that the writer has internalized the precursor's lexical hierarchization for the context of poetry. To advert to Joyce's example, if the precursor's lexicon puts *opal* and *hush* high on the list when writing poetry, the younger writer's lexicon will do the same and will result in an uncommonly frequent use of these words.

This is not all there is to it, however. Writing poetry is what cognitive scientists refer to as a multistage process (see, for example, Johnson-Laird 258–59). An author produces a line, reconsiders it, revises it. When producing the line, the author draws upon the internal lexicon, as hierarchized for the context of writing poetry. However, when rereading the line, he or she judges whether the words are the right words (also whether the sentence structure is right, and so on). "Right" here means a number of things—for example, thematically relevant. Most important, however, it means aesthetically effective in the explicit or implicit judgment of the author. An author writes a line or develops a story or creates a character. He or she then reexperiences that line, story, character and judges whether it produces the right effect. Ultimately, the author judges the entire work in this way, deciding whether it is complete, whether the whole is aesthetically effective.

Note that the bulk of this judgment is subconscious. It is not as if authors have a checklist of properties that will make the work complete. Indeed, they probably could not explain why they feel that a line must be revised, a plot element reworked, why slightly changing a character's attitude is "right," why one word or one order of words is better than another. Their decisions on these matters are the result of an extensive process of evaluation involving many subconscious components.

In the present context, perhaps the most important of these components are tacit adjudications relative to internalized aesthetic constructions. These constructions are of two sorts. First, authors have schemas, prototypes, and exempla that define aesthetic excellence for given communities or markets. One group prefers ironic distance (part of a schema) and Marguerite Duras (an exemplum); another group prefers patriotic sentimentalism and Sly Stallone. These cognitive structures provide a sort of aesthetic audience outside of the writer. Whether one construes success in economic terms or not, successful writers are clearly writers who reach an audience. To reach an audience, their evaluations cannot be idiosyncratic. The risk of aesthetic evaluation is that it will be too personal. I may write a poem and decide that it is aesthetically effective and finished, but find myself alone in this judgment. The evaluative use of such community-aesthetic schemas, prototypes, and exempla is, in part, to limit that idiosyncrasy by drawing on more commonly accepted principles.

Second, authors have various structures—the same or different—that manifest their own literary response. There are exempla that they find particularly aesthetically effective, prototypes and schemas that abstract features from their own aesthetic preferences. These too are crucial in subconscious evaluation. (Sometimes we have the feeling that a work is well made, but insincere. In part this is the result of authors evaluating their work relative to communal aesthetic structures, and not relative to personal aesthetic structures. One common problem with student writing is the precise opposite; the writer has evaluated it personally, but not communally. In fact, sometimes student poets have not yet internalized community-aesthetic structures for the community toward which they are aiming their poems; they are aiming toward readers of Adrienne Rich, but their community-aesthetic structures are drawn from Hallmark.)

More exactly, in the case of lyric poetry and diction, both personal- and community-aesthetic exempla would include clusters of words or lines from the works of precursor poets—lines from AE in the case of the opal-hush crowd. In judging whether a line of poetry is or is not right, then, the poet subconsciously compares the effect of the new line with that of the precursor lines, either in its direct, personal impact, or as a gauge of community or market response, or both. This is also where novelty enters, for at another level that subconscious judgment must not only compare the line in question with prior exempla, it must perform a more complex, second-order task. In the simplest terms, authors must subconsciously evaluate a homology: their line/the precursor's line//other contemporary lines of poetry/their precursor's lines. They must judge community-appropriate novelty as well.

The same considerations apply at the level of sentence construction. We all speak and write according to certain subconscious, internalized rules. These include rules of sentence formation. Some of these rules are optional and context-bound—for example, various rules of decorum limit the use of contractions in certain formal contexts. To be influenced at the level of sentence formation is to internalize optional rules peculiar to the sentence formation of the precursor. Milton frequently placed the direct or indirect object at the beginning of the sentence, inverted the order of nouns and adjectives (for example, "Ten paces huge / He back recoil'd" [*PL* 6.193–94], rather than "He recoiled ten huge paces"). To be influenced by Milton at the level of sentence structure is to internalize his principles of word-order inversion as optional rules, applicable in certain (poetic) contexts. As with diction, this will result in subconscious, automatic production. And these productions too will be reconsidered and revised, in part by comparison with exempla—in this case, lines from Milton. This too will be primarily subconscious. A poet does not look at a line and reject it, saying, "That just doesn't sound like Milton." Rather, the poet rereads a line, unreflectively considering it through particular schemas and in connection with various—Miltonic and other, communal and personal—exempla and prototypes, reacting to the properties and relations rendered salient by those cognitive structures. Ultimately, the poet will decide, for reasons that can be only partially articulated, that the line is or is not right.

The same is true for the larger structures of character and plot. Here too we are dealing with the internalization of rules that function productively and are combined with a revisionary use of exempla, and so on, in a multistage process. In the case of character and plot especially, this is primarily a matter of clusters of properties arranged by typology, as our previous instances of betrayer and rebel indicated. In these cases too, both production and evaluation make reference to a range of structures, with the new character subconsciously evaluated by reference to exempla (for example, Milton's Satan and Byron's Satanic Manfred), and so on.

Plot is, in a way, the most obviously schematic of all these categories. At the highest level of abstraction, we find universal schemas involving such general principles as causal connection between events. We have various more fully specified structures, ranging from the broad schemas of comedy and tragedy, through the more specific schemas of lovers separated and reunited, and the one just person destroyed by an unjust society. A plot schema of particular interest to us is that of the Fall of humankind. This schema typically includes a couple and some seductive interloper. It most often involves the seduction of the woman and leads, not to a specific loss, but to a transformation of the couple's relation to the world and to one another—a sort of alienation from or pervasive sadness regarding all of life, perhaps relieved by hope for redemption in the future. *Paradise Lost* provides one crucial exemplum of this plot. But various other works take up the same story, some based on Milton, some not. These are all exempla and they collectively define a prototype for the Fall. These structures also contribute to the generation and evaluation of new narratives. For example, such structures guide the way Joyce sets out the plot of *Exiles*, the details he chooses, and so on; they determine why he considers the conflict to be a conflict and the ending to be an ending. And this too is primarily subconscious. Although Joyce was no doubt aware of rewriting the Fall in *Exiles*, he was probably not aware of most of the details of this connection. Here too, much of what he wrote probably just seemed "right" and he would have been hard put to explain why.

All of the examples cited thus far concern positive influence. However, every aspect of literary production that is open to positive influence is equally open to negative influence. By producing a work that is ineffective or otherwise faulted, a precursor may provide a younger writer with an example of what he or she should not do. For example, Moore's locomotive error, denounced by Joyce, no doubt in combination with other instances of the same sort by Moore and other writers, exerted a negative influence on Joyce—something that can be seen in his almost obsessive concern with accuracy in particulars when composing *Ulysses*. These too are open to the same sort of cognitive explanation just discussed; the author constructs schemas to avoid the faults in question, revises the work in light of these schemas, along with exempla and prototypes that render salient what should be avoided (rather than what should be done). (For a discussion of negative influence, see Hermeren 42–50.)

The preceding examples are one-sided in another, more important way as well. Thus far, we have been looking primarily at the ways in which aesthetic creation is the same as ordinary cognition. However, it is not the same in every way. Specifically, the exempla of precursors, as well as various broader prototypes and schemas, have an important function in aesthetic response. This returns us to the difference between popular and elite literature. Elite literature, again, is written to be read in the context of an entire history of elite literature. In this way, Stephen is a character who demands to be read in the context of Milton's Satan, Byron's Manfred, and so on. In other words, the schemas, prototypes, and exempla drawn from precursors are important not only in the author's multistage creation and evaluation of a work, but in the reader's reception and appreciation of that work as well. Indeed, this is what gives aesthetic interest to a study of influence. When properly done, a study of influence does not merely recount a causal sequence that led to the production of a novel, poem, or play. Rather, it places the novel or poem or play in a literary context that aesthetically enriches it.

We may better understand this aesthetical aspect of literary cognition by further considering the *rasadhvani* theory of the Sanskrit aestheticians and by developing that theory, in part by reference to the cognitive structures we have been considering. Abhinavagupta maintained that a work of art is to be savored repeatedly. Specifically, Abhinavagupta argued that what should be savored in a work is dhvani, or suggestion (*Aesthetic Experience* xxxii). Ānandavardhana, the great theorist of suggestion, stressed that dhvani is not some sort of allegorical meaning or some paraphraseable implication of a literary work (see Ānandavardhana 204 and Abhinavagupta's comment in *Locana* 206). It is something more like a penumbra of associations, prominently literary associations. Indeed, the sahṛdaya is, by definition, familiar with the range of literary works that provide such associations. However, the sahṛdaya is not merely or even necessarily a scholar. *Sahṛdaya* literally means someone "with heart." A sahṛdaya is someone who can attune his or her feelings to the work, to the characters in the work, the events, and so on. Knowledge of past literature is important precisely to the degree that it contributes to this sympathy of feeling. It is for this reason that the most important form of dhvani is rasadhvani, the suggestion of rasa, or sentiment—whether that sentiment be love or anger or remorse.

As a complex of association and feeling, dhvani is linked with a sort of implicit memory. Abhinavagupta says that dhvani is the activation of "memory traces" (see *Locana* 116–17, 192, 225)—the tacit or subconscious stimulation of ideas, sensations, and associated emotions from long-term memory. Yet in experiencing dhvani, in "activating" these traces, we do not think of the ideas as such, reexperience the sensations, directly feel the emotions. Indeed, we only experience, unselfconsciously, a hint of the idea, an inkling of the emotion. If we fully recalled the memory, fully reexperienced the emotion, we would be distracted from the work of art. But the suggestion, the dhvani, becomes part of our literary experience, extending and enriching it. The echo of a phrase from Milton brings the phrase and the emotion of the phrase to the back of the reader's mind. The emotion bleeds into the poem. A Byronic image brings Manfred to the back of the reader's mind, and the emotion evoked by this subconscious recollection inflects the reader's experience of the new work.

This has parallels in ordinary life that help to clarify the process. Suppose I walk into a store and am suddenly sad, but do not know why. Later, I remember that on my last visit to that store I met a friend who died not long afterward. In this case, my entering the store activated the memory trace of that death. This activation did not bring the memory fully into consciousness; nonetheless, the emotion did seep through, in an attenuated form. There are experimental instances of the same sort. As Johnson-Laird points out: "people given two seemingly identical pictures of the same person reliably prefer one picture to the other, though they cannot say why. In fact, the person in the preferred picture has eyes with dilated pupils." Why do we prefer this picture? "When you see someone with dilated pupils it may be a sign that they are taking an interest in you, and your perceptual system can unconsciously register the fact, but signal to consciousness only an emotion with the person as its object" (379).

This process, though it involves emotion, is also best understood in terms of cognitive structures, and in relation to the lexicon. Whenever we interpret language, we access certain lexical entries, and "prime" a range of related entries (see Garman 494; Holland et al. 57), which is to say, we bring a range of related entries (including schemas, prototypes, and exempla) to the top of the lexicon, making them readily accessible, but not actually accessing them. Suppose I am writing about a university. Upon reading the word *university*, my readers will access the entry for "university" and prime such related entries as "college," "student," "professor," and so on. They will not actually access the entries in this semantic field, but they will (subconsciously) make them directly accessible.

In ordinary interpretation, we access only as much of the lexical entry as we need in order to interpret the utterance (that is, we do not access a range of literally nonrelevant ambiguities or associated memories; see Schreuder and d'Arcais 416). Thus, in interpreting the preceding sentences, readers presumably accessed enough of the entry of "university" to give a bare definition—institution for post-secondary education. It is unlikely that they accessed such cultural associations as Newman's "Idea of a University" or personal memories of their own university experiences. Ordinarily, our accessing of lexical entries is "shallow" in this sense. Related to this, in ordinary interpretation, priming fades quickly (see Garman 360–61). Though three sentences ago, all readers primed such entries as "student," by the beginning of this sentence, that priming had long faded. In other words, in ordinary interpretation, lexical activation is minimal.

If Abhinavagupta is right, however, in aesthetic reading, or savoring, our activation is far from minimal. First of all, our access to lexical entries is deeper—a plausible notion, for as Garman points out "almost certainly the lexicon allows for *degrees* of involvement of its component parts in the process of lexical access"; such access "is not an all-or-nothing affair" (298–99). In this case, it is not that we become conscious of more of the entry, but rather that more of the entry is brought near to consciousness. When Joyce refers to the university, we may or may not think of Newman. But our lexical entry for Newman and that for "The Idea of a University" are more likely to be primed if we are approaching Joyce's work in the aesthetic attitude (or "dhvani attitude" as Amaladass appropriately calls it). Similarly, in the course of aesthetic reading, fewer of the associatively primed lexical items will fade quickly.

This is not to say that everything we access or prime remains part of our aesthetic experience. Most of it must fade if there is to be an aesthetic experience at all, rather than some confused jumble of incoherent ideas and emotions. However, when the work is well made, and the reader sensitive ("with heart"), some memories and associations will repeatedly effect and thus sustain a pattern of primed entries. The emotion of these primed memories and associations will then accumulate, until the reader feels it as rasa: tragic pity, comic joy, romantic love, and so on. The experience of rasadhvani, then, is the experience of a coordinated set of lexical items that are primed but not accessed—lexical items that include literary and personal memories and all their associated feelings. (Note that these lexical items are not simply the single words mentioned in the text, but all those items that are triggered by situations, events, and broader structures as well.) The study of influence is aesthetically relevant insofar as it enriches the associative context in which we experience a work. We can now understand this as a matter of establishing cognitive networks that will allow the priming of entries for precursor works, and thus enhance the rasadhvani of the work at hand.

It is important to note that the preceding theory should be subjected to rigorous testing along the lines of standard research in cognitive psychology. However, there is already some supporting empirical evidence in the studies by Halasz, Larsen, Laszlo, and Seilman indicating that literary works give rise to more personal recollections than nonliterary works. There are many methodological problems with this research (primarily, it fails to control adequately for the content of the literary and nonliterary works and it fails to recognize the subject-relativity of aesthetic experience). Nonetheless, it does lend at least some prima facie support to the preceding development and extension of the rasadhvani theory, especially when considered in connection with related, nonliterary studies, such as that reported by Johnson-Laird.

Allusion, Influence, and Tradition

At the center of our cognitive analysis of influence is the notion of idiolect, a system of internalized rules. Before turning to psychoanalytic aspects of influence, it is worth pressing this notion into further service as a model for conceptualizing the various types of relation that may obtain between a writer and a precursor, or a new work and a precursor's work. One important distinction, relevant to cognitive issues and usefully viewed in linguistic terms, is that between allusion and influence. Allusion is something like quotation in ordinary language. It is not the assimilation of aesthetic or linguistic principles, but the partial repetition of another utterance. Allusion is certainly aesthetically important. It functions to call up for the reader a complex of associations from the literary context in which the author wishes to place his or her work. It directs and to a degree forces the reader's intertextual understanding. Related to this, allusions frequently derive from exempla important to the construction and reception of the later work. For this reason, we shall pay attention to Joyce's allusions to Milton. But allusion is not influence any more than quotation is rule-generated utterance.

Similarly, influence must be distinguished from self-conscious imitation, including structural imitation. Although imitation is usually more significant than allusion, it too is not the result of an assimilation of aesthetic principles from a precursor. It implies a more intimate relation between author and precursor than does mere allusion, but that is only because the self-consciously designed connections are more extensive and systematic. One could think of imitation in terms of translation according to fixed templates—for example, the sort of translation students are asked to do in elementary linguistics textbooks. Extending the analogy, we could think of allusion as the quotation of a foreign phrase. In the case of quotation/allusion and in that of translation/imitation, actual internalization of the rules of the foreign language is absent. (Imitation is, however, a common step in the internalization of rules, linguistic or aesthetic.)

This division is in accord with common, if most often vaguely formulated, views on influence. Thus, for example, Harold Bloom emphasizes that "[b]y 'poetic influence' I do not mean the transmission of ideas and images of earlier to later poets," but rather "a poet's stance, his Word, his imaginative identity," which, while "unique to him . . . is as much also his precursor's" (*Anxiety* 71). In a somewhat obscure way, Bloom is focusing on the same sorts of difference just outlined. Goran Hermeren draws similar distinctions and points out that whereas imitation is not influence *stricto sensu*, it is in some sense closer to influence than allusion. Indeed Hermeren adds several distinctions to the preceding list (see the table on 92), though not all seem significant. Of these, however, it may be worthwhile mentioning Hermeren's notion of "paraphrase." In literary terms this would be a retelling, such as Lamb's version of Homer or the various eighteenth- and nineteenth-century retellings of *Paradise Lost*. To recur to our model, this may be comparable to a free translation. In any case, it clearly does not involve the internalization of rules and is thus relevantly distinguished from influence in the narrow sense.

At another level, Hermeren distinguishes between the influence of individuals and the influence of groups (15), a distinction well worth considering in this context. Certainly writers are influenced by other writers individually and by schools. Prima facie, this may appear difficult to explain. However, once we understand aesthetic production and reception as principled activities, as matters of internalized schemas, etc., the nature of group influence becomes perfectly clear and, indeed, expected. When an author is influenced by a single precursor, he or she has abstracted certain principles from that precursor's work (and critical writings, perhaps) and assimilated them, possibly in a somewhat altered form; the author has, in addition, drawn exempla from that person's work, and so on. An author influenced by a school does the same thing, only he or she abstracts and assimilates principles from the works of a number of similar authors, rather than one only, forms prototypes out of exempla from a number of authors, and so on. This is a particularly simple matter when those authors themselves share schemas, prototypes, and so on—which is precisely what defines them as a school or movement. A good example of this is the Byronic hero, a prototype synthesized out of a range of exempla in a number of romantic authors.

Indeed, we could isolate several levels of influence here, extending from that derived from individual writers, through schools, to periods or genres, to the entire body of literature—for all of this contributes to the formation of aesthetic or literary idiolect. We tend not to speak this way only because, above the level of schools, "influence" becomes so diffuse and general that it appears more useful to separate it out as "education" or, in Eliot's usage, "tradition." Influence and tradition, then, are different in degree only, not in kind—just as local, regional, national, and international forms of a "language" are different in degree, not in kind. Moreover, in both cases the lines defining these distinctions are not fixed.

More generally, the assimilation of aesthetical principles involves a considerable range of factors and cannot be reduced simply to the relation between a writer and a single powerful precursor (though of course such singular relations are very important and indeed it is only from individual precursors that a new writer may abstract and assimilate even traditional principles—again, there is no language beyond idiolect). Claudio Guillen points to this broad complexity of influence when he writes that "[t]he genesis of a poem is, if not an endless process, an endlessly complex one—as extensive, within certain temporal limits, as our knowledge of the individual's inner life may be. Certain events or conditions are crucial in it, and others trivial; but of course no single event or condition controls, shapes, or elucidates the final dimensions of the work of art" (57).

In this context, it is worth turning for a moment to the work of Hans Robert Jauss. Jauss is one of the few writers to have understood influence in terms of rules. From a phenomenological and historical perspective, Jauss has sought to study the "interrelations of production and reception" in terms of the "continuous establishing and altering of horizons" (15, 23), which is to say the continuous synthesis of different aspects of a work and the continuous alteration of expectations that go along with this, both productively and receptively. Jauss sees reading as a process in which the rules learned in earlier readings are confirmed or altered. "A literary work," Jauss points out, "even when it appears to be new, does not present itself as something absolutely new in an informational vacuum, but predisposes its audience to a very specific kind of reception by announcements, overt and covert signals, familiar characteristics, or implicit allusions. It awakens memories of that which was already read, brings the reader to a specific emotional attitude, and with its beginning arouses expectations for the 'middle and end,' which can then be maintained intact or altered." Calling for a "textual linguistics" that could isolate the "specific rules of . . . genre or type of text," Jauss continues by explaining that "[t]he new text evokes for the reader (listener) the horizon of expectations and rules familiar from earlier texts, which are then varied, corrected, altered, or even just reproduced" (23).

Jauss bases his conception of reading on Husserl's notion of constitution. Constitution is a sort of synthesis. To take an example I have used elsewhere, imagine that you approach a statue. You see one aspect only—say the front. As you move around the statue, the visible aspect of the statue varies constantly. But you do not take all these different aspects as completely isolated. Rather, you synthesize them, combine them into a whole. From the moment you see the statue initially, you form expectations about what there is on the other sides of the statue, what you would see if a different aspect were presented to you. These projected aspects are the "horizons of expectation." (There is an amusing case of indeterminate horizons in *Ulysses* when Leopold Bloom, the "distinguished phenomenologist" [12.1822], seeks to ascertain anatomical details about the backside of a statue.) These horizons themselves derive from patterns constructed from past experiences of art and of life. Thus, if we see the front of an apparently human form, we expect the back to be human also, for the simple reason that we have a pattern—or schema—of the human form that we have built up out of art and life.

Clearly, the same sort of thing happens in literature. As Jauss points out, the "beginning arouses expectations for the 'middle and end'" (23). Certain events set up expectations for other events, certain behaviors for other behaviors, and so on. Let us suppose for the moment that the reader we are discussing is an author. Moreover, he or she is reading the work of an earlier author for the first time. (In fact, this seems to be the sort of situation Jauss has primarily in mind.) In this case, the sorts of expectation at issue are clearly more matters of "tradition" than of "influence." However, influence can enter when such expectations are disappointed, when the rules governing expectation are violated. Indeed, it is precisely this sort of deviation that makes influence isolable from tradition, for influence is precisely the assimilation of rules perceived as transgressive or in excess of or exterior to tradition. It is their difference from tradition that makes the principles of a school or an individual stand out as a potential influence.

Jauss discusses this difference or idiosyncrasy of one writer's principles in terms of "aesthetic distance," which he defines as "the disparity between the given horizon of expectations and the appearance of a new work, whose reception can result in a 'change of horizons' through negation of familiar experiences or through raising newly articulated experiences to the level of consciousness" (25). Jauss's point is that a given author's violations of standard or common principles may be slight or extreme—so extreme, indeed, as to cause utter incomprehension in readers. The later works of Joyce provide paradigm examples.

Interestingly, the sort of incomprehension Jauss points to can in certain cases be greater for the aficionados of elite art than for others. For both cognitive and economic reasons, those immersed in the tradition will have a firmer sense of standard or "professional" principles and a greater investment in these. Thus they will frequently be confined in their openness to innovation. An amusing example of this is to be found in a story about John Constable, recounted by E. H. Gombrich. At a time when the normative principles of painting favored brown foregrounds, Constable began to break with common practices and insert some green; he was, after all, depicting grass. One day, Constable was "sitting on the jury of the Royal Academy, of which he was a member, when by mistake one of his own paintings was put on the easel for judgment, and one of his colleagues said rashly, 'Take that nasty green thing away'" (48). In literature, many writers have argued that their work was rejected due to the distorting influence of standard views. For example, Shaw frequently claimed that his plays were seen as unrealistic precisely because he had characters act realistically and thus radically undermined the expectations of critics who had formed their conceptions of human character on the basis of fundamentally unrealistic drama (see Shaw 44). In a similar vein, it is perhaps not accidental that many of Joyce's earliest admirers were not "professionals," and it is certainly not accidental that for most of his career he had great difficulty in finding presses willing to publish his work. In any case, the important point for our purposes is that it is precisely the nontraditional principles of precursors' works that can function influentially; it is the principles that defy, or at least exceed tradition that can be understood to be assimilated from individuals or schools.

This brings us to a final distinction relevant to the cognitive aspect of influence—that between influence and derivativeness. This is, obviously, a normative issue and thus in some ways difficult to pin down. However, a normative judgment of derivativeness is based on a descriptive judgment concerning the degree and nature of influence, and I think it is possible to say something about this that might add a degree of descriptive precision and go some way toward explaining the distinction. Most obviously, a writer P is derivative of a writer Q if the influence of Q on P is in some sense "too extensive" or "stifling of P's individuality." This is the vague sense in which we most often use the notion of derivativeness. We can recognize it, but we find it hard to say precisely what it is.

In order to begin to gain a better understanding of this distinction, we need first of all to recognize degrees of derivativeness. Indeed, it is best to think of derivativeness not as something opposed to influence, but rather as a degree of influence. In other words, derivativeness and influence are not two different things. Rather, as the weight of influence increases, we begin to judge a work more derivative. However, this is not a simple calculation. Thus two authors may share many aesthetic principles and the later author may not be considered derivative of the earlier author. In contrast, two authors may share a relatively small number of aesthetic principles and the later author might still be considered derivative. Why is this?

The first thing to consider in examining derivativeness is what principles the author and his or her precursor share. However, mere shared principles are not enough. First of all, the shared principles must not be merely local. There are principles that are fundamental to style or narrative development, and others that govern only marginal phenomena. Thus an author who takes preferences for setting, character types, and plot structures from another author is more likely to be considered derivative than an author who takes a preference for having one or another character use tag questions (for example, "you know what I mean?"). An author who writes about nothing but people in obscure landscapes crawling through mud for no evident reason is more likely to be considered derivative of Beckett than an author who happens to put pomeranians into a lot of his or her works. Even a great many principles of the latter sort would not make the later author derivative. This is, of course, widely recognized.

Just as obviously, the relevant shared principles must be extratraditional. Clearly, one author cannot be considered derivative of another if the rules they share are shared by everyone—after all, he or she cannot even be considered genuinely influenced if the shared principles are traditional. However—and this is perhaps the most interesting, because least obvious point—not all extratraditional principles are equal in their nontraditionalism. To return to our linguistic model, we can think of traditional principles as "unmarked" and extratraditional principles as "marked," as contrary to tendency, as involving "aesthetic distance." As Jauss indicates, there are many degrees of aesthetic distance, and thus there are many degrees of markedness for extratraditional principles. For example, the extratraditional principles of *Finnegans Wake* are more marked than those of *Ulysses*, which are themselves more marked than those of *Dubliners*. Derivativeness, then, also varies with the degree of markedness of shared principles. As the interior monologue of *Ulysses* developed in an obvious way out of previous refinements in point of view, it is less marked (less aesthetically distant) than the partial creation of new language, the fusing of character and setting that appears in *Finnegans Wake* seemingly without precedent. Thus using interior monologue will contribute less to a judgment of derivativeness than creating a new language, à la *Finnegans Wake*.

But this is not all there is to the matter. Part of the reason for our judgments in these cases is not only that such language creation was not traditional before Joyce and involved great aesthetic distance then but also that it did not become traditional after Joyce and, therefore, still involves great aesthetic distance. Derivativeness is a partial function of degree of markedness both during *and after* the composition of the precursor's work. Indeed, the degree of markedness at the time of the younger writer and, even more important, at the time of the evaluator seem to be the crucial factors, not the degree of markedness at the time of the precursor. In other words, were Jane Doe to publish a novel in a created, wakean language right now, the book would most likely be judged derivative. However, were many people to publish wakean novels, Doe's book would come to appear less and less derivative. (There are economic as well as cognitive reasons for this, having to do with the way in which innovations can be marketed.)

Thus derivativeness is a function of two scales: the degree of pervasiveness of common principles (that is, the degree to which principles common to author and precursor govern the larger structures of their works, as opposed to governing merely local elements) and the degree of markedness of those common principles, primarily at the time of evaluation. (I assume throughout, of course, that the principles of the later author have been actually derived from the precursor, that we are not dealing with mere accidental parallels.) A high degree of both will guarantee a judgment of clear derivativeness; a low degree of both will exclude such a judgment; other combinations will yield less certain evaluations.

The Psychoanalysis of Influence

As already noted, affective factors in influence have been more widely discussed than the cognitive factors to which we have been attending. Moreover, as we have already addressed certain issues of affective influence in connection with the theories of Harold Bloom, and more importantly in relation to the Sanskrit writers, there is less to say about this topic—though affective considerations will be of great importance in the following analyses.

The first distinction that it is important to draw in this context lies on the border dividing psychology from economy: the distinction between the textual manifestation of influence and the author's statements about influence. Especially in a culture that values innovation in art, an author may be highly motivated to deny influence even when, perhaps especially when, it is clearly manifest in his or her work. This is particularly true when the influence is extensive. But it may occur even when the influence is minor—especially when the influencing figure is in some way a competitor. Perhaps Joyce's relations to figures such as Synge and Moore fall into this category. For example, while Synge was alive, Joyce had hardly a decent thing to say about him. However, Joyce's behavior showed that he admired Synge greatly. Moreover, Joyce was clearly influenced by Synge, though in a very limited way. After Synge's death and Joyce's own partial success, Joyce could speak more generously of Synge. In contrast, Joyce could unproblematically affirm the more considerable, though still limited, influence of, for example, Ibsen. Presumably this is because Synge was considered the young genius of the Irish literary revival, whereas Ibsen was barely known in Ireland. Synge was competition. And Ibsen, far from being competition, was a figure who could be invoked against competitors.

A more important distinction is that between conscious and unconscious affective relations. An author may deny influences dishonestly, while being well aware of the presence of those influences in his or her own work. However, an author may equally be unconscious of influence. Moreover, an author may consciously deny influence for conscious, rational reasons or for unconscious reasons. Thus, for example, Joyce might deny the influence of Synge or Milton or any other given writer, while being perfectly conscious that Synge or Milton has indeed exerted an influence. On the other hand, Joyce might equally be completely unaware of that influence. Finally, he may recognize the influence and deny it either for reasons of rational self-interest (for example, fear of competition) or for unconscious reasons (for example, because of a negative transference onto Synge, Milton, or whomever).

More generally, I would understand the unconscious affective component of influence primarily in terms of transference and identification, including what might be called identificatory idealization. Very simply, transference is the assimilation of some contemporary figure to an infantile construction or "imago," especially an Oedipal construction of a parent. In the transference, we have unconsciously identified some person from our present life with our infantile conception of someone with whom we had a psychologically conflicted relation in a critical period of childhood. Or, rather, with one part of that infantile conception. Typically, we "split" our imagoes into positive and negative, and specify them according to their role in various (unconscious) fantasies. Thus the mother imago may be split into virginal and lascivious, the father imago into protecting and punishing. Transference of any sort—positive or negative, virginal or lascivious, admiring or fearing—distorts our relations with the object of the transference by systematically biasing our actions toward, reactions to, and fantasies about him or her (including our interpretations of the person's speech and behavior).

Once again, it is my view that there are no special literary transferences—and thus no special literary Oedipal struggles. There are only ordinary transferences and, granted the general outlines of psychoanalytic theory, the burden of proof is on those who would wish to claim differently. In any event, authors can and do enter into ordinary transferential relations with precursors, and these distort the later author's relation to that precursor—including the response to that author's work. Moreover, precursors are not the only objects of an author's transferences. Characters enter into the fantasy life of readers, including those readers who are authors, in what is, in effect, a transference relation. Indeed, part of the effect of literature may be necessarily transferential. For example, it may be that the transferential assimilation of literary characters and struggles to our own Oedipal or other unconscious conflicts is a necessary part of our aesthetic experience of plot structure.

It may seem odd to speak of transference relations with fictional characters. However, it does not matter whether the object of transference is real or not. In relevant respects, our relation to fictional characters is much the same as our relation to real people. After all, when reading a novel, we suspend disbelief and respond to the characters as if they were real. (Who would cry over the tragic fate of a mere cluster of words or an image in the author's fancy?) Indeed, we most often have a greater sense of a character's reality than we do of an author's—or of most other real people's. Indeed, we understand real people and fictional characters in terms of the same cognitive structures, through which we encode properties and relations, model new constructions, and so on. Transference, either to real people or to fictional characters, is merely a special case of this sort of activity. Specifically, it is the case in which the schemas, prototypes, and exempla are infantile, are implicated in profound psychosexual conflicts, and are not merely subconscious but "dynamically unconscious," which is to say, repressed.

Like transference, identification and identificatory idealization also appertain to both characters and authors. Specifically, a reader may assimilate an author or character not only to a fantasy about someone else (for example, an infantile imago of a parent), but equally to a fantasy about him- or herself. This sort of "mirroring" connection with a precursor or character may take one of two forms; it may involve assimilating that precursor or character to one's ego image (including unconscious and infantile elements of that image) or to one's ego ideal. In the first case, the character or precursor is seen as a version of the self, and the self is reviewed through the character or precursor. In the second case, the character or precursor is seen as an ideal that the reader/later author might imitate. (This is more properly considered a complex phenomenon involving identificatory and transferential components. I classify it with identification because that aspect is more important in the present context.)

Switching to cognitive principles, we would say that in identification one comes to understand oneself through the exemplum of someone else and one comes to understand the other person/character through one's exemplum of oneself. In identificatory idealization, in contrast, one comes to understand the other person/character in terms of schematic and prototypical ideals and to see the other person/character as an exemplum of those ideals. Moreover, one comes to judge one's potential accomplishments, to guide one's decisions, in part, by reference to this new exemplum. Thus I may identify with someone and, say, buy gifts for that person based on my own personal preferences, which I tacitly (and perhaps incorrectly) assume to be shared. Or I may idealize a person and, for instance, unreflectively follow that person's voting patterns on the tacit assumption that his or her views and interests are an ideal version of my own. Clearly, there are degrees of both identification and identificatory idealization, and either may operate within a broader or a narrower context. I might identify with and idealize someone in a variety of areas, mimicking clothing, taste in music, mannerisms, work patterns, or intellectual preferences. However, I might equally identify with and idealize someone only in the narrow context of political attitudes, not extending this to aesthetic preferences.

In terms of literature, a younger author may come to identify with a precursor, and especially to idealize him or her in that identification. This most often involves the younger author assimilating him- or herself to the precursor and imitating the precursor in any number of things from literary style to personal appearance. When this occurs, it is clearly significant for the study of influence. And it does occur: sometimes in a flamboyant manner, where the young writer engages in an elaborate, adolescent mimicry of the precursor; sometimes in a quiet and rather private manner, which may be far more significant. Moreover, an idealizing identification may be repressed in a roughly Bloomian manner and resurface in an altered form, distorted by defense mechanisms. For example, it might reappear in a "reaction formation," turned into its opposite, the younger poet now inverting the style, life, preferences of the precursor, point for point. One could argue, for example, that Samuel Beckett's spare and lucid prose style, as well as his (evidently) more or less regulated later life, constitute such a reaction formation against an earlier identificatory idealization of Joyce. However, it is important to keep in mind that personal identification with a precursor and the cognitive assimilation of aesthetic principles employed by that precursor are independent processes. Cognitive assimilation can and most often does proceed without such identification. An author might personally identify with and even idealize a relatively minor aesthetic influence and not personally identify with a strong aesthetic influence. Moreover, even the most intense identificatory idealization is insufficient to produce the internalization of rules: identification with Joyce does not, in and of itself, result in the ability to write Joycean prose.

Identifications with characters are in some ways more important for literary production (and reception) than identifications with precursors—perhaps unsurprisingly, as they already involve a literary object. Moreover, here identifications are not so commonly idealizing. No doubt readers, including authors, can and do seek to become like certain characters about whom they read, just as they can and do seek to become like certain authors. But they equally come to see themselves in characters and to see or understand themselves through characters. Indeed, Joyce appears to have been more likely to relate to characters as ego images, and, as I shall argue, did so significantly in the cases of Milton's Satan and, later, Milton's Adam. Here and elsewhere, it is important to emphasize that this identification with an ego image is bidirectional (like all cognitive construction); it involves the author seeing him- or herself *in* the character and, at the same time, seeing him- or herself *through* the character. Thus, when Joyce identified with Milton's Satan, he simultaneously used himself as a model for the character and the character as a model for himself.

Transference too can apply to characters as well as authors. And the same bidirectionality we have been discussing obtains there also. I suggest, for example, that Joyce transferred one part of a split mother imago (the sexual or lascivious mother) onto Milton's Eve, and the other (virginal) part onto Dante's Beatrice. But this was not a simple transference where Joyce projected completely fixed unconscious fantasies onto the literary characters. The literary characters themselves, especially in their relation to characters with whom Joyce himself identified (Satan, Adam, and Dante), reacted back on Joyce's fantasies and to a degree altered, developed, redirected, respecified his imagoes. The analysis of transference and identification in influence is comparable to the analysis of repression in psychoanalysis. There it is not merely the "primary" or initial infantile repression that is important but the primary repression as reconstrued and reelaborated in a series of secondary repressions, subsequent experiences, and fantasies, which have been repressed precisely because they are linked with the primary repression. So too, in the analysis of influence, it is not merely the initial transferential fantasy that is important, but that fantasy as reconstrued and reelaborated in a series of literary transferences.

In cognitivist terms, we could say that repressed structures are elaborated through subsequent experiences, including literary experiences, which they in part encode. The initial exemplum or prototype or schema would be unspecified for a large number of properties and relations; subsequent experiences would serve to elaborate these, at least as possible alternatives. To take a banal example, a repressed maternal prototype may come to be triggered by a certain sort of clothing (for example, a nun's habit), deriving not from one's mother, but from subsequent transferences (for example, onto primary school teachers). Similarly, in literature, an author's expression of an unconscious prototype (or imago) may incorporate a wide range of properties drawn from literary characters that the author has unconsciously assimilated to the initial, parental exemplum—as in the cases of Beatrice and Eve for Joyce.

It is important to stress here that both transference and identification, though standardly spoken of in terms of persons and imagoes, are equally matters of fantasies. In other words, they can be construed in terms of plot just as they can be construed in terms of character. The two are, in fact, inseparable. For example, maternal imagoes are maternal imagoes precisely insofar as they have a place in particular fantasies. Thus we could say that Joyce understands the story of Beatrice in relation to one complex of fantasies surrounding his mother, and reelaborates that complex in relation to that story. Similarly, we could speak of the story of Manfred or the story of Satan in connection with Joyce's fantasies about himself, rather than speaking of Joyce's identification with these characters. It does not really matter which phrasing we adopt, for the two are in effect equivalent. What is important, however, is that we recognize this equivalence and the inseparability of imagoes and fantasies.

Finally, these transferences to and identifications with characters have an aesthetic function. They tie an author's own characters and stories to unconscious imagoes and fantasies and thus to the most powerful and significant elements of his or her psyche. Through the usual procedures of revisionary evaluation relative to subconscious communal aesthetic structures, the author may create a work that establishes the same type of (unconscious) link in the minds of the readers—and such a link defines the most intense sort of rasadhvani. Unconscious imagoes and fantasies have precisely the same indirect emotional impact as primed, but unaccessed, memories. Only, in the case of imagoes and fantasies, the feelings are stronger and more fundamental to our psychological life. (For a developed theory of literary response along roughly these lines, see Norman Holland.)

In summary, influence involves cognitive and affective elements. As to the former, all aesthetic production, all production guided by aesthetical intent, is rule-governed in the way in which linguistic production is rule-governed. Internalized, idiolectal rules defining schemas, prototypes, and exempla—organized hierarchically in cross-indexed lexical entries—guide the entire range of aesthetic productions, from prose rhythm to characterization to plot causality. *Tradition* refers to the rules common to a large body of writers. It is only extratraditional individual rules that are properly considered under the heading of influence (along with rules peculiar to a certain school or movement, which provide a transitional case). The idiosyncrasy of the rules and the pervasiveness of their function in the new artist's work determine the degree to which the new artist may or may not be considered derivative. All such rules operate in a multistage process involving revisionary evaluation by reference to both personal and communal exempla, etc. An aesthetically successful work primes but does not access a range of relevant memories and associated emotions in a reader's mind. The patterning of these memories and emotions is the rasadhvani of the work and forms the basis for a reader's aesthetic experience of that work, when the reader approaches the work in the aesthetic attitude, which is to say, as an object of beauty to be savored or lingered over. This savoring or lingering over may be defined as a subconscious deepening of lexical activation and prolonging of lexical priming.

Affectively, authors may accept or deny influence. And they may do so honestly or duplicitously, for conscious or unconscious motives. The unconscious aspects of influence may be divided into those based on transference and those based on identification, with identificatory idealization as an intermediate case. These transferences and identifications derive from unconscious, split imagoes along with associated fantasies and operate in the usual psychoanalytic manner. They may take as their object either the author or one of the author's literary characters. Of these, the relations to characters appear to have a more central function in the development of influence. Such transferences and identifications serve to link literary characters and narrative sequences with powerful unconscious imagoes and fantasies, and to further specify these imagoes and fantasies. This link, freed of idiosyncrasy through revisionary evaluation, may become a crucial part of the rasadhvani of a new work.

Finally, this entire psychological scenario is located within a historical economy of literary production. This economy organizes the field of literature and determines necessary conditions for literary success relative to targeted markets—for literary success is nothing other than one form of market success. Though various sorts of affinity (for example, gender, region, class, profession) define important markets, one particularly significant marketing distinction in late capitalist society is that between readers who presuppose a canon with historical depth and those who do not; marketing to the former relies primarily on product innovation, whereas marketing to the latter relies primarily on obsolescence—or, equivalently, the mere disappearance—of old products. This difference has two consequences. First of all, novelty (or at least the convincing appearance of novelty) becomes an imperative for the former (elite literature), but not for the latter (popular literature). Thus elite literature comes to value a maximal difference from precursors, a maximal evasion of influence. Yet at the same time, the broader context of elite literature determines that relations with precursors form a crucial part of the dhvani of a new work. Insofar as it operates aesthetically, the new work must in part activate relevant memory traces of cohort works, patterning them in such a way as to enhance its own rasa. These two factors make influence in elite literature a crux of particular conflict and particular importance, both intellectually and aesthetically.

Chapter 2

Joyce Agonistes: Reading Milton in Contexts

Joyce, even more than many other writers, sought from a young age to crush his competitors. He stole and criticized, incorporated and ridiculed. And he often praised lavishly those who could never compete with him. Extending a common modernist practice, he had a particular tendency to parody important precursors, as a number of critics have indicated. Discussing Joyce and Ibsen, Tysdahl notes that "Joyce often parodies what he makes important use of. Parody, in Joyce, very rarely amounts to an abnegation of the thing parodied" (13). Ellmann points out that *Ulysses* is in some ways "a great joke on Homer," but, he adds, "jokes are not necessarily so simple, and these [uses of Homer] have a double aim." Joyce's parodies are both "mock-heroic" and "the ennoblement of the mock-heroic" (*James Joyce* 360). Mary Reynolds, in her study of Joyce and Dante, points out that "Joyce's own transformations, like the comments on Dante he made to friends, often have elements of burlesque and frequently of irony, but they never imply a reductive view of [*The Divine Comedy*], its purposes, or its author" (4). Joyce similarly burlesqued Aristotle, refashioning his most influential poetic concepts into implicit puns and in-jokes, while at the same time making serious use of less-known Aristotelian ideas (see Hogan "Influxes").

But there is more to Joyce's defensive response to both influence and competition than parody. Indeed, Ibsen, Homer, Dante, and Aristotle are among the rather small number of truly important writers whose influence Joyce acknowledged. And in the cases of Ibsen and Aristotle, we have already seen the degree to which the invocation of these authors served to displace threatening contemporaries—primarily the antirealist mythographers and Platonists of the Celtic revival.

Tysdahl captures Joyce's response to influence best when he writes:

> Joyce does acknowledge some literary debts readily—and indeed with some *bravura*. It is interesting to note, however, that the authors whom he thus acknowledges are so widely different from him in most respects that no one would ever suppose their influence to be something that was not completely under Joyce's own control. He pointed to Edouard Dujardin's *Les Lauriers sont coupes,* for instance, as the source of the interior monologue. But nobody knew of Dujardin except as a minor symbolist poet; he was clearly not a writer whose reputation could overshadow Joyce's; and, despite the device of the interior monologue, which Dujardin had certainly made use of many years before Joyce, the differences between *Les Lauriers sont coupes* and *Ulysses* are enormous. Moreover, the stream of consciousness method is only one among many novel stylistic devices in *Ulysses.* In short, Joyce's claim to originality was in no danger here. (212)

Tysdahl goes on to cite Joyce's contrasting treatment of Freud and Vico, thereby hinting at a response to influence quite typical of Joyce: the pairing and opposing of a repudiated figure and a lauded figure, the latter providing the value against which the former, a possible competitor, is devalued. Sometimes this appears to be purely a matter of competition; at other times, it is probably a matter of genuine preference. Perhaps most important, in certain cases—and the case of Milton and Dante is one of these—the conjunction appears to have deeper roots, both psychological and political. Before going on to Milton, however, I will briefly overview Joyce's relations with some other important precursors and contemporaries.

Predecessors and Competitors

As is well known, there are almost countless instances of Joyce repudiating precisely the authors he used. Because Joyce saw his project, in part, as one of realism, his relation to realists is a good place to start. Gustave Flaubert, probably the most influential and highly esteemed writer associated with the realist movement, provided Joyce with several elements of his early technique. Joyce derived from Flaubert his ideal of the author as a god present everywhere in the work, but visible nowhere (see Gifford *Joyce*

Annotated for 215:15–18 and citation). In line with this, Flaubert was perhaps the great master of unintrusive narration. And when Joyce rewrote *Stephen Hero* into *A Portrait*, he sought to follow Flaubert in eliminating authorial interventions. Moreover, Joyce's interest in combining realism with symbolism was, if not derived from Flaubert, at least confirmed by him. No less than Joyce in his epiphanies, Flaubert sought symbols in reality, and was not averse to arranging them in the manner we have come to think of as typical of *Ulysses*—as for example in the famous agricultural fair, where Rodolphe is making love to Emma, and the announcer, speaking of manures, is providing an unwitting commentary on Rodolphe's less than sincere expressions (see 167–69). Ezra Pound noticed similarities right from *Dubliners* and maintained that with this collection "English prose catches up with Flaubert" (quoted in Cross 17). Budgen remarks that Joyce "knew by heart whole pages of Flaubert" (176). And critics from Pound to Gilbert to Cross have noted the influence of Flaubert's *Tentation de Saint Antoine* on the Circe episode of *Ulysses* (see Cross 126; Stuart Gilbert 320–23). However, when Edmond Jaloux once praised the *Trois Contes*, Joyce petulantly took up the book, insisted that it was a flawed work, and began to isolate what he averred, incorrectly, were errors in Flaubert's French (see Ellmann *James Joyce* 492, 492n). If it had come from a lesser author, the response would simply be embarrassing.

Joyce's fellow Irishman George Bernard Shaw is another case in point. Ellmann tells us, in a note to Joyce's essay on A. E. W. Mason, that Joyce "followed [Shaw's] career attentively" (*CW* 131n). The second performance of Joyce's English Players in Zurich included Shaw's *Dark Lady of the Sonnets* and their second season began with *Mrs. Warren's Profession* (see Ellmann *James Joyce* 440, 445). More important, Joyce fairly clearly modeled *Exiles* in part on Shaw's *Candida*. However, in writing and speaking about Shaw, Joyce regularly denounced him as a "preacher" (see, for example, *CW* 208) and a "mountebank" (Ellmann *James Joyce* 440). (For a fuller discussion of the influence of Shaw on Joyce, see Black.)

Similarly, in Trieste in 1908, when attending a play by Turgenev, Joyce exclaimed, "Nobody back home has any idea there are artists like these" (Ellmann *James Joyce* 266). Moreover, Joyce's portrait of Stephen in *Ulysses* seems to owe at least something to Turgenev's Bazarov from *Fathers and Sons* (as Anne Graziano has argued in unpublished work). But Joyce disparaged Turgenev, refused to share Stanislaus's admiration for him (235), and compared him unfavorably with Lermontoff (207n).

Joyce called George Moore "stupid" for his errors in realism. But in his youth, Joyce so admired Moore and Edward Martyn's *Bending of the Bough* that he set out to write his own play for the Irish Literary Theater, *A Brilliant Career* (see Ellmann's note to Joyce's "Day of the Rabblement," *CW* 68). Only one year later (in 1901), Joyce referred to the two as "not writers of much originality" (*CW* 71). In Trieste, Joyce and Francini Bruni began to translate Moore's *Celibates* (Ellmann *James Joyce* 187). They translated only the first few chapters, but one of these, "Mildred Lawson," "ends with a woman ruminating in bed," rather like *Ulysses,* as Ellmann has pointed out (*James Joyce* 188). Reed Dasenbrock has argued that *Hail and Farewell* was an important, unacknowledged precursor of the "mythic method" of *Ulysses* (see 198–99). Peter Costello has maintained that *Vain Fortune* contributed to the climactic confession scene in "The Dead" (172). And Ellmann notes that Joyce used the ending of Moore's *Lake* when writing the ending of chapter 4 of *A Portrait* (*James Joyce* 234), though this evident admiration did not keep Joyce from denouncing precisely that ending: "Yerra, what's good in the end of *The Lake*? I see nothing," he wrote to Stannie (234).

Joyce was equally unforthcoming about other contemporaries. As to Marcel Proust whom, on their one meeting, he followed like a lost puppy (see Ellmann *James Joyce* 508–9)—he said "I cannot see any special talent" (488). Perhaps fearing comparison, Joyce refused to allow "seedcake" to be translated as "madeleine" in the French version of *Ulysses* (508). Despite his close associations with Ezra Pound, when asked for a comment on Pound by the editor of *This Quarter,* Joyce confined his praise of Pound to a discussion of how kind and brilliant Pound had been *in helping Joyce* (*CW* 253–54). In a more narrowly literary context, Jane Ford has maintained that "[t]he textual affinities between *The Secret Agent* and *Ulysses*—both manifest and latent—juxtaposed against the subtly deprecatory references to Conrad himself embody the anxiety of influence" (14). And Daniel Mark Fogel has argued similarly regarding Joyce's relation to Henry James.

Returning to the Irish competition, Joyce referred to James Stephens as "my rival, the latest Irish genius" (Ellmann *James Joyce* 333). When they first met, Joyce insisted that Stephens should give up writing, and, in a criticism akin to those he leveled against Flaubert, insisted that Stephens "did not know the difference between a semi-colon and a colon" (Ellmann *James Joyce* 333). He later claimed that Stephen's masterpiece, *The Crock of Gold,* was inferior work, something "anybody" could have written (591). Yet when he thought (however melodramatically) of abandoning *Finnegans Wake* to another writer, Stephens was the only writer he could imagine taking his place (591–92). Indeed, *The Crock of Gold* is one important influence on the *Wake* and on other of Joyce's works—Pan providing an important sexualization of Milton's Satan and thus contributing to Joyce's schema of the seducer, Caitilin serving as one model for Issy, and so on.

Joyce's antipathy for Lady Gregory is well known. He publicly criticized her *Poets and Dreamers*. Like his criticisms of Yeats, this was in some ways brave and necessary if he was to preserve his intellectual independence. Indeed, Joyce's criticisms of most authors are quite reasonable. The point is not that Joyce's criticisms are always or even usually wrong; rather, the point is that he rarely acknowledges his debts to those he criticizes. In line with this, one wonders if *Cuchulain of Muirthemne* might not have had a more positive effect on Joyce. For example, it is difficult to read Stephen's transformative slang "God becomes man becomes fish becomes barnacle goose becomes featherbed mountain" (*U* 3.477–79) without recalling the similarly constructed speech in the dialogue of Cuchulain and Emer (37ff.). More important, it might have provided Joyce with one model for Emma in Emer (not only in name, but in her qualities—see Gregory 36).

Staying within the circle of the Irish revival, we find a more noteworthy case in John Millington Synge. Joyce first met Synge in Paris in 1903 and borrowed the manuscript of *Riders to the Sea*. Yeats had praised the play as "Greek" (quoted by Joyce in his "Pola" notebook, in Scholes and Kain 85). Joyce relentlessly criticized the play, on Aristotelian grounds, both to Synge himself and to Stannie. Demonstrating the play's Aristotelian flaws was no doubt a way of undermining Yeats's praise. Later, Joyce refused to take Synge's part in the playboy riots (Ellmann *James Joyce* 240), and later still he ridiculed Synge in "Gas from a Burner," envisioning him flying aloft, angel-like, clad in pilfered women's undergarments (*CW* 244). But from the very first reading, Joyce took the trouble to memorize large sections of Synge's play (Ellmann *James Joyce* 124). Later, he sought to translate the play into Italian (282), put it on his second playbill for the English Players, and many years after, again in Paris, he borrowed the play from Sylvia Beach's lending library (489). He also incorporated elements from Synge's *Shadow of the Glen* into Davin's encounter in *A Portrait* (a connection noted by Phillip Herring [45] and developed by Chris Congdon [in unpublished work]).

Perhaps the most striking case of denunciation is that of Yeats. It is well known that Joyce as a young man told Yeats that he was a lost cause, that he was too old to learn anything from Joyce's teaching (Ellmann *James Joyce* 101n). He also referred to Yeats as "a tiresome idiot" (*SL* 147), and at one point sneered at him as Lady Gregory's gigolo (Ellmann *James Joyce* 491).

He denounced the Yeatsian "world of faery" in "Drama and Life" (*CW* 45). After Yeats died, Joyce did refer to him as the greater writer of the two (Ellmann *James Joyce* 660n), but this was atypical. As with Synge and Flaubert—and, as we shall see, Milton—Joyce could recite a good deal of Yeats from memory (Ellmann *James Joyce* 661n; see also Magalaner and Kain 68). More important, Yeats was a major influence on Joyce both early and late. Joyce's early poems repeatedly show the presence of Yeats. For example, "Come out to where the youth is met" (Ellmann *James Joyce* 150) is not only influenced, but derivative—though, of course, Yeats would never have been guilty of such bizarre mixed metaphors as "Your feet have woven many a maze." The title of Joyce's first, lost collection of verse, *Moods*, "suggests the influence of W. B. Yeats," as Ellmann remarks (*James Joyce* 50). Even in *Chamber Music*, lines, cadences, stanzas repeatedly echo Yeats's early lyrics. "Pale flowers on his mantle / Dark leaves on his hair" of *Chamber Music* 1 draw on such poems as Yeats's 1889 "Ephemera," as do the otherwise Yeatsian lines "Be not sad because all men / Prefer a lying clamor before you" of 19 and the couplet "Nor grieve because our love was gay / Which now is ended in this way" of 33 (excepting the artless rhyme); and both stanzas of 32. *Chamber Music* 20 contains echoes of "The Lake Isle of Innisfree"; 31 recalls "Down by the Sally Gardens," and so on (compare Kenner's discussion of 21 and "To His Heart, Bidding It Have No Fear," in *Dublin's Joyce* 40–41, and the more general discussion 37–43). In *Ulysses*, Yeats provided Joyce with one leitmotif for Stephen's mourning through the lyric "Who Goes with Fergus?" And the world of faery that Yeats articulated, employed, and urged on others—and that Joyce denounced—is profoundly important for Joyce's final work. Perhaps "influence" is not the appropriate word for Yeats's relation to *Finnegans Wake*. But whatever the extent of specifiable influence, clearly Yeats's work was a necessary condition for Joyce's great Irish myth. It is not an exaggeration to say that without Yeats's work there could have been no *Finnegans Wake*. Indeed, there probably would have been no James Joyce at all.

Sometimes Joyce's denunciations take on a comic character. Thus Joyce criticizes one writer because "[t]he form he chose to write in, diffuse, overloaded with minute and often irrelevant observation, carefully relieved at regular intervals by the unfailing humorous note, is not the form of the novel which can carry the greatest conviction" (*Padua* 33). Though it might seem Joyce is here describing the author of *Ulysses*, in fact the reference is to Charles Dickens. Joyce denounces another author because he "stinks of sex" (Ellmann *James Joyce* 382) and because he finds one of this author's heroes shifting between a desire for purity and a desire for lasciviousness in his beloved (619). Again, this sounds like a criticism of Joyce—indeed, Joyce was criticized in much these terms. However, it is in fact a criticism of Richard Wagner, of whom Joyce made significant use in "Circe" (often by way of George Moore—see chapter 10 of Dasenbrock; for an extended examination of Joyce's relation to Wagner, see Timothy Martin).

But again, Joyce not only denounced but also praised—and he often praised one author precisely to denounce another. One contemporary whose work Joyce actually championed was Edouard Dujardin. As Tysdahl pointed out, no doubt this reflected, in part, Joyce's judgment that Dujardin was no competition. And, in private, Joyce himself admitted as much (see Ellmann *James Joyce* 520n).

A particularly interesting case of this sort is that of Italo Svevo. When Svevo was an unknown Triestine, Joyce praised his work, encouraged him, and helped him in the advancement of his art (see references in Ellmann *James Joyce*). When Svevo died, Joyce wrote to his wife saying that "he would be glad to do anything for Svevo's memory," as Ellmann puts it (*CW* 269). However, when an English translation of *Senilita* appeared and Joyce was asked to write an introduction, he demurred. Indeed, in replying to the publisher's request that he comment on Stanislaus's introduction (which the publisher had procured after Joyce's refusal), Joyce wrote a letter mocking *The Confessions of Zeno*, reducing it to a sort of how-to book on stopping cigarettes. It is perhaps not accidental that Joyce's enthusiasm for Svevo declined as Svevo's success increased, and even turned to mockery when Svevo's work received an English language publisher and the approval of Stanislaus.

As Tysdahl indicates, one interesting invocation of an obscure figure to dismiss a powerful competitor and influence is to be found in Joyce's use of Vico to disparage Freud. Joyce claimed that Vico anticipated Freud (Ellmann *James Joyce* 340). He denounced Freud as "mechanical," referring to the universal symbolism (382). He argued with Mary Colum about psychoanalysis, and Mary Colum challenged him, asking, "why deny your indebtedness to Freud and Jung?" Joyce, who referred to Jung and Freud as "the Swiss tweedledum and the Viennese tweedledee" (*SL* 282), replied, "I hate women who know anything" (Ellmann *James Joyce* 634). Colum was certainly correct. Joyce was deeply indebted to Freud for his conceptions of association and parapraxis, as evidenced massively in Ulysses (a point developed by Melanie Savage in unpublished work). Joyce himself said to Djuna Barnes, "In *Ulysses* I have recorded, simultaneously, what a man says, sees, thinks, and what such seeing, thinking, saying does, to what you Freudians call the subconscious." However, he added, "but as for psychoanalysis, it's neither more nor less than blackmail" (quoted in Ellmann *James Joyce* 524). His own attempts at dream interpretation were straightforwardly Freudian (see 436ff. and 524ff.). But although he celebrated the influence of Vico, he only rarely and obliquely acknowledged any debt to Freud.

Another case along the same lines is Ibsen and Shakespeare. From early on, Joyce invoked the imprimatur of Ibsen to criticize his Irish competitors and to valorize his own work. But although he frequently used Shakespeare as a model—for example, in the opening chapters of Ulysses—Joyce hardly celebrated the English dramatist with the same enthusiasm with which he celebrated the Norwegian. In *Stephen Hero*, Joyce has Stephen dismiss Shakespeare and Goethe (who later provided one model for "Circe"—see Gilbert, who refers to that episode as Joyce's "Walpurgisnacht" [7]). Specifically, Stephen finds in Ibsen, "and not in Shakespeare or Goethe ... the successor to the first poet of the Europeans" (*SH* 41). In "Drama and Life," Joyce contrasts "the respective grades of Macbeth and The Master Builder" clearly to the benefit of the latter (*CW* 42). In 1915 he still sought to prove "Ibsen's superiority to Shakespeare" in conversation with Siegmund Feilbogen (Ellmann *James Joyce* 398), and in the late thirties he insisted to Ole Vinding that Ibsen "towers head and shoulders above" Shakespeare (694).

There are many other examples of this sort of ranking in Joyce, such as his elevation of Lermontoff over Turgenev. His deprecation of Wagner is paired with an elevation of Bellini (Ellmann *James Joyce* 382). At one point, he placed Crabbe above Goldsmith (*CW* 128), though later he did come to praise the latter. And in a particularly amusing passage of "Drama and Life," he deprecates Corneille and Calderón in comparison with Haddon Chambers and Hermann Sudermann (*CW* 40—though on the same page he reverses his judgment of Wagner and Bellini, perhaps due to the audience). Certainly some of this is just contrariness. Some is an honest effort to force people to think for themselves and to see worth in neglected writers. But much is no doubt defensive, an attack, once again, on potential competitors.

In many ways, the most interesting case of disparagement and hierarchization comes with Joyce's relation to his own brother Stanislaus. Richard Ellmann's biography of Joyce gives ample testimony to Joyce's repeated derogation of Stannie, his use of Stannie's money, ideas, and so on, combined with a campaign of discouragement and insult (though, admittedly, much of this information comes from Stannie himself—hardly a disinterested observer). Stanislaus notes in his diary that Joyce "thought the man [in Turgenev's *Diary of a Superfluous Man*] very like" Stannie (62)—hence, superfluous. But Stannie was far from superfluous to Jim; he was absolutely essential. Jean Kimball has maintained, not without reason, that "without his younger brother's quite extraordinary contribution, both practical and psychic, to James Joyce's life, there might never have been enough of that life to have produced the work we have from Joyce" (232–33).

In addition to providing practical help, Stannie exerted literary influence on Jim. At the level of allusion or borrowing, Stannie was the one who came up with the titles, "A Portrait of the Artist as a Young Man," "Stephen Hero," and "Chamber Music." He also coined a number of characters' names (see *Diary* 12, 28). The most important way in which Stannie influenced Jim, however, and the most brutal way in which Jim sought to crush his possible competitor, concerned Stannie's diary. Jim read Stannie's diary regularly. As Stannie reports it, perhaps exaggerating, Jim said that he "would never write prose and that [his] diary was most uninteresting except in the parts that were about [Jim]" (*Diary* 20). Jim "frequently" told Stannie that he was a "thick-headed bloody fool" and a "commonplace youth" (20). Despite this, in 1903 Joyce remarked that Stannie's diary "would have been of great use to him in writing his novel" (148). And in 1905 Jim wrote to Stannie from Pola asking to receive the diary for the same purpose (148n).

The diary was certainly not without literary merit. The dialogue between John Joyce and two friends (*Diary* 105–6), later reworked by Jim into a section of "Grace," is very effective, and shows a good ear and sense of character. Jim, who ranked drama above the other verbal arts, must have found this a powerful indication of Stannie's potential talent, and thus his potential threat. Even more important, on 18 July 1904, Stannie engaged in a literary exercise. He tried to write down all the thoughts coming into the mind of someone falling to sleep (165ff.). While it lacks polish, the interior monologue is in many ways remarkable—especially in the way it foreshadows Molly Bloom's soliloquy of 16 June 1904. The movement in and out of the bed, thoughts of the time, recollections, ellipses—all these recur in *Ulysses*. It is hard to believe that they were not in part thieved from Stannie, who according to Jim's pronouncement "would never write prose."

Thus Jim/Stannie takes its place in a series of oppositions that defined Joyce's relation to many of his influences, including Ibsen/Shakespeare, Lermontoff/Turgenev, Vico/Freud, Bellini/Wagner, Crabbe/Goldsmith,

Chambers and Sudermann / Calderón and Corneille. A complete list would also include Schoeck/Stravinsky (Ellmann *James Joyce* 669), Mangan/Swift (545n), and, of course, Dante/Milton, among others.

In *Stephen Hero,* Joyce writes of Stephen that "above all things he hated to be compared with others" (66). Evidently this aversion of Stephen's was shared by Joyce. When he chose his nom de plume of Daedalus in 1904, this was no doubt in part because Daedalus had fabricated wings of escape, wings to take him away from his island prison. But Daedalus was exiled for killing his nephew Talus out of jealousy for Talus's promise as a maker. Whether Joyce thought of this or not, it is apt. Few other figures could represent so well Joyce's attitude toward precursors or contemporaries who threatened to dispute his art and achievement. In *Finnegans Wake,* Joyce was cagier, but his choice of name had the same resonance. Aptly, he chose for his fictional self-portrait the name "Shem the Penman," not only after James Joyce the writer, but equally after Charles Young's play concerning a forger, Jim the Penman (see Ellmann *James Joyce* 550).

The Place of Milton

It is a commonplace to observe that the high moderns disliked Milton. Judging from the paucity of direct references in his letters and essays in particular, it would appear that Joyce too harbored no special fondness for England's greatest epicist. Perhaps this accounts for the relative dearth of critical commentary on the relation between Joyce and Milton. Occasionally, influences are acknowledged, as when Harry Levin links the theme of the Fall in *Finnegans Wake* and *Paradise Lost* (699), when Bernard Benstock asserts that "Joyce meant for a definite affinity between [*Finnegans Wake*] and the classical epics . . . with *Paradise Lost* primarily" (*Wake* 164; see also 167), when Daniel Schwarz places Milton (along with Blake, Swift, and Wilde) in the third and final circle of influences on *Ulysses* (63), or when Harry Blamires avers that "the shadow of Milton . . . hangs over Joyce" ("Influence" 200). However, even the acknowledged connections are rarely expounded.

This is unfortunate. After all, Joyce set out in *Ulysses* to write an epic, a fact that would appear to make inexorable his encounter with Milton. Indeed, quite generally, Milton's influence seems inevitable (a point recently illustrated by John Shawcross in *John Milton and Influence*). Harold Bloom has argued that if "one examines the dozen or so major poetic influencers before this century, one discovers quickly who among them ranks as the great Inhibitor, the Sphinx who strangles even strong imaginations in their cradles: Milton" (*Anxiety* 32). It is worth pausing for a moment to recall the unique status held by Milton among English poets, and indeed among English writers in general. As Havens notes, Milton was far more popular than, for instance, Shakespeare up through the middle of the nineteenth century. His works went through many editions, and *Paradise Lost* in particular was imitated, simplified, explicated for the common reader, and redone into children's versions (see 25–26, 34–36, 69). In keeping with this, Samuel Johnson picked out sections of the great epic that were the "favorite of children" (Havens 185). In more elite circles, Milton's influence on eighteenth- and nineteenth-century writers in all genres was unparalleled—as is indicated, for example, in Gilbert and Gubar's discussion of Milton as the great precursor against whom nineteenth-century women novelists had to define their art. Indeed, it is no exaggeration to say that Milton was effectively deified. Havens lists a range of writers whose attitude genuinely approaches idolatry (see chapter 1). Even Johnson—viewed by Milton partisans as an unkind, even slanderous critic—thought it not "indecent hyperbole" to call *Paradise Lost* "a book of universal knowledge" (183). And this appears slight praise when compared with the effusions of the romantics. In *The Excursion,* Wordsworth hailed the "divine Milton" (1.250) and in "At Vallombrosa," a poem recounting his pilgrimage to one of Milton's residences, he called Milton the "holiest of Bards" (l. 26). Iconoclastic Shelley celebrated "sacred Milton" in the preface to *Prometheus Unbound* (982 in Perkins). John Keats and Leigh Hunt actually wrote poems on the occasion of seeing a relic of Milton's hair (both are printed in Perkins; see 710, 1149). As these examples make clear, it would be difficult to overstate the towering stature of Milton in English letters in the eighteenth and nineteenth centuries. (Indeed, it would be difficult to overstate his stature even outside England; for example, as Boss has discussed, *Paradise Lost* deeply influenced a range of Russian authors and virtually assumed the status of a sacred text among Russian Masons.)

Moreover, Milton's pervasive literary presence was not merely an abstract matter of general reverence. We can observe its concrete manifestations in Joyce's reading and schooling. Joyce owned in Trieste at least two copies of Milton, one corrected in such a way as to indicate the possession of yet a third and primary copy (see appendix). The two copies are heavily annotated for language instruction as Stanislaus and, perhaps, James used Milton's poetry in teaching their Berlitz students (a fact that provides still further evidence of the degree to which our attitudes toward Milton have changed in the course of the past century). As Bruce Bradley and Kevin Sullivan point out, the presence of Milton in Joyce's formal education was, if anything, greater than might be expected. For example, the 1897 Intermediate Middle examination at Belvedere involved knowledge of "Lycidas," "L'Allegro," and "Il Penseroso," and a paper with a section on "Outlines of English Literature from Chaucer to Milton, both inclusive" (Bradley 129). Moreover, after the Intermediate examinations, Joyce "had probably gone on to read the rest of Milton's poetry" (Sullivan 129). And in his matriculation course essay of 1898–99 on the study of languages, Shakespeare and Milton are the two writers Joyce cites to illustrate the necessity of humanistic education (*CW* 27).

Indeed, from as early as 1904—perhaps the critical year in Joyce's literary development—there is direct evidence of Joyce's engagement with Milton in relation to his own work. In his "Pola" notebook, he twice quotes Milton. The first phrase, "[t]he artillery of heaven" (*PL* 2.715) is a Miltonic reference to thunder (Scholes and Kain 85). The second—"the world will not willingly let die" (Scholes and Kain 90)—derives from "The Reason of Church Government Urged against Prelaty" and was incorporated by Joyce into Gabriel Conroy's speech in "The Dead." More important, in the same notebook, Joyce's first entry under "S.D.," his first entry explicating his own autobiographical character Stephen Dedalus, links Stephen as an artist directly with Milton: "Six medical students under my direction will write Paradise Lost except 100 lines" (Scholes and Kain 91). Joyce saved this phrase for almost two decades, reworking it, and placing it in *Ulysses*. In doing this, he appears quite explicitly to have affirmed the connection, positive or negative, between what he himself no doubt viewed as the two great epics in the English language. Finally, years later, in his late thirties, Joyce was able to recite from memory all of "Lycidas" and "L'Allegro" (and presumably much else of Milton as well), as he did one night in a Locarno cafe for an admiring Frank Budgen (see Budgen 176).

There are, of course, many levels on which Joyce's relation to Milton worked itself out. Before going on to an examination of specific works, I will consider the following in more general terms: (1) Joyce's personal relation to Milton the man and his circumstances; (2) Joyce's relation to Milton as a public figure, both in his religion and in his politics; (3) the effect of Milton's work on Joyce's aesthetic development; (4) Joyce's transferential relation to Milton's work; (5) the mediation of Milton's work through Joyce's reading of other authors.

Milton's Life

Tysdahl claims that "[i]nfluence is . . . like a plant that will only strike root in soil similar to that from which it comes. If Joyce's circumstances had not in some ways been analogous to those of Ibsen, influence from the one to the other would seem inconceivable" (10). I cannot follow Tysdahl in viewing social or personal similarity as a precondition for influence (in part for reasons already noted in connection with identification). But in the case of Milton the similarities nonetheless exist—social similarities and personal similarities that are striking. They are coincidental, of course, but Joyce was always fascinated by such coincidences. For example, when he chose James Stephens as a potential inheritor of *Finnegans Wake,* he seemed in some ways less concerned with Stephens's writing than with the fact that they shared a Christian name and a birth date, that Stephens's surname was the same as the given name of Joyce's fictional alter ego, and so on. But there is a difference between the coincidental relation of Joyce and Milton and that of Joyce and Stephens, for the similarities between the former writers frequently assume almost antithetical meanings. In many ways, Joyce and Milton, Joyce's Ireland and Milton's England, were remarkably alike. But the latter was colonizer and the former was colonized, the latter had means and the former was brutalized by poverty. Given these circumstances, very few things could have the same meaning for both men.

The most obvious personal connection linking Milton and Joyce is blindness. Though Joyce's sight was never fully lost, it was exceptionally poor from his youth, and, like Milton's, declined rapidly in middle age. As Hodgart points out, in the *Wake* Joyce refers to his blindness (*FW* 182) in a Miltonic phrase that clearly links the sightlessness of these two Homeric poets (Hodgart 149). Joseph Schork has expanded Hodgart's observation, uncovering a larger complex of similar connections. But Milton went blind from excessive unillumined labors as Latin secretary for the Council of State, as an assiduous worker for a government that was notorious for its cruelty in the western colony of Ireland. Joyce went blind from poverty and drink.

The case is similar with the coat of arms. Joyce's somewhat pathetic concern with his coat of arms is well known. He found romance in the idea of a noble paternal past. Oddly, as Michael O'Shea points out, "the Joyce arms are remarkably similar to those of John Milton" (154). It is hard to say whether Joyce knew the Milton coat of arms—or even, for that matter, the correct Joyce coat of arms. (The reproduction he owned, O'Shea explains, was faulty.) But given his remarkable interest in heraldry and its function in works such as *A Portrait* (as discussed by O'Shea), it is certainly not impossible. Again a noteworthy link, a connection encouraging identification. But the context impedes the identification. For Milton's coat of arms was "genuine" and meaningful. He was the conqueror, the propertied

Sassenach. Joyce's coat of arms was a dubious attempt to uncover a shred of nobility behind squalor, an attempt without social or political consequence. Whatever Joyce's Norman ancestors may have been, he was now the conquered, ignoble Celt.

Other personal similarities are less starkly oppositional. For example, Saintsbury (an author Joyce greatly admired, see *Letters* 1.195) points out in his *Short History of English Literature* (owned by Joyce in Trieste) that the "only other member of the [Milton] family who is remembered was the poet's younger brother Christopher," a judge and a Royalist, in many ways the opposite of John. Not only is Stanislaus, James's younger brother and opposite, the only other member of the Joyce family who is remembered, James must have been well aware from early on that this would be the case.

One of the best-known anecdotes about Milton's life provides a further connection. The elaborate treatment given by Joyce to Stephen's pandying by Father Dolan—not only in *A Portrait,* chapter 1, but in the "Circe" episode of *Ulysses* as well—is no doubt due in part to the powerful impression made on Joyce by a real incident of this sort in his own life. But it also recapitulates a famous incident in the life of Milton, when, as Samuel Johnson puts it in his *Lives of the English Poets* (owned by Joyce in Trieste), Milton "suffered the public indignity of corporal correction" at school (58). Whether this event in Milton's life provided a selection principle for Joyce's writing is not so important here as the fact that when Joyce learned of Milton's punishment, he could hardly have avoided connecting it in his mind with his own humiliating experience.

A further and deeper similarity may be found in the fact that Milton, like Joyce, considered entering the clergy after leaving school. But like Joyce he ultimately decided against a religious life. Moreover, he came to this decision for the Joycean (that is, Satanic, Miltonic) reason that he could not agree to obey, to "subscribe slave" as he put it (quoted in Johnson 91). As Johnson explains, "the thoughts of obedience, whether canonical or civil, raised his indignation" (91; see also 157). Milton might well have adopted Stephen's creed: "obedience" only "in the womb" (*U* 14.336–37).

Also like Joyce, Milton went to Italy after his mother's death and there developed his first serious poetic ambitions. Indeed, these ambitions and their relation to the sojourn in Italy are expounded in "The Reason of Church Government" in precisely the passage from which Joyce quotes in the "Pola" notebook and, subsequently, "The Dead." But, unlike Joyce, Milton's poetic ambitions were fired by literary success, and not by the oppression, censorship, and grinding poverty that Joyce suffered.

Finally, for some time after returning from Europe, Milton served as instructor "vapour[ing] away" his time in "a private boarding school" (Johnson 98), a fact to which Joyce alludes when he has Stephen, more than a year after returning from Europe, similarly vaporing away his time by teaching "Lycidas." Unlike Joyce, however, Milton left his teaching, not to travel again across the channel, but to take part in the turmoil that was then rending English society. Unlike Joyce, he set aside his poetic aspirations to engage himself politically—turning ultimately to a highly didactic art of precisely the sort Joyce denounced in "Drama and Life" (CW 43), *A Portrait* (205ff.), and elsewhere. The very fact that each had to make such a decision between politics and art, the fact that each wrote in a time of civil war and Anglo-Irish war, indicates that the similar soil claimed necessary by Tysdahl was, to a degree, present. And yet, once again, the identities here are reversed like images in a mirror, oppositions as much as identifications, common properties rendered irreconcilable, for not only did Milton join in the political fray, he joined the enemy. And perhaps if Milton's side had not been victorious, however briefly, Joyce would never have been faced with a political decision. Perhaps the country into which he was born would not have been placed just beyond the margin of European civilization, Europe's odd European colony, and one of its most brutalized.

Milton's Religion and Politics

Personally, Joyce's relation to Milton could only have been one of profound ambivalence, identification combining with repulsion. Joyce's understanding of Milton's religious and political views and actions no doubt rendered this ambivalence even more powerful. The popular vision of Milton, in grim Puritan uniform firmly buttoned at the neck, the corners of his lips tightening downward in a frown of dour moral disapproval, would hardly have been one in which a young libertine such as Joyce could have seen an image of himself. Like one of his subtle heresiarchs, Joyce warred throughout his life against Irish Catholic suppression of sexuality—a suppression widely viewed in Ireland as a direct result of the diffusion of Puritan thought, its gradual almost unperceived entry into the Catholic teachings prevalent on the island. As Stanislaus put it in *My Brother's Keeper*, "the Irish Catholic Church . . . [is] a hybrid form of religion produced by the most unenlightened features of Catholicism under the inevitable influence of English Puritanism" (234).

And yet Milton, the militant Puritan, was hardly a puritan in this sense. Certainly the abuses and degradations of exploitative lust are, for Milton, lapsarian. Before the Fall, Adam "rode not rutted" (*U* 3.386) as Stephen has it in "Proteus." For Milton, the true connubial bliss of sexual congress preceded the Fall. But clearly, then, such congress is not in and of itself execrable. Indeed, Milton even sets forth the unorthodox doctrine of angelic intercourse, as red-faced Raphael tacitly admits to a teasing Adam. ("Love not the heav'nly Spirits, and how thir Love / Express they, by looks only, or do they mix / Irradiance, virtual or immediate touch? / / To whom the Angel with a smile that glow'd / Celestial rosy red, Love's proper hue, / Answer'd. Let it suffice thou that thou know'st / Us happy, and without Love no happiness" [8.615–21].)

Moreover, Milton's Puritanism was vigorously antagonistic to church hierarchies. In his various antiprelatic tracts, such as "The Reason of Church Government," "An Apology for Smectymnuus," and so on, Milton argues powerfully against precisely the clerical structure that, in its Catholic incarnation, was one chief enemy of Joyce the artist, one chief impediment to his freedom. One of the major themes of *A Portrait* is the absolute necessity of freedom for artistic creation. Stephen insists that he will "discover the mode of life or of art whereby [his] spirit could express itself in unfettered freedom" (246) and thus he "will not serve that in which [he] no longer believe[s] whether it call itself [his] home, [his] fatherland or [his] church" (246–47). Joyce and Milton are at one in their denunciation of a clerical hierarchy that can fetter the minds of a citizenry.

But Joyce's first disillusion with the ecclesiastical structure came with the fall of Parnell; it came with the near destruction of the Home Rule Party; it came when the Irish Catholic Church followed the English lead and decried Parnell; it came when the Irish Catholic clergy sided with Gladstone in his split with Parnell, a split provoked in large measure by the pressure of English nonconformists (see Lyons 196–98), spiritual descendants of John Milton. In *A Portrait*, Simon Dedalus inquires concerning Parnell and the sermons of the clerics, "Were we to desert him at the bidding of the English people?" (32). And later Mr. Casey enumerates the political infamies of his "priestridden race": "Didn't the bishops of Ireland betray us in the time of the union when bishop Lanigan presented an address of loyalty to the Marquess Cornwallis? Didn't the bishops and priests sell the aspirations of their country in 1829 in return for catholic emancipation? Didn't they denounce the fenian movement from the pulpit and in the confessionbox? And didn't they dishonour the ashes of Terence Bellew MacManus?" (38).

Milton's writings had an entirely different orientation. As Samuel Johnson stresses, Milton retreated, late in life, from his criticisms of Anglicanism, singling out Catholicism for condemnation and insisting that the "papists" must not be "permitted the liberty of either publick or private worship" (quoted in Johnson 148). But even in his early writing, Milton viewed prelaty as wrong and dangerous, in part because it provided an improper example for the Irish; it was too papist and served only to encourage the western barbarians in their superstition and atavism, which it was the burden of Milton's more advanced civilization to eradicate. Joyce quotes from one of Milton's major antiprelatic tracts, "The Reason of Church Government Urged Against Prelaty," in the "Pola" notebook and, ultimately, in "The Dead." I discuss the literary function of this quotation below, but for the present it is important to note that in this essay Milton is explicit about the frightening connection between Protestant prelaty and Irish national aspirations. He denounces "these murderous Irish, the enemies of God and mankind" (in Milton *John Milton* 663), but then goes on to take the liberal and gentlemanly view of things, explaining that the fault for Irish evil lies not with the poor misguided children themselves, but rather with the English church that has failed to fulfill its mission of education and reform.

The colonial and chauvinist attitude expressed in this is wholly characteristic of Milton's references to the Irish question quite generally—which takes us to Joyce's relation to Milton in his political role. Though Joyce loathed what he viewed as parochial and sometimes xenophobic Irish nationalism, he always remained faithful to Eire, in his fashion. In *My Brother's Keeper*, Stanislaus maintains that the "two dominant passions of [Joyce's] life were to be love of father and of fatherland" (234). Peter Costello's biography makes clear that Joyce's family was deeply connected with the Fenians, that Joyce developed strong Fenian sentiments in his youth—and retained them. For example, the character of Mr. Casey was based on John Kelly, an active Fenian and organizer for the Land League, who was repeatedly incarcerated and was even condemned to hard labor. Kelly lived for a time with the Joyces (Costello 94) and was godfather to one of their children (112). In Paris, Joyce sought out Patrick Casey, another Fenian, notorious for his part in the Clerkenwell explosion. A connection through John Joyce, Casey was enough of an intimate that he recognized John's voice in James (201–2).

Joyce's deep, if not unambivalent, affection for Ireland, island of saints and sages, surfaced regularly, and sometimes importantly, self-consciously in his fiction. However, what is perhaps the most touching expression of his relation to Ireland as a country crushed by foreign domination, as a people degraded by centuries of racial hatred, is to be found in an Italian lecture, delivered in 1907 at the Universita Popolare of Trieste: "Irlanda, Isola dei Santi e dei Savi." In this lecture, Joyce defends at length the Irish character and appears almost desperate to debunk the racist view of Celtic inferiority. Joyce explains, not without bitterness, that the "English now disparage the Irish because they are Catholic, poor, and ignorant." But, he says, "Ireland is poor because English laws ruined the country's industries ... because the neglect of the English government in the years of the potato famine allowed the best of the population to die from hunger" (CW 167). He continues, "Nor is it any harder to understand why the Irish citizen is a reactionary and a Catholic, and why he mingles the names of Cromwell and Satan when he curses. For him, the great Protector of civil rights is a savage beast who came to Ireland to propagate his faith by fire and sword. He does not forget the sack of Drogheda and Waterford, nor the bands of men and women hunted down in the furthermost islands by the Puritan, who said that they would go 'into the ocean or into hell,' nor the false oath that the English swore on the broken stone of Limerick" (168).

Later in this lecture, Joyce seeks to disprove the view that "the Irish are ... the unbalanced, helpless idiots about whom we read in the lead articles of the *Standard* and the *Morning Post*" (CW 171) by listing the names of great Irish writers and translators. Finally, in a gesture that now can seem little more than pathetic, he pleads, "in the field of practical affairs this pejorative conception of Ireland is given the lie by the fact that when the Irishman is found outside of Ireland in another environment, he very often becomes a respected man" (171).

To understand Joyce's sad apologia, we must recall the racist environment in which Joyce grew to maturity. In the late nineteenth century, the problematic that defined mainstream discourse on the Irish presupposed Irish inferiority—only the evitability of this inferiority was at issue. Thus the terrain of debate was marked out by those who saw Irish degradation as biological, as rooted in their racial constitution, and those who saw it as historical. As F. S. L. Lyons explains, quoting L. P. Curtis, debate on Ireland was divided between

> "the Anglo-Saxonists, who argued that Irish character made the Irish unfit for self-government, and the environmentalists, who believed in the potential equality of mankind and contended that historical circumstances had made the Irish what they were." ... Considerable evidence has been adduced to indicate that such ideas were more

widely held by Victorian intellectuals than has generally been supposed, but of course racism was no monopoly of the educated classes. . . . It was by no means impossible for ordinary British citizens, whatever their politics, to feel at one and the same time that the Irish were deeply to be pitied for their poverty and sufferings, but also that because of their backwardness, their illiteracy, their supposed domination by their priests, they were fundamentally unsuited to have charge of their own affairs. (187)

In *Apes and Angels* and elsewhere, Curtis has explored the nineteenth-century pseudosciences that linked closely the Celt and the ape (a lingering vision in our own century; recall T. S. Eliot's image of Apeneck Sweeney in "Sweeney among the Nightingales" [*Poems* 49]). Dogfaced or simian, illustrations of animalized Paddys filled the pages of popular English magazines and newspapers throughout the nineteenth century. In *Punch,* one waggish racialist conjectured that the Irish were in fact the missing link, the intermediate species that provided the transition from monkey to African: "A Creature manifestly between the Gorilla and the Negro is to be met with in some of the lowest districts of London and Liverpool by adventurous explorers. It comes from Ireland." The writer goes on to elaborate: "It is, moreover, a climbing animal, and may sometimes be seen ascending a ladder with a hod of bricks" (quoted in Curtis 100). (It is not, perhaps, by accident that the hero of Joyce's final masterpiece was a fallen Irish hod carrier.)

Milton was more liberal. Two centuries earlier, he held to a version of the environmental thesis. (Biological racialism had not developed so far in those days.) Specifically, he believed that Irish inferiority—which he considered indisputable—was contingent, a social and historical product. But he also believed that the English, and specifically the English Puritans led by Oliver Cromwell, had the divine obligation to lead the Irish onto the True Path, as they were incapable of such progress themselves. Milton seems never to have wavered in his hatred for the Irish or in his profound commitment to urging the fulfillment of the Saxon man's burden. In his "Observations on the Articles of Peace," Milton denounces the "abhorred *Irish* rebels," the "inhumane Rebels and Papists of *Ireland*" (*Works* vol. 6, 243). In his first *Defense of the People of England,* Milton calls the Irish, "our most savage and inhuman enemies" (*Works* vol. 7, 525).

Milton also proved himself an able propagandist against the Irish and in the service of the Council of State. He repeatedly insisted that the Irish had slaughtered more than six hundred thousand innocents (see, for example, *Eikonoklastes* book 12, *Works* vol. 5, 188). In the *Eikonoklastes,* he again generously places the ultimate blame on the English for failing to provide adequate guidance to the benighted natives (*Works* vol. 5, 190). But elsewhere he retreats from such liberality and claims that Eire is "a nation cursed and set apart for destruction . . . whose godless fellowship . . . [is] stained with the blood of so many harmless citizens" (*Works* vol. 5, 39). In "Observations on the Articles of Peace," he even goes so far as to claim that "though all these many years shown and taught" by their enlightened English caretakers, the heathen Celts "preferre their own absurd and savage Customes before the most convincing evidence of reason and demonstration: a testimony of their true Barbarism" (*Works* vol. 6, 245).

Perhaps more important than Milton's cultural intolerance, was his absolute, practical political opposition to Irish independence and his vigorous advocacy of the use of harsh penal measures to secure English domination of Ireland. In "Observations on the Articles of Peace," Milton clearly finds the idea of Irish self-rule, equal to England, appalling. He explains, with good Calvinist logic, that "by their own . . . demerits and provocations" the Irish have been "justly made our vassals" (*Works* vol. 6, 244). Subsequently, he maintains that Charles's admittedly opportunistic advocacy of some degree of Irish independence would in and of itself be adequate reason for his dethroning.

Finally, Milton was an active and vocal supporter of Cromwell's campaign in Ireland and of the land confiscations resulting from his cruel successes. As Joyce noted in the passage quoted above, Cromwell's campaign is and has been notorious in Ireland for its savagery. Aidan Clarke explains that, "when Oliver Cromwell landed at Dublin with a puritan army in 1649, his mission was not only conquest, but also revenge. The indiscriminate inhumanity with which that revenge was exacted upon the royalist garrison and many of the townspeople of Drogheda, and upon the defenders of Wexford, became indelibly impressed upon the folk memory of the Irish" (202). Moreover, in terms of British domination, this campaign marks one major turning point in the development of Ireland's colonization. As Clarke explains:

> When the treaty of Mellifond brought the nine years' war to an end, most of the land in every province was in the possession of Catholics—some of them the descendants of early English settlers, but most of them the native Irish themselves. By 1660, Catholics, whatever

their origin, were allowed to own land only to the west of the River Shannon, in the province of Connaught and the county of Clare. Elsewhere, there were new landowners—Scots and English who had come to Ulster in the first decades of the century, and, in Leinster and Munster, more recent settlers who had arrived in the wake of Cromwell's armies in the 1650s. (189)

Milton, again in his Calvinist vein, repeatedly claimed that English victories over the Irish were a sign of God's favor (see the "Apology for Smectymnuus," *Works* vol. 3, 340), and in the *Declaration of 1652*, he saw the defeat of the Irish as an instance of divine providence (*Works* vol. 18, 13, 21). In the First Defense he praised the "Irish Campaign (so acceptable to Almighty God)." He also recognized and fully endorsed Cromwell's use of the campaign to exact revenge on the loyalist Irish (see *Eikonoklastes*, *Works* vol. 5, 197). And in what is perhaps his most hideous and reprehensible statement on the "Irish question," Milton in *Eikonoklastes* approves the parliamentary policies that "brought [the Irish] every where either to Famin, or a low condition" (*Works* vol. 5, 199).

Joyce had probably not read most of Milton's pronouncements on the Irish. But one or two, indeed his commitment to and engagement in the Cromwellian cause, suffice. It is difficult to imagine that Joyce had nowhere in his mind regicide Milton, when he wrote in his first essay on the Irish poet James Clarence Mangan, "the poet who hurls his anger against tyrants would establish upon the future an intimate and far more cruel tyranny" (*CW* 82).

But, once again, there was more to Milton. His libertarian views—betrayed when in government, but cogently defended in his earlier writings—must certainly have struck a sympathetic chord in Joyce. Joyce was deeply influenced by the anarchist or libertarian socialist thought of writers such as Kropotkin, Proudhon, and Bakunin, as Dominic Manganiello has argued at length in *Joyce's Politics*. And Stanislaus maintained in *My Brother's Keeper* that Joyce "believed in individual freedom more thoroughly than any man" he had ever known (120). The most obvious point of contact between Milton and Joyce in this arena lies in the area of censorship. "Areopagitica" is one of the earliest defenses of a free press, and remains one of the most powerful. Joyce no doubt read this work and appreciated it—perhaps increasingly as with time he was repeatedly subjected to censorship himself. Indeed, one, perhaps the only political passion Joyce maintained throughout his life was to the cause of freedom of the press, for this freedom is in some ways even more fundamental for the artist than the freedoms from family, nation, and religion.

Indeed, this was one aspect of Milton's work greatly stressed by the romantic writers who mediated Milton's influence on Joyce. Coleridge saw Milton (along with Dante, Chaucer, and Pindar) as an instance of the "close connection of poetic genius with the love of liberty" (Wittreich 221), even going so far as to set up a contrast between Milton on the one hand and a "stern and prejudiced Puritan" on the other (Wittreich 209). Shelley too saw Milton as the great hero of liberty. He was part of "that fervid awakening of the public mind which shook to dust the oldest and most oppressive form of the Christian religion" (Perkins 982).

But here the ambiguity in Milton redoubles itself in his followers. Coleridge and Shelley were not ignorant of Milton's intolerance, his connection with Cromwell. One reason for their nonetheless unqualified enthusiasm was that in England, liberty and progress came to be associated exclusively with Whiggism, an opposition to monarchy, and it was in this context that Milton's liberalism was usually celebrated (see Good 224ff.). Things could not have been so simple for an Irishman and a Fenian—especially one who kept in mind the images of Charles and Cromwell.

Many Romantic writers, despite their revolutionary politics, also shared Milton's racist views. Shelley opposed the Act of Union and supported Catholic emancipation. But his youthful "Address to the Irish People," where he expresses these opinions, is condescending in almost every phrase, patronizing in tone and content. Moreover, it assumes unselfconsciously that the Irish are a passionate rather than a deliberative race and that this predisposes them to alcoholism (see 41, 47). And as Joyce would have known from Arthur Symonds, Shelley in private admitted to considering the Irish a people "of scarcely greater elevation in the scale of intellectual being than an oyster" (quoted in Symonds 60).

Byron was perhaps the sole exception to this tendency. He was a good friend of Thomas Moore, the Irish poet and historian, and a constant advocate of Irish rights. In Parliament, he spoke forcefully and bitterly against English rule in Eire: "Some persons have compared the Catholics to the beggar in 'Gil Blas;' who made them beggars? Who are enriched with the spoils of their ancestors? And cannot you relieve the beggar when your fathers have made him such?" Recognizing the implicit racism in paternalistic philanthropy, he added, "If you are disposed to relieve him at all, cannot you do it without flinging your farthings in his face?" ("Speeches" 345). He went on to denounce the injustice of the judicial system, etc. In

Don Juan, he cited the brutal suppression of the United Irish Rebellion as one reason for his exile in Italy, and he painted a damning portrait of the English foreign minister, Viscount Castlereagh, a "Cold-blooded, smooth-faced, placid miscreant.... Dabbling ... sleek young hands in Erin's gore" and panting "for wider carnage" (Dedication lines 89–91). And in "The Vision of Judgment," the major accusation he brought against George III was that he was a "bigot" who suppressed the rights of five million Irish men and women (lines 377–80, 395).

What is crucial for our concerns is that Byron too regularly associated his position with that of Milton. Stressing Milton's opposition to tyranny, Byron (much in the manner of Joyce) established an opposition between Milton and George III's poet laureate, Robert Southey. For every collaborationist trait Byron found in Southey, he saw its opposite in Milton. Indeed, in the dedication of *Don Juan*, Byron insisted that Milton would never have obeyed Castlereagh and George III in their execrable treatment of the Irish (lines 81ff.). Joyce would, of course, have recognized this as a wild overestimation of Milton's character. But he would also have recognized that it was not an overestimation of Milton's principles.

Thus the figure of Milton, the figure of this great precursor poet so highly esteemed by Joyce's teachers and by the literary tradition in which Joyce found himself, must have blurred and split, cracked and divided in Joyce's mind, formed itself into two irreconcilable figures—the libertarian Milton and the imperialist and Puritan Milton, Milton the enemy of tyrants and Milton the apologist for tyranny, both temporal and spiritual. It is the latter Milton with whom Joyce struggled in his earliest works. But it is the former Milton—and, of course, Milton the artist—that gave these early struggles their urgency.

Milton's Work: Ideas of Beauty

There is evidence that from early on Milton served Joyce as one in a handful of poetic models. The earliest extant poem by Joyce is a translation of Horace's ode, "O fons Bandusiae" (see Ellmann *James Joyce* 50–51). Stuart Gilbert compares this early effort of Joyce to Milton's juvenile translation of the fifth ode, "Ad Pyrrham" (Gilbert 88n). Gilbert's point is to assert the superiority of Joyce. But the connection drawn by Gilbert may reflect a deeper affinity than he himself recognized. It is striking that both Joyce and Milton turned to the translation of Horace in their poetic youth. But it is perhaps more striking that Horace's fifth ode is addressed to Pyrrha, a presence in Joyce's work, and one perhaps associated with Milton (see

Hogan "Drowning"). Furthermore, the poem addresses the Lycidasian theme of drowning and includes a reference to the beloved's "golden Hair," which may recur in the "goldenhair" of *Chamber Music* 5—perhaps coincidentally the same number as the Horatian ode. One source for Joyce's poem is probably Wilde's "Requiescat," to which it is particularly close metrically. However, the scholarly scene of the poem—a student lured from the gloom of his study by the singing of a "merry air"—recalls the situations of "L'Allegro" and "Il Penseroso" enough to make a Miltonic context plausible. Finally, it is worth pointing out that the most striking stylistic feature of Joyce's translation is its extensive use of enjambment. This is a noteworthy feature not only of Milton's translation, but of Milton's poetry in general—as Saintsbury notes in his *Short History* (399).

Further Miltonic connections may be glimpsed in the dismal adolescent collection "Shine and Dark." Though for the most part the poems are aestheticist in nature and more reminiscent of Swinburne, early Yeats, Dowson, Symons, Johnson, and others than of Milton, their titular and structural division into the chirpingly gay and the groaningly miserable calls to mind the "L'Allegro"/"Il Penseroso" dichotomy. This connection is reenforced by the opening line of the single extant shine poem: "Let us fling to the winds all moping and madness," which recalls the opening exorcisms of both Miltonic mood poems. Less strikingly, the reference to "the seventeen devils with sapient sadness" in the same poem (Ellmann *James Joyce* 82) may refer to the pandemonic convocation in *Paradise Lost*, though the number seventeen has no basis in Milton.

Miltonic references recur in Joyce's later poetry as well. There are the possible influences on *Chamber Music* 5. And when Joyce turned to the topic of "Flood" in *Pomes Penyeach*, he recurred to Milton once again. Specifically, the third line of this poem reads, "Vast wings above the lambent waters brood," recalling the famous lines from *Paradise Lost*, "with mighty wings outspread / Dove-like satst brooding on the vast Abyss" (1.20–21).

Other hints of a more significant conceptual connection with Milton are biographical rather than artistic. For example, early in his diary, Stanislaus explains, "I have nick-named myself 'Il Penseroso'" (57). He later points out that his brother was a self-proclaimed optimist (85). It is difficult to say whether James took up Stanislaus's Miltonic schema of personality types, and saw himself as "L'Allegro." However, he certainly viewed his differences with Stanislaus in terms consistent with Milton's division. Indeed, in the context of Joyce's insistent denial of the influence of Stanislaus, even the fact that Stanislaus thought of himself as "Il Penseroso" is interesting. Recalling the evening when Joyce recited Milton to Frank Budgen by a Swiss lake, his brother far away, prisoner in a war camp, one may wonder if it is wholly accidental that he recited "Lycidas" (with whom he connected Stephen) and "L'Allegro" (with whom he, perhaps, connected himself), but he passed over the obvious companion, "Il Penseroso," both poem and brother. Joyce's relation to Milton was quite possibly bound up, at least in certain respects, with his relation to Stanislaus.

The most obvious and powerful incorporations of Milton's work into Joyce's aesthetic cognition, however, occur elsewhere: first and most obviously in the prototype of brave rebellion—Satan; second in what Joyce conceived to be the prototype of seduction—Eve. For his entire life, these two figures served to organize, focus, structure the diverse perceptions, fantasies, dreams, and recollections that clustered around his idea of himself and his ideas about the women he loved and desired. He himself struggling with brave hopelessness against a cruel and insuperable enemy; she at once seductive and easily seduced, always on the verge of betrayal, ready to fall.

Joyce's relation to the figure of Eve involved deeply unconscious elements. However, his conception of himself as rebel-poet Satan is simpler, more obviously cognitive, more self-conscious. Indeed, as a literary identification, it is explicit. In *A Portrait*, Stephen makes the Satanic proclamation, "I will not serve" (246). As Father Arnall explained at the horrific retreat, "the sin of pride, the sinful thought conceived in an instant: *non serviam:* I will not serve. That instant was his ruin" (117). Stephen defines himself with the same phrase of defiance that hurled Satan and his crew forever into unceasing torment.

Certainly Joyce's Satanic self-conception was not purely Miltonic. Nor, indeed, was it initially Miltonic. As a tender youth, Joyce arranged Adam and Eve plays utilizing familial talent and casting himself in the role of the serpent (Ellmann, *James Joyce* 26). At the very beginning of his diary, Stanislaus remarks on Joyce's "satanic irony" (*Diary* 2), later asserting that God expelled the angels from the seat of bliss because he found Mephistopheles "too ironical" (96). Moreover, Stanislaus was not the only one to find in Joyce the Satanic strain. In 1904, when homeless, Joyce lived briefly with James and Gretta Cousins. From the latter, he took the name for his first literary re-creation of Eve-like Nora, Gretta Conroy. He also found his own Lucipherine identity confirmed by the Cousinses, who viewed him as the "lost angel of a ruined paradise" (Ellmann *James Joyce*

171). When Joyce was refuged in Zurich, fourteen years later, his landlady spied the similarity as well—no doubt in part due to the self-consciously satanic beard and costume characteristic of Joyce at the time. She called him "Herr Satan" (435).

The most important person who came to identify Joyce with the Prince of Darkness was Joyce himself. At times, he appears to have held to Stanislaus's ironic view. For example, in his oracular essay "A Portrait of the Artist as a Young Man," Joyce proclaims that "he saw between camps his ground of vantage, opportunities for the mocking devil in an isle twice removed from the mainland, under joint government of Their Intensities and Their Bullockships" (Scholes and Kain 67). At other times, his diabolic self-identification was more whimsical. For example, in 1936, Joyce sent to his grandson, Stephen, a tale about the little town of Beaugency and the Devil. In a postscript, Joyce identified himself with the feline-befriending Beelzebub. Much like the author of *Finnegans Wake*, "The devil," Joyce informed Stephen, "mostly speaks a language of his own." In addition, the name of this language sounds rather like a Wakean pun of babbling syllables on Beelzebub, "Bellsybabble." Finally, this Joycean devil, much like his creator, could "speak quite bad French very well" though he had "a strong Dublin accent" (*SL* 384).

Most often, however, the Satan through whom Joyce saw himself was the prideful Satan who fell instantly from divine grace giving birth to sin through the momentary thought "I will not serve," the Satan whom Stephen's mother saw when, in *Stephen Hero*, she accused Stephen bitterly, "You suffer from the pride of the intellect" (134). When Joyce thought of rebellion seeking the absolute freedom that was for him the necessary condition of imagination, he thought by way of Satan, most often and most deeply the Satan of John Milton.

Here too politics and ambivalence entered. Even before composing his great epic, Milton implicitly linked Satan with Charles and the rebel Irish with the demon crew. Employing a phrase commonly used to characterize the devil in Eden, Milton wrote in *Eikonoklastes* that Charles's defense of the Irish was the clever rhetoric of "a plausible deceiver" (*Works* vol. 5, 195). And yet later writers drew on this identification as an image to strengthen and inspire the Irish. In "The Vision of Judgment," Byron puts the defense of the Irish into the mouth of the devil and ends the poem with George III passing through the pearly gates. And when Shelley wrote his "Declaration of Rights," a broadside addressed to the Irish and calling on them to recognize their rights and struggle against oppression, he ended it with the words: "Awake!—arise!—or be forever fallen" (72). These are the words of Satan, calling to his cohorts still dazed on the fiery gulf, to stir themselves from the torpor of defeat and struggle further against the tyranny of masters (*PL* 1.330). Gilbert and Gubar have shown us the ways in which a nineteenth-century woman writer almost necessarily found herself located in the Miltonic position of a fallen angel. If anything, this was even more obviously true of the Irish writer, for in that case the link was not merely analogical, but historical as well. Joyce was drawn to identify with Satan, not only by temperament and profession, but by national origin.

Milton and Transference

But Joyce did not understand himself only as Lucifer. As he aged, he increasingly came to view himself through the figure of Adam and in relation to the imago of a faithless "whorish" Eve. Robert Adams has argued that "Joyce's interest in the fall and redemption of man was pervasive" (*James Joyce* 80), and he is certainly correct at least with regard to the former. But in this case, Joyce's focus does not seem to have been on his own role as Adam. Rather, his attentions in this regard appear to have centered on Eve as promiscuous seductress, as both lure and lured. In *Stephen Hero*, Stephen contrasts virginal Emma with the "woman in the black straw hat" (192). He plumps for the latter. By the time Joyce comes to *Ulysses*, Emma has disappeared, Stephen's mother has died, Stephen himself has ceded pride of place to Adam-like Leopold Bloom, and the main female character, Molly Bloom, has a black straw hat resting on her lapsarian commode of apple design (see 17.2102–3).

It is well known that Joyce, like Stephen, tended to split his image of sexual womanhood. As Mark Shechner has pointed out, Joyce suffered gravely from the "virgin/whore syndrome" (90). Joyce imagined under both aspects all the women to whom he was attracted, in life and in fiction, but one aspect predominated in each case. Shechner links Mary Sheehy, Emma Clery, and Beatrice Justice in the first category, along with the Blessed Virgin and Mary Joyce, James's mother (186, 244; in light of Costello's discoveries, we should substitute Mary Cleary for Mary Sheehy in this list). He classes Gretta Conroy, Bertha Rowan, and Molly Bloom with the Joycean nightwomen (209)—to whom we should add Nora, the most important biographical instance of this category.

Some feminist critics have disputed this division in Joyce's relation to women. For example, in their introduction to *Women in Joyce*, Suzette Henke and Elaine Unkeless maintain that "The time-honored dichotomy between 'virgin and whore,' 'mother and temptress' may provide an oversimplified and radically deceptive schema" (xv). There is certainly much more to all of Joyce's female characters than these imagoes. However, this is always true in a transference relation. The so-called virgin/whore dichotomy simply indicates the schemas and associated prototypes through which Joyce unconsciously encoded, understood, responded to women in the context of sexuality. Moreover, even in relation to sexuality, the relevant exempla were multiple and the prototypes and schemas incomplete, open to differing specifications. To deny the validity of this division on the basis of characters' complexity is directly parallel to denying transference on the grounds that our understanding of other people is always more complex than a simple imago. Henke and Unkeless are certainly right that this transferential dichotomy does not tell the whole story about women in Joyce. However, they are, I think, mistaken in implying that it does not tell any of the story at all or only an unimportant part of the story.

It is a psychoanalytic commonplace that both figures in such a split have their source in the mother, as Shechner, for example, emphasizes in the case of Joyce (see 95). This is no doubt true. Joyce, too, split his mother into virgin and whore. But his virginal imagination of Mary Joyce predominated. It was when he came to substitute Nora for his mother that the more degraded and enticing image came to the fore. Shechner goes so far as to claim that "Nora was May Murray Joyce reborn" (87). Perhaps Joyce felt something of the kind. His mother's illness had recalled him from the continent, returned him to the prison of Ireland whence he had fled like Daedalus from Sicily. But on 16 June 1904, Joyce met Nora, and four months later returned with her to the continent, evading the nets of nation, religion, and family. Ellmann maintains that when Joyce met Nora "he entered into relation with the world around him and left behind him the loneliness he had felt since his mother's death" (Ellmann *James Joyce* 156). Perhaps this relation with the world was a necessary condition for Joyce's art as well. Though he had already begun to compose *Stephen Hero,* Joyce began *Dubliners* only after meeting Nora—publishing the first story, "The Sisters," on the first anniversary of his mother's death. Many readers of *Ulysses* have the sense that Stephen has been subdued by his three masters, by drink and by hopelessness. If so, it may be that the difference between Joyce and Stephen, or one crucial difference, is that, unlike Joyce, Stephen did not meet Nora Barnacle on 16 June 1904. (At the end of "Circe," Stephen, drunken and battered, lying on the roadside—abandoned by all but Bloom—doubles himself like a foetus and mutters the words of an air sung to his dying mother; his lone, maternal protector mishears, thinking: "A girl. Some girl. Best thing could happen him" [16.4950–51].)

Even otherwise the connection between Mary Joyce and Nora Barnacle is clear enough. But, once again, while each has for Joyce virginal and wanton characteristics, the former predominate with the mother who drew him back to the dungeon of Ireland and corpselike haunted his dreams (and whose brownclad spirit Margaret Joyce claimed to see rising heavenward on the eve of the Assumption of Our Lady—see Ellmann *James Joyce* 136), while the latter predominate with the spouse who fled with him to illicit union on the continent. Thus, when Joyce was in Paris, before his mother had fallen ill, she had already "come to him in a dream confused in his sleeping brain with the image of the Virgin Mother," as Stanislaus explained (*My Brother's Keeper* 226). Joyce recorded this dream and fashioned it into Epiphany 34. In the Scholes and Kain numbering, the immediately following Epiphany 35 concerns an incestuous prostitute named Eva. In this conjunction, we glimpse a religious opposition of Eve and Mary overlying the psychological opposition of whore and virgin—both of which will later be linked to the literary opposition of Eve and Beatrice. Moreover, this appears to be a hint of Joyce's ambivalence toward his mother, his split imago—the virginal aspect to the fore, but the promiscuous aspect only partially concealed in the directly conjoined incestuous prostitute.

Joyce's attitude toward Nora, however, was different. While he certainly adopts a reverential attitude at times, in some ways this worship seems to function primarily as a foil to his obscenities, rendering them bolder and more titillating by contrast. In 1909, Joyce wrote ambiguously to Nora, "You have been to my young manhood what the idea of the Blessed Virgin was to my boyhood" (*SL* 165). Two days later, he confided, "I feel I would like to be flogged by you. I would like to see your eyes blazing with anger" (166). He continued to a bald assertion of his dichotomous feelings: "One moment I see you like a virgin or madonna the next moment I see you shameless, insolent, half naked and obscene" (166–67). Several months later, Joyce recurs to this theme: "inside this spiritual love I have for you there is also a wild beast-like craving for every inch of your body, for every secret and shameful part of it, for every odour and act of it. My love for you allows me to pray to the spirit of eternal beauty and tenderness mirrored in your eyes or to fling you down under me on that soft belly of yours and fuck you up behind, like a hog riding a sow, glorying in the very stink and sweat that rises from your arse," and more poetically "[m]y prick is still hot and stiff and quivering from the last brutal drive it has given you when a faint hymn is heard rising in tender pitiful worship of you from the dim cloisters of my heart" (181). More obviously viewing Nora as a prostitute, Joyce wrote on the following day, "I have such a wild lust for your body that if you were here beside me and even if you told me with your own lips that half the red-headed louts in the county Galway had had a fuck at you before me I would still rush at you with desire," and then continued, "God Almighty, what kind of language is this I am writing to my proud blue-eyed queen" (183). Elsewhere, Joyce wrote, "The smallest things give me a great cockstand—a whorish movement of your mouth" (184).

In keeping with the less-elevated view of his blue-eyed queen, Joyce evidenced a deep fear of cuckoldry. For example, in one letter he cautions Nora not to allow their masturbatory letters to overarouse her—"you might get so hot that you would give yourself to somebody" (*SL* 187). A more obvious example may be found in a famous incident that occurred during Joyce's trip to Ireland in 1909. One week before the sixth anniversary of Joyce's mother's death, Vincent Cosgrave ("Lynch" of *A Portrait*) told Joyce that he had dated Nora in 1904. This caused Joyce to write a series of despairing and accusatory letters to Nora, crying out melodramatically (but, it appears, sincerely), "O Nora is all to be over between us? Write to me, Nora, for the sake of my dead love. I am tortured by memories. Write to me, Nora, I loved you only: and you have broken my faith in you" (158). Ultimately, Joyce demanded "Is Georgie my son? The first night I slept with you . . . there was very little blood" (158). He went on to lament, "In Dublin here the rumour here is circulated that I have taken the leavings of others. Perhaps they laugh when they see me parading '*my*' son in the streets" (159). Fortunately, Joyce, weeping and fainting, paid a visit to J. F. Byrne, then resident at 7 Eccles Street (subsequently occupied in fiction by the cuckolded Leopold Bloom). Byrne convinced Joyce that the whole thing was a lie and a conspiracy. But still Joyce returned to accusations a few weeks later, though in a milder tone.

I have discussed one point at which Joyce appears to have connected prostitution and the figure of Eve. More generally, sexuality and the Fall came to be closely associated for Joyce. In part, this is Miltonic, for in *Paradise Lost* Milton emphasized the degradation of Adam and Eve's sexual commerce following their defiance of divine will. Moreover, the sexual ripeness of Milton's Eve was stressed by such commentators as Hazlitt (see 372 in Wittreich). However, the connection occurs elsewhere as well, most importantly in the Kabbalah, which influenced Joyce greatly. As to Joyce's view of sexual womanhood in all this, Stanislaus publicly lamented Joyce's inability to free himself from the Christian view of woman as *radix malorum* ([root of evil], perhaps with a pun on *mala,* apple; *My Brother's Keeper* 46), a view well illustrated in *Paradise Lost.* Similarly, in his "Pola" notebook, Joyce wrote enigmatically, "A woman is a fruit" (Scholes and Kain 91); in this image, Joyce combined the fruit offered by Eve in the biblical and Miltonic Fall with the sexual favors of a woman—called the "juice of the fruit" by Lynch in *Stephen Hero* (202). Interestingly, this is also the image used by Hazlitt in his effusion on Eve's naked sexuality.

Joyce, then, had a deeply transferential relation to the women he desired and this transferential relation linked them with the figures of fallen Eve and Immaculate Mary. I discuss below the degree to which Eve becomes specifically Miltonic—especially in relation not to the Blessed Virgin, but to her more literary associate, Beatrice. First, however, let us consider one contingent event that may have helped to link Joyce's virgin/whore syndrome to the name and writings of John Milton. Joyce experienced sexual union for the first time in his middle teens. He was stopped by a prostitute as he walked home from a play he had attended with his family. The play was entitled *Sweetbriar* (Ellmann *James Joyce* 48) or *Sweet Brier* (Costello 151). It is hard to imagine that either then or later Joyce did not associate this title with the well-known lines of "L'Allegro"—"Through the Sweet-Briar, or the Vine, / Or the twisted Eglantine" (47–48). Indeed, in his minor conflict with John Eglinton in "Scylla and Charybdis"—a conflict begun by Eglinton's ironic comparison of Stephen with Milton—Joyce has Stephen recollect a truncated version of these lines (9.873), internally mocking the man he was used to call "the terrible virgin" (see Stanislaus Joyce *My Brother's Keeper* 253). Assuming this likely, though admittedly conjectural association, the incidental context of Joyce's first sexual encounter might well have helped to link forever in his mind degraded sexuality with the writings of John Milton. This connection was no doubt strikingly reenforced when, several years later, in transit to Paris, Joyce purchased the services of a particularly vulgar English prostitute named Eve (Costello 204).

Joyce and Milton through and against Other Authors

Once again, Joyce did not read Milton alone, in innocence of the history of other readers and writers for whom Milton was also a precursor. Of Milton's interpreters, several had special importance for Joyce, particularly in their contributions to his construction of prototypes out of Satan, Eve, and Adam, and the encompassing story of the Fall. These intermediaries prominently include John Dryden, Daniel Defoe, William Blake, Lord Byron,

Percy Shelley, and Marie Corelli. Dryden, though not in general an important precursor for Joyce, literally rewrote Milton's epic for the stage and thus provided a historically critical interpretation of that epic. Defoe and Blake were the objects of Joyce's 1912 lectures at the Universita Popolare of Trieste, "Verismo ed idealismo nella letteratura inglese (Daniele De Foe—William Blake)." The former was Milton's cynical, realist reviser, the latter his visionary, idealist re-creator. Byron was, of course, Joyce's boyhood idol; for Joyce, Shelley was a flawed, but aesthetically powerful extension of Byron. It was they who refashioned Satan into what T. S. Eliot was later to call "Milton's curly-haired Byronic hero" (quoted in Gilbert and Gubar 201). Corelli was the best-selling author of her time or any preceding, and took up the Miltonic and romantic strains, revising and reorienting them for a mass market.

Joyce conjoined and contrasted Milton with one of Milton's precursors as well: Dante Alighieri, the most sublime and spiteful demonologist in the history of the Catholic church. Dante was, for Joyce, primarily an alternative to Milton, not a means for revising him. Unlike Dryden and others, the exemplum of Dante did not so much refashion *Paradise Lost* as render salient for Joyce the particularity or difference of Milton. Finally, Joyce saw the myth of the Fall not only through Milton (and, of course, the Bible), but through Kabbalistic lore as well. This tradition—which, like the *Divine Comedy*, did not revise Milton, but was rather revised by him—also significantly redirected and reorganized Joyce's understanding of and response to Milton.

The State of Innocence and the Fall of Man: An Opera, Dryden's dramatization of *Paradise Lost*, was the earliest significant literary revision of Milton's epic. Though Joyce made few direct references to Dryden in his literary work or elsewhere, this opera altered or reoriented Milton in three ways that were to become very important for Joyce, either directly or indirectly. First, Dryden excised God from the text and centered it on Adam and Eve, rather than Satan. This is the least radical and least significant of these alterations, for it functions primarily to bring the poem into the mainstream of retellings of the Fall. On the other hand, this shift parallels Joyce's removal of God from both *Ulysses* and *Finnegans Wake*, and his shift of focus from the Satanic Stephen of *A Portrait* to the Adamic Bloom in *Ulysses*.

Second, and more important, Dryden was the first interpreter of Milton to stress Eve's sexuality and the sexual nature of the Fall itself. Before the Fall, Eve frankly describes to Adam the bliss of carnal union:

> When your kind Eyes look's languishing on mine,
> And wreathing Arms did soft embraces joyn,
> A doubtful trembling seiz's me first all o'r;
> Then, wishes; and a warmth, unknown before:
> What follow'd, was all extasie and trance;
> Immortal pleasures round my swimming eyes did dance,
> And speechless joys, in whose sweet tumult tost,
> I thought my Breath, and my new Being lost. (438)

Hearing this, Lucifer becomes aroused and, resolving on her seduction, wishes to "Enjoy and blast her in the act of love" (439). Certainly, this sexuality is not absent from Milton's work. But it is far more salient in Dryden's play and becomes more clearly visible in Milton's poem when viewed through this play.

Finally, Dryden is perhaps the first author to foreground the condition of Adam as one of homelessness and, in particular, exile, and he does so in some of the most affecting lines in the play:

> Adam. Heav'n is all mercy; labor I would chuse;
> And could sustain this Paradise to lose:
> The Bliss; but not the place: here could I say
> Heav'n's winged messenger did pass the day;
> Under this Pine the glorious Angel stay'd:
> Then, show my wondring progeny the shade. (459)

Exile was obviously an important element in Joyce's self-understanding and literary self-reconstruction through Satan; this connection has its literary origins in Byron. But in Leopold Bloom and Humphrey Chimpden Earwicker, Joyce reconfigured himself through Adam as well. And they too are exiles—Earwicker directly and literally, Bloom indirectly and metaphorically. Bloom's father was a literal exile from Hungary—and, before that, folded away in the memory of nature, his farther ancestors were exiled from Palestine, dispersed from the land of Eden.

Joyce's debt to Defoe is perhaps less than that to Dryden, but it is better documented. In his lecture on Defoe, Joyce evidences great respect for this "sensible barbarian" who was the "father of the English Novel" and "the great precursor of the realist movement" (18, 7, 13). Milton rears his grim visage at several points in this essay, but his presence looms in the social and political background of this study even when Joyce does not mention him. For example, it is hard not to connect and contrast Milton and Defoe when Joyce emphasizes that Defoe was born just after the Restoration and that he was an advocate of free speech, but, more like Joyce than Milton, he was subject to the whimsy and censorship of publishers and lacked skill and prudence in financial matters. (For a brief discussion of some connections between Joyce and Defoe, see Seidel 102ff.)

More important, Joyce discusses directly Defoe's *History of the Devil*—in part, a revision of Milton. As Joyce explains, "Defoe's devil has few things in common with the strange son of Chaos who enters upon eternal war against the purposes of the Supreme Being" (18). Joyce continues, noting that Defoe, like Joyce himself, "puts himself in the Devil's place . . . [and] boldly quarrels with the conception of the majestic protagonist of *Paradise Lost*" (18). Following this, Joyce lists a series of points from the work, a number of which are significant for our understanding of Joyce's relation to Milton. Specifically, Defoe "wonders how many days it took the Devil to fall from heaven into the abyss, how many spirits fell with him, when he became aware of the creation of the world, how he beguiled Eve, where he prefers to live, why and how he made himself wings" (18). The number of days that lapsed following the demonic fall is of considerable interest in *Ulysses*, as are the questions of Eve's beguilement, the demonic abode, and so on. Defoe also maintains that Adam was "effeminated" (73), a point relevant to Joyce's re-creation of Adam in Leopold Bloom, "the new womanly man" (*U* 15.1798–99). Perhaps most interesting of Defoe's concerns, however, is that relating to flight. In positing that Satan fabricated his own wings, Defoe directly connects Satan with Daedalus, thereby linking two of the figures most obviously crucial to Joyce's literary self-understanding and transformation. Indeed, in this context one might wonder if Stephen Dedalus's aim of uninhibited flight in art might not also allude to Milton whose "advent'rous Song / . . . with no middle flight intends to soar / Above th'*Aonian* Mount, while it pursues / Things unattempted yet in Prose or Rhyme" (*PL* 1.13–16)—surely Joyce's ambition as well.

But, though he was not unself-critical, Joyce celebrated Satan, and he warred, and had Stephen war, against the paralyzing conformities of religion, state, and family, all represented in the hierarchy of Milton's divine abode of bliss—religion and family obviously, but state as well, if one recalls the connections of Satan with Charles and of the Satanic hordes with the "murderous Irish, the enemies of God and mankind" (Milton *John Milton* 663). Moreover, Stanislaus explains in *My Brother's Keeper* that Joyce's "interpretation of the Fall" was that "the soul is awakened to spiritual life by sinning" (160). And in his "Trieste" notebook comments on Stephen, Joyce wrote, "He came to the knowledge of innocence through sin" (Scholes and Kain 95). In some ways these last are Miltonic views. After all, our first parents gained knowledge not only of evil but of good in eating the forbidden fruit, and through Divine Providence the world will be better for it. But surely Joyce did not have this in mind. Milton hardly conceived his doctrine of Providence as justification for drunkenness, lechery, and irreligion. And he did not see himself as favoring the Devil in his war with all things good and right. Joyce did take this view of Satan and of the Fall from *Paradise Lost*, but from *Paradise Lost* by way of the romantic poets, first of all William Blake.

Blake was no doubt mistaken in claiming (in a famous phrase) that Milton was "of the devil's party," but many modern readers feel that he "was a true poet" primarily because of his portrait of Satan (178). In remaking *Paradise Lost* from the perspective of Satan, Blake provided Joyce with a way of separating Milton's character of Satan from Milton's view of that character, and from the stifling political and religious ideology that defined that view. Joyce and Stephen tacitly affirm the Satanic dicta evoked by Blake—"Energy is eternal delight" (178). "The road of excess leads to the palace of wisdom" (179). "You never know what is enough unless you know what is more than enough" (181). "Prisons are built with stones of law, brothels with bricks of religion" (180). "He who desires, but acts not, breeds pestilence" (180). And, most important for an artist who aspires to fly with the wings of imagination, an artist who risks falling like Icarus, but insists that an artist's "errors are volitional, and are the portals of discovery" (*U* 9.229): "No bird soars too high if he soars with his own wings" (Blake 180)—all proverbs gathered by Blake "walking among the fires of hell, delighted with the enjoyments of genius, which to angels look like torment and insanity" (179).

In addition, though Milton's God is absent from Joyce's work, Blake's revision of Milton's stern deity—in the figure of Urizen—provided Joyce with a way of structuring that absence. Specifically, in *A Portrait* and *Ulysses*, the place of Milton's God is taken by an abstract principle of authority, stifling to the young artist. This abstract principle is manifest variously in the institutions of church, state, and family; it is a principle of structure and hierarchization that, in the Aristotelian manner, has no existence outside such material incarnations. It is this concrete, manifest principle against which Stephen cries out defiantly that he will not serve. And it is this principle that casts out the nets that would trap him in his intended flight "Above th'*Aonian* Mount," the nets he must evade. The image is

Blake's. In the prophetic books, this malign principle is found incarnate in Urizen:

> . . . Urizen
> Walked over the cities in sorrow;
>
> 7. Till a Web, dark & cold, throughout all
> The tormented element stretch'd
> From the sorrows of Urizen's soul.
> And the Web is a Female in embrio.
> None could break the Web, no wings of fire,
>
> 8. So twisted the cords, & so knotted
> The meshes, twisted like to the human brain.
>
> 9. And all call'd it The Net of Religion.
> ("The Book of Urizen" lines 460–69)

Finally, just as Milton's God clashes with a rebellious Satan, Urizen battles with the rebellious, Satanic Fuzon—ultimately killing him, stoning him to death with the tables of the law ("The Book of Ahania" lines 87–94). This first death recalls that of Stephen Protomartyr, the first Christian stoned to death by the old law. Blake thus links Satan and Stephen, not merely by association, but by analogy. It hardly needs to be pointed out that this connection found its way to the very center of Joyce's self-portrait. (For a discussion of some other possible links between Joyce and Blake, see McArthur.)

Blake's importance to Joyce as a reviser of Milton is equalled only by that of Byron. Both were important to Joyce primarily as poets, but there was more to his sympathy in each case. Yeats had championed Blake and traced or claimed to trace his lineage back to Ireland. More important, Byron was one of the very few English authors who avoided both oppressive and paternalistic racism toward the Irish. Byron was Joyce's great poetic ideal in youth. But Joyce retained his interest in, even love of, Byron to the end of his life. In the 1930s, for example, Joyce tried to collaborate with George Antheil on an operatic version of Byron's *Cain*, to be sung by the Irish tenor John Sullivan, whose cause Joyce was championing. The collaboration failed, in part because Joyce refused to change any words of the "great English poet" (quoted in Steffan 473).

It was through Byron and Shelley that Joyce came to reconstrue the

Satanic rebel as a poet, or the poet as a Satanic rebel. This is true not only in general terms, but in details of character, action, and setting drawn from *Childe Harold, Manfred, Cain,* "Alastor," *Prometheus Unbound,* and other works of "the Satanic School." Milton had, in passing, characterized Satan as an exile (*PL* 1.632). Byron elaborated this and made exile the condition of his heroes. In doing so, he rendered these heroes more isolated as well: "Proud though in desolation; which could find / A life within itself, to breathe without mankind" (*Childe Harold's Pilgrimage* 3.107–8). Even more important, he further articulated this Satanic hero's mind and heart: brooding, remorseful, despondent, struggling with a memory of sin, tottering on the edge of suicide—all characteristics employed by Joyce in making Stephen. Moreover, all this misery was not without self-ironizing wit and parody. Joyce also drew from Byron a sense that irony and sincerity, even ridicule and sympathy, not only can, but most often do coincide. (Again, realism: "Confess, confess—you dog . . . is it not *life*, is it not *the thing?*" Byron wrote of *Don Juan* to a friend [quoted in Perkins 829].) The Byronic hero is often parodied in the very works where his or her suffering is most sincerely and sympathetically put forth. Here too Stephen Dedalus is a late exemplum of the schema.

Shelley reenforced and elaborated Byronic tendencies (for the most part, minus the irony). In addition, he has distinct importance due to his critical development of the romantic view of Milton's Satan. In "A Defense of Poetry" (from which Joyce quotes in *Ulysses* [see 9.381–82]), Shelley maintains that "Milton's Devil as a moral being is . . . far superior to his God," for the one is a hopeless but perseverant rebel, whereas the other is an imperturbable torturer (1081). Indeed, Shelley even goes so far as to argue that *Paradise Lost* exhibits a "bold neglect of a direct moral purpose," which neglect "is the most decisive proof of the supremacy of Milton's genius" (1082). On the other hand, it is difficult to imagine that Joyce ever accepted Shelley's rather implausible view that Milton strove for a Joyceanly static art, rather than a kinetic art of the church militant, an art consistent with Milton's stated purpose to "justify the ways of God to men" (*PL* 1.26). It is also worth noting that, in the preface to *Prometheus Unbound,* Shelley described Satan as morally tainted and contrasted his flawed character with "the highest perfection of moral and intellectual nature" to be found in Prometheus (981 in Perkins). Though Joyce was deeply influenced by *Prometheus Unbound,* he did not follow Shelley in this enthusiasm for moral perfection. In this respect Joyce remained Byronic.

Marie Corelli holds a somewhat different position from the other writers discussed. Corelli—or, rather, Mary Mackay, a woman of Celtic extraction who wrote under an Italian nom de plume (for a discussion of Corelli's obscure origins, see chapter 1 of Bigland)—must have combined many characteristics Joyce detested, not the least of which was her deep concern with pleasing what Joyce would call "the rabblement." But Joyce read at least two of her books—*The Sorrows of Satan* and *Ziska* (see *SL* 55)—and included a number of allusions to the former in *Ulysses* and *Finnegans Wake*. The most important, and most explicit reference occurs in "Scylla and Charybdis." When Stephen's unusual project of rewriting *Paradise Lost* minus one hundred lines is broached at the National Library, Eglinton mocks Stephen's mournful Satanism, as Mulligan had done earlier in the book, and announces that the aspiring poet will entitle his epic masterpiece *The Sorrows of Satan*. The title is inappropriate to *Ulysses*, but perhaps not inappropriate to the sort of work Joyce might have written, had he not learned—in part from the negative example of Corelli—the aesthetic importance of ironic distance in self-portraiture.

On the whole, Corelli's novel is melodramatic and moralistic. It concerns a young man, Geoffrey Tempest, who cannot make ends meet, because his novels are not "indecent enough" to find a publisher—a fiction that Joyce must have found highly amusing. Fortunately, or so it seems, Tempest inherits a large sum of money from an uncle who has sold his soul to the devil. In consequence, he makes friends with Satan in the guise of Prince Lucio Rimanez and under his influence sinks into a life of mild decadence (for example, he overeats, a vice for which Corelli has particular animus). Eventually Tempest's spouse, Sybil, her character degraded by "Ibsenism" (201), makes a play for Rimanez—before the wedding, she told Tempest that she had "lax morals," but he ignored her. Rimanez delivers a rousing discourse on female fidelity, roundly denouncing not only Sybil, but the "majority" of women, and affirming that "[i]f women were pure and true, then the lost happiness of the world might return to it" (355). He contrasts Eve-like Sybil with the excruciatingly chaste Mavis Clare (Marie Corelli's self-portrait in the novel), and Sybil's fallen state with "the cottage of Mavis Clare," which he equates with a new "Eden" (358). Unhappily, Tempest overhears. Sybil does herself in, ending her tortured life with a badly written (though at times touching) suicide note, which, despite stylistic lapses, manages to affirm that "God EXISTS!" (409). Tempest fails to catch the drift of Sybil's exclamations. Subsequently, he is shipwrecked, he is rescued, his money is stolen, and he reforms himself, at last finding the Lord. Meanwhile, Satan has been called briefly heavenward. In Corelli's view, Satan is kept in hell by the evil of humankind. Each time a good soul resists his temptations, he is rewarded with a few moments of heavenly bliss. If the world were good, he too would be redeemed.

The most important influence of the novel on Joyce was no doubt negative. Marie Corelli felt herself misunderstood and maligned by hostile critics. She used *The Sorrows of Satan* in part to take revenge. Joyce's situation and goals were not dissimilar. Indeed, the exchange with Eglinton is at the very center of Joyce's attack on those Irish arbiters of taste who failed to recognize his talent. It would have been easy for him to turn this into a manichean struggle between the poet and the boor. But he resists this temptation. He is careful to make Stephen faltering and self-critical (like Milton's Satan, in fact), and to emphasize the slimness of his youthful accomplishments—a mere handful of delicate verses redolent of aestheticism. (Another link with Milton: Johnson stresses that Milton's juvenilia showed no special promise and did not warrant the poet's lofty expectations of himself: "the products of his vernal fertility have been surpassed by many" [87].) Corelli, in contrast, did not resist the manichean temptation. Her self-portrait provided an exemplum against which Joyce could evaluate his own self-portrait, an exemplum that functioned to render salient the artistic flaws that can result from wounded narcissism. As Kershner put it, "if Dedalus is a triumph of ambiguous self-portrayal, Mavis Clare is a horrible warning against the novelist's autobiographical impulse" (57).

On the other hand, the novel is not at all as ridiculous as this might imply, and it had other effects on Joyce as well. There are some very nice moments, and the characterization of Sybil—despite Corelli's self-conscious aims—is very sympathetic, sometimes moving, and often effectively Ibsenist. (A Miltonic case of the evil character stealing the show, despite the author's best intentions.) Joyce would have felt a certain affinity with Geoffrey Tempest, an impecunious writer in a struggle with publishers and his landlady (as Kershner has noted, see 55–56). More important, Corelli's Lucio Rimanez—an artist and a tragic figure, far superior to those who condemn him—stands with the heroes of Blake, Byron, and Shelley at the apex of the romantic elevation of Satan. Joyce must have been particularly struck by Corelli's iconic identification of Rimanez/Satan and Stephen Protomartyr, a link more fully explicit than that to be found in Blake. During Sybil's ill-fated attempt at seduction, both the first sinner (Rimanez/Satan) and the first saint (Stephen, represented in stained glass above Sybil and Rimanez) evidence "great and terrible anguish" (353). In the context, we seem to have little choice but to infer that Satan is a martyr like St. Stephen—though more long-suffering and even more tragic, in Corelli's unorthodox angelology.

Finally, Joyce surely took a keen interest in the theme of marital infidelity, the wife who would betray her husband with his friend—as Joyce later imagined Nora had done with Cosgrave. Perhaps for Joyce the major function of *The Sorrows of Satan* was to link definitively spousal betrayal with diabolic seduction and with the myth of the Fall—a connection suggested, but not developed, by Milton's other revisers. (For the connection between Sybil and Eve, only suggested, but relatively clear, see Corelli 350–51). The revision of the Fall in terms of marital infidelity is central to both *Exiles* and *Ulysses*.

If Corelli provided to Joyce one further basis for expressing and understanding his images of the whore and faithless wife in the figure of Eve, it is Dante who provided him a way to express and understand his image of the virgin in a literary figure—specifically in Beatrice. Certainly Joyce's interest in Dante was of long standing. Stanislaus maintained that "[i]n early youth," Joyce's "gods were Blake and Dante" (quoted in Ellmann *James Joyce* 53). Later on, Gogarty nicknamed Joyce "the Dante of Dublin" (75) and barbered him into a resemblance of the Florentine poet (131). More important for our purposes, Richard Ellmann tells us that Joyce as a young man "exalted Dante at the expense of Milton, whom he fiercely rejected" (59). In his lecture on Daniel Defoe, Joyce went so far as to claim that "*Il Paradiso Perduto* di Milton e una transcrizione puritanica della *Divina Commedia*" [Milton's *Paradise Lost* is a puritanic transcription of the *Divine Comedy*] ("Verismo" 144).

In claiming Dantean influence on Milton, Joyce is not alone. Milton admired Dante and certainly drew on the *Divine Comedy* and other works in writing *Paradise Lost* and other poems. Indeed, Joyce is not alone in claiming supremacy for Dante. As Irene Samuel points out in *Dante and Milton*, "critics have generally preferred to exalt the one poet or poem at the expense of the other" (31). Voltaire, Landor, and Eliot were among those in the Milton camp; Macaulay, Carlyle, and Ruskin were among those joining Joyce in the advocacy of Dante. On the other hand, some influential writers have linked Dante and Milton toward less partisan ends. In *A Portrait*, Stephen takes his tripartite division of the arts—lyric, epic, and dramatic—and his valorization of the dramatic above the lyric and the epic from Victor Hugo; and for Hugo, the three prime examples of dramatic poetry were "Shakespeare, Dante, and Milton" (quoted in Gifford 254). Similarly, in his "Defense of Poetry," Shelley praised Milton as the third great epic poet after Homer and Dante, and he closely connected *Paradise Lost* with the *Divine Comedy* (1081–82). Indeed, in the same section of the "Defense," Shelley maintained that "the superstructure of English literature is based upon the materials of Italian invention," which parallels not only Joyce's claim about Milton and Dante, but also his more general claims about English literature before Defoe, "the first English writer" (Joyce "Verismo" 144), the others (for example, Chaucer and Shakespeare) being for the most part Italian, in Joyce's view.

In any case, though he no doubt drew on Shelley and other writers in considering the issue, Joyce's most important reasons for pairing the two authors and for celebrating Dante while denigrating Milton were, it would seem, quite different from those of his literary mentors. As Bernard Benstock has noted, Joyce's enthusiasm for Dante was, at least in part, a way of avoiding the English literary tradition, the tradition of the oppressor (*James Joyce* xv). More exactly, Joyce could find in Dante many of the virtues he admired in Milton, but without the racism, imperialism, and hypocrisy about freedom. For example, though he was a monarchist, Dante vigorously criticized the interference of the Catholic church in secular matters and not only when the church was represented by a corrupt and dissolute hierarchy. In his treatise *De Monarchia*, Dante argues vigorously for the strict separation of church and state, maintaining that the political actions of the church have been the major source of civil strife in recent times. This latter view would have struck a profoundly sympathetic chord in Joyce, given his deep bitterness against the Catholic hierarchy for its role in the fall of Parnell. Moreover, Joyce no doubt viewed quite differently criticism of the Catholic Church coming from a Catholic and such criticism coming from an advocate of the dispropriation and vengeful execution of his Catholic compatriots and ancestors. Joyce, who remained thoroughly pacifist for his entire life, must have found himself likewise in accord with Dante's view that "The Goal of Mankind is Universal Peace," a view to which Dante devoted an entire section of his treatise, and a view opposed to the protestant militancy of the more muscularly Christian Milton. Finally, Joyce agreed with Dante's advocacy of freedom, an advocacy again shared by Milton in theory, yet betrayed by Milton in practice.

But perhaps the most important reason Joyce paired Milton and Dante, and elevated the latter above the former—beyond what was no doubt in part an honest literary evaluation—involved his own split relation to the women he loved. Joyce split his beloved, whether mother or wife, into a virgin and a whore. Dante and Milton (by way of Dryden, Corelli, and

Kabbalistic lore) provided him with literary models to which he could relate his split imagoes and through which he could, consciously or unconsciously, rethink them. Eve was the lustful seductress of *Paradise Lost* 9, "*Eve*, whose Eye darted contagious Fire" (1036), who precipitated Adam's uxorious Fall, and who sealed their lapsarian pact in brute carnality. Beatrice was the virginal savior, pure in thought and deed, who intervened on behalf of the spiritually disoriented Dante in order to guarantee his salvation.

In both life and art Joyce expanded these types. I discuss the art below, but the function of these twin literary types in Joyce's romantic life is neither unimportant nor irrelevant. Nora is to a degree assimilated to the whorish Eve. Her incarnation as Molly Bloom will make this identification more evident. More interesting than this, however, was Joyce's tendency to assimilate the other women he desired to Beatrice, sometimes quite explicitly. This is especially clear with the woman of *Giacomo Joyce* (perhaps Amalia Popper, perhaps not [see Costello 308]) and with Marthe Fleischmann—at least when he was only admiring her from afar, before he had, on 2 February 1919, "explored the coldest and hottest parts of her body" (Ellmann 451).

The woman of *Giacomo Joyce* is straightforwardly connected with Beatrice: "She walks before me along the corridor and as she walks a dark coil of her hair slowly uncoils and falls. Slowly uncoiling, falling hair. She does not know and walks before me, simple and proud. So did she walk by Dante in simple pride and so, stainless of blood and violation, the daughter of Cenci, Beatrice, to her death" (11). This connection is further emphasized by Joyce's description of her as "virgin most prudent" (9), and his association of her (in "A Flower Given to My Daughter"—see Ellmann *James Joyce* 345) with "the white rose," an image he invariably linked with Dante's white rose of heaven. In connection with this, she is almost disembodied, like the spiritual Beatrice. Indeed, she does not blow her nose, Joyce tells us (2), and "[h]er body has no smell" (13). In contrast to this "stainless" Beatrice, Joyce finds himself aroused by "a little brown stain on the seat of [Nora's] white drawers" (*SL* 184) and delights in imagining her grunting defecations. Quite unlike the former, who has no odor and whose hair, uncurling at the back of her head, attracted Joyce's affectionate attentions, Nora was for Joyce a "little farting . . . brown-arsed fuckbird" (186), and in her case his affectionate attentions were drawn by a very different sort of curling and uncurling behind: "a sudden immodest noise made by [her] behind and then a bad smell slowly curling up out of [her] backside" (184).

Finally, there is a peculiar passage late in *Giacomo Joyce*, in which a serpentine woman "coils" toward Joyce. Her lips suck at his left armpit, "a coiling kiss.... I burn! ... A starry snake has kissed me: a cold nightsnake. I am lost!" (15). Clearly, the imagery is that of the Fall. But who is this demonic seductress? At first it appears to be the new Beatrice, suddenly transformed—"She coils towards me" and previously "she" has always been the same. But this Beatrice has been distant, and now the snakecoiling woman addresses Joyce intimately, "Jim, love!" Then the kiss, a hellish "fang of flame leaps out." Jim responds: "Nora!" With the appearance of Nora, the serpent-seduced and seductive Eve, *Giacomo Joyce* spirals swiftly to a close.

In relation to the Beatricean beloved of *Giacomo Joyce*, and before the more demoniacally seductive appearance of Nora, Joyce seems to have seen himself primarily in his role as Satan. Thus, for example, just after comparing the loved one to Beatrice, he explains "Surely hell's luck will not fail me!" (11). In the case of Marthe Fleischmann, however, Joyce seems rather to have seen himself as Dante. In only his second letter to Marthe Fleischmann, Joyce, reducing his age by two years, claimed that he was thirty-five, "the age of Dante when he entered into the night of his being" (*SL* 233)—in other words, the age when salvationary Beatrice intervened on his behalf. A few days later, Joyce sent Fleischmann a copy of his *Chamber Music* and subsequently wrote to her, in part expressing his melodramatic fear of her imminent death. Perhaps he felt that such morbid solicitousness, coming hard on the heels of her perusal of his poetry, would have an aphrodisiac effect. In any event, his concern for her early demise was no doubt in part the result of his assimilation of her to Beatrice, whose early death (alluded to in *Giacomo Joyce*) clearly haunted Dante for his entire life and made possible her virginal-salvationary position in Dante's imagination, and thereby in Joyce's.

Eventually, of course, Joyce's relationship with Marthe Fleischmann took quite a non-Dantean turn. Moreover, Joyce's relation with Amalia Popper—or whoever inspired *Giacomo Joyce*—no doubt had many aspects, not all of them related to Beatrice. What is important here is that his relation to each was initially defined in connection with Beatrice and in opposition to Nora, who for Joyce took on even more the character of Eve through the contrast. This highly literary splitting was not confined to Joyce's biography and autobiographical writing. It was of central importance to his more fictional efforts as well—especially "The Dead," *A Portrait,* and *Exiles.*

But there is a change between *Exiles* and *Ulysses*. In *Ulysses*, the importance of Beatrice fades, and a new division enters—or, rather, a division only hinted at before becomes prominent, a division that is not precisely an opposition and that Joyce drew from the Kabbalah—the division between Eve and Lilith. And this brings us to the final filter through which Joyce saw Milton, a final set of principles that complicated, modified, and reordered those that Joyce drew from *Paradise Lost*. Jackson Cope and Sheldon Brivic have discussed at length the importance of Kabbalistic writings in both *Ulysses* and *Finnegans Wake*, emphasizing the mystical elements of this tradition. In a related vein, Ira Nadel has discussed Joyce's considerable interest in Talmud and his "partial knowledge of Hebrew" (127). However, it is Kabbalistic myth and folklore that are most relevant to our purposes, for it is the tales of Lilith and Samael that entered into Joyce's understanding of the Fall, refashioning *Paradise Lost* and Genesis, and being refashioned by them, until these and the other works we have discussed combined into a new structure, a Joycean story of the Fall, both concealed and elaborated in *Ulysses* and *Finnegans Wake*.

Linking Milton and Kabbalah is not as strange as it might seem. In his discussion of Samael and Lilith, A. E. Waite—one of Joyce's major sources on Kabbalistic lore (see Cope 78–79)—explains the Fall in part by reference to Milton, reading the Kabbalistic tale through the filter of *Paradise Lost*: "[T]he seduction of Adam by Lilith and of Eve by her companion Samael caused our mortal condition. This is the sense in which death was brought into the world, 'and all our woe'" (*Secret Doctrine* 102 n. 4, quoting the famous opening lines of *Paradise Lost*, lines to which Joyce himself repeatedly alluded). Moreover, a number of critics have seen a strong Kabbalistic influence in *Paradise Lost* and an even stronger Kabbalistic influence on Blake's interpretation of *Paradise Lost*. Indeed, in the early part of this century, Milton's rabbinical studies were a significant focus of criticism (see, for example, Fletcher for an overview and citations; see also Denis Saurat's article, published in Paris as Joyce was finishing *Ulysses* in the same city). And in *Die Entstehung des Talmuds* (owned by Joyce in Trieste) Funk mentions Milton's "deathless work" as a prime example of literature influenced by Jewish legends of Adam and Eve. More generally, in the opposition between the Hellenic and the Hebraic (brought up at several points in *Ulysses*), Milton was located in the latter camp: "a Hebrew in Soul" Wordsworth called him in the preface to *Lyrical Ballads* (quoted in Wittreich 130).

The influence of Kabbalistic material on Joyce was in part mediated by later writers as well. Some elements of Kabbalistic lore had worked their way into late nineteenth-century popular culture. Because of this, Kabbalistic revisions of biblical tales and the weaving of Kabbalistic motifs into contemporary fictions became almost commonplace, the character of Lilith being particularly prominent. In the half century before *Ulysses*, Robert Browning, Ada Collier, Anatole France, Rémy de Gourmont, Isolde Kurz, George MacDonald, E. D. E. N. Southworth, George Sterling, and Marie Corelli published works referring to Lilith directly in their titles; many others, including Dante Gabriel Rossetti, brought Lilith into their works without announcing her presence on the cover (see the list in Koltuv 126–27).

Joyce, however, made his own direct use of Kabbalistic materials. Perhaps most important, as the quotation from Waite indicates, Lilith and Eve are not opposed as are Beatrice and Eve. In effect, they are for Joyce different versions of the same imago, different versions of the same lasciviousness that characterized Joyce's transferential view of sexual womanhood. In some ways, they represent only a further articulation of Joyce's earlier whore imago, with the Madonna imago suppressed. But in some ways they represent a less pathological view of women, a healthier acceptance of shared human physicality—an acceptance that develops and deepens over the course of the last two works.

Chapter 3

A Romantic Milton Masked with Dante Alighieri's Face: Joyce and Milton before *Ulysses*

1906 was, as Ellmann reports, a dry year for Joyce, and he did virtually no new writing. *Dubliners* had almost achieved its present shape, but still ended with the story "Grace"—which, as Ellmann has pointed out (following Stanislaus), "employed the tripartite division of the *Divine Comedy*, beginning with the Inferno of a Dublin bar, proceeding to the Purgatorio of a drunkard's convalescence, and ending in the Paradiso of a highly secularized Dublin church" (*James Joyce* 229). In this Paradiso, the stern spiritual guidance of virginal Beatrice is replaced by the worldly direction of a priest who has sold his spiritual principles for donations from the wealthy and who aptly takes his name from one of the streets in Dublin's brothel district: Father Purdon.

But Joyce felt something was missing in the collection (see *SL* 109–10) and projected two further stories—"Ulysses" and "The Dead." He completed the latter and placed it after the Dantean "Grace." As far as I am aware, this is the first of Joyce's prose fiction that incorporates a direct reference to Milton. And it follows what are evidently his first borrowings from Dante into that genre as well.

Dubliners, Milton, and the Imperial British State

Parts of "The Dead" seem strongly if implicitly Miltonic. Most obviously, the names of Gabriel and Michael recall Milton, though these names are by no means exclusive to *Paradise Lost*. While the connection between the two Gabriels does not appear to go beyond their common name, and perhaps a common ineffectualness, there is a striking inversion or irony relating Michael Furey and Milton's archangel Michael. Michael Furey dies after being kept outside "at the end of the garden . . . at the end of the wall where there was a tree" (221). In a contrasting role, but in a similar scene, Milton's more furious Michael, the archangel, guards the gate in the wall at the end of the garden in order to keep Adam and Eve outside, precisely so that they will die, so that they cannot reenter Paradise and eat from the tree of life. In this respect, Gabriel and Gretta are akin to Adam and Eve, and Michael Furey—though only a memory—prevents them from regaining a bliss they once enjoyed.

In a different form and related to different but still deeply personal events, a parallel situation recurs at the end of *Exiles,* between Richard, Bertha, and Robert. And even more strikingly, it is recapitulated toward the end of *Ulysses*—now in the relation between Leopold and Molly Bloom. In each case, our original expulsion from the garden is revised. In this revision, Adam and Eve do not go, but remain. Someone else—Michael or Robert or Stephen (or Blazes)—leaves through the gate or is kept out in the garden by the wall. Moreover, rather than being reconciled and "hand in hand . . . wand'ring," these Adams and Eves are to some degree estranged. Some third figure, more like Satan than like the bearer of God's burning sword, some interloper, some serpentlike usurper has seduced the new Eve. The concluding reconciliation of the spouses, like that in *Paradise Lost,* is uxorious. But it is marred by deep mistrust and a profound sense of betrayal, a feeling that is, in effect, the fruit of the Fall, the result of the expulsion from Eden. Such triangulation and disillusion is clearly present in all three works. It almost counts as Joyce's typical ending and it certainly had profound personal significance for Joyce himself—a personal significance expressed in transformational, even inverse, relation to a Miltonic structure.

Indeed, in "The Dead," as in *Exiles,* it is more quadrature than triangulation, for there is a clear alternative to Eve—a virgin, unapproachable, even forbidding, the other half of the split imago: Miss Ivors. Like the other virgin figures in Joyce's writings—Emma Clery of *A Portrait* and Beatrice Justice of *Exiles*—Miss Ivors is partially modeled on Mary Cleary, the object of Joyce's unrequited adolescent love. Here she draws her name from a title of Mary Immaculate: "Tower of Ivory," a title used by Stephen for his earliest virginal love, Eileen (see *A Portrait* 36). A woman of this sort— whether Miss Ivors, Miss Justice, Miss Clery, or Miss Cleary—was, almost by definition, a woman Joyce could not attain. Like anyone else, Joyce resented this fact. And he expressed this resentment in literature, though he did so with more than ample self-irony. Thus for Gabriel Conroy to praise the hospitality of Ireland is at the same time to damn the frigid national conscience of Miss Ivors: "and sometimes I fear that this new generation, educated or hypereducated as it is, will lack those qualities of humanity, of hospitality, of kindly humour which belonged to an older day" (221). "Very good: that was one for Miss Ivors" (209). But the sally is feeble, and Miss Ivors is not there to hear it anyway. Moreover, the other woman—Gretta, or Bertha, or Molly, or Nora—had, in Joyce's mind, too much of that hospitality praised by Gabriel, and thus with her there was always in the background a shadow, some third party, a ghost like Michael Furey. For Joyce, at this time, there were in the sphere of sexual love only the two women: the one who would never be his, the exalted and unapproachable, the tower of ivory; and the hospitable woman who would be his, but only at intervals (every other night, if Cosgrave was truthful), only in part and uncertainly.

Beyond these hints of a narrative connection with the story of the Fall, and the related manifestation of split maternal imagoes in Gretta and Miss Ivors, there is an explicit reference to Milton in "The Dead." It is here that Joyce's political relation to Milton emerges. This reference comes toward the beginning of Gabriel's after-dinner speech, as he praises the manners of the past at the expense of the present generation. "Those days," he opines, "might, without exaggeration, be called spacious days: and if they are gone beyond recall let us hope, at least, that in gatherings such as this we shall still speak of them with pride and affection, still cherish in our hearts the memory of those dead and gone great ones whose fame *the world will not willingly let die*" (203; emphasis added). Mr. Browne "loudly" responds "Hear, hear!" (203).

Gabriel's allusion derives from Milton's "The Reason of Church Government Urged against Prelaty," an antiepiscopal work of the sort that provided ideological underpinning for the Puritan revolution—and, thereby, the Cromwellian confiscation and related terrors. In this essay, Milton denounces "these murderous Irish, the enemies of God and mankind" (*John Milton* 663), but liberally explains that the fault lies, in fact, with the English bishops who have failed to educate and reform these misguided heathens. Milton's discussion of reforming the brute Irish ends book 1 of the tract. The phrase quoted by Gabriel is taken from the immediately following preface to book 2, where Milton discusses his vocation as a poet and how he came to be convinced, by the Italians who appreciated his work, that he "might perhaps leave something so written to aftertimes, as they should not willingly let it die" (668). Moreover, he goes on to discuss his decision to follow the example of Ariosto in pursuing an epic in the vernacular, "to be an interpreter and relater of the best and sagest things among mine own citizens throughout this island" (668), and thus to establish himself as the national poet of England. This odd "digression" functions to establish Milton's authority and his "right" to address religious and political topics (671).

It is certainly no accident that Gabriel conceives of his speech in part as a rebuke to the nationalist Miss Ivors. Earlier in the evening, she had criticized him for engaging in a mild form of collaborationism in writing book reviews for a unionist newspaper. Gabriel is in many ways a version of Joyce and, like Gabriel, Joyce too was highly critical of insular Irish nationalism—including its lack of hospitality or broad humanity (compare his portrait of the Citizen). Yet by inserting this allusion into Gabriel's speech, Joyce indicates the degree to which Miss Ivors was right. Gabriel no doubt conceives of this allusion as purely literary, as entirely apolitical—much like his book reviews. But, much like his book reviews, it is not apolitical. It is, however mildly, collaborationist in its unquestioning acceptance of colonial hegemony, a hegemony manifest in those literary discourses, such as Milton's, that have aimed to justify and sustain the political, economic, and cultural dispropriation of the Irish. When Joyce initially conceived the need for a final story in his collection, he aimed to capture and praise precisely the gracious generosity of Irish society that it is Gabriel's goal to emphasize and appreciate in this speech (*SL* 110). Joyce felt that his stories before 1907 were too harsh and left out the beauties of Irish society and of Ireland itself. When he repented of his unrelievedly brutal criticism of his homeland and compatriots and when he chose to add an appreciative story to the end of *Dubliners*, perhaps he did so in part because he saw a hint of unwitting collaborationism in himself as well.

Parallel to this, it is also no accident that Joyce has Mr. Browne, the protestant in the group, respond enthusiastically to Gabriel's allusion to Milton. This recalls the adamantly protestant, and anti-Catholic, argument of Milton's work, however literary the passage in question may be. Moreover, it indicates once again the ambivalence with which Joyce must have responded to writings such as Milton's. We heard of Mr. Browne's religion a few pages earlier when Mary Jane had interrupted Aunt Kate during a harangue against the pope's decision to turn women out of the choirs. Mary Jane complains that Aunt Kate might give "scandal to Mr. Browne who is of the other persuasion." In response, Aunt Kate insists that she doesn't "question the pope's being right," going on to say that she is "only a stupid old woman and . . . wouldn't presume to do such a thing" (194–95). Mr. Browne's protestantism cannot help but remind us of the intellectual servility encouraged by a prelatic hierarchy of the sort Milton condemns. But in the context of Milton's treatise, it also cannot help but remind us of the brutalization of Irish Catholics by those who opposed such a hierarchy, and of the associated racist ideology that made it imperative for Joyce also "to be an interpreter and relater of the best and sagest things among mine own citizens throughout this island"—the task he self-consciously took up in this story.

This one quotation, then, crystallizes many concerns Joyce must have had about Milton, and brings up several of the associations that cluster about Milton in Joyce's subsequent writings. In context, it also recalls the striking contradictions in Milton's political and social thought, and hints at the ambivalence Joyce certainly felt toward England's premier poet. Once again, one clear source of Joyce's ambivalence toward Milton was his conflict with Milton's political and cultural imperialism. Joyce's avowed distaste for Milton was at least in part a political distaste, a distaste for an ideologist. Needless to say, this distaste made it all the more important for Joyce to remake Milton's great English epic—announced in the very passage from which Gabriel quotes—as a great Irish epic. The tension produced by Joyce's sense of political and cultural oppression virtually guaranteed that he would reject Milton. But it also guaranteed that Milton would be a poet he would seek to outdo.

Beatrice, Eve, and a Portrait of the Artist as a Young Man

Joyce's relation to Milton is expressed somewhat differently in *A Portrait*. It is more thoroughly personal, but at the same time the political, or politico-religious concerns are more fully developed, and more obviously damning. As in *Dubliners*, Joyce's direct references to Milton are localized. The first two parts of the novel, and a quarter of part 3, make no direct reference to Milton. But the speeches of the retreat and the elaboration of Stephen's traumatic conversion incorporate numerous unmistakable references to *Paradise Lost*, thereby linking Milton with the harsh moral rigorism of Irish Catholic doctrine, which Joyce deplored.

On the other hand, unlike in *Dubliners*, the presence of Milton in *A Portrait* far exceeds such direct references. Most important, Joyce made repeated use of Miltonic models, particularly the prototypes of Eve and

Satan. As to the former, the virgin/whore opposition is clearly important for Stephen through much of the book and, in most cases, it is modeled on the religious opposition of Mary and Eve or the literary opposition of Beatrice and Eve. In earliest youth, Stephen explicitly connects his beloved ivory-fingered Eileen with Mary Immaculate, the "Tower of Ivory" (36), his golden-haired Eileen with the Blessed Virgin, the "House of Gold" (43). Later, his love shifts to the imaginary Mercedes living in "a small whitewashed house" (63). He imagines a meeting, a "magic moment" in which he, Christlike, is "transfigured . . . [in] supreme tenderness" (65)—a lovely image of preadolescent spiritualized eros, far from Stephen's later degraded, obscene diabolism. In adolescence, the split character of Stephen's fantasies surfaces. Echoing Joyce's own masturbatory dreams, Stephen at night in "dark orgiastic riot" imagines a different transfiguration, Satanic and animal, when a "figure that had seemed to him by day demure and innocent" now comes "towards him . . . through the winding darkness of sleep, her face transfigured by a lecherous cunning, her eyes bright with brutish joy" (99)—the first hints of Lilith, who seduced men to spill their seed in the crime of Onan or in the lesser crimes performed unwittingly in sleep. Shortly after this, Stephen abjures Lilith for her successor, Eve; he experiences his first sexual congress, encountering a prostitute in a daedalian "maze of narrow and dirty streets" (100) and undergoing the bestial rights of the Fall, "darker than the swoon of sin" (101). From that "evil seed of lust all other deadly sins had sprung forth" (106), Stephen reflects, making clear the connection with the original sin. Satisfied, his soul sinks, like Milton's Satan, into the cold waste of chaos (103). This encounter with a physical incarnation of the lascivious imago—a seductive Eve—leads directly to the intellectual elaboration of its virginal counterpart: "[t]he glories of Mary held his soul. . . . His sin, which had covered him from the sight of God, had led him nearer to [Mary] the refuge of sinners" (104, 105).

At another level, from at least the time of his 1904 essay "A Portrait of the Artist as a Young Man," Joyce conceived of his muse in contradictory terms—"a witch" and yet a "sacramental . . . grace" (166). Perhaps most interesting in the present context are his characterizations of her as angelic "envoy from the fair courts of life" and lapsarian "Lady of the Apple Trees" (66). She finds her way into *A Portrait* as the highly ambiguous bird girl, the "angel" yet "mortal" (172), a spiritual principle with her legs bared to the thigh, frills of underpants visible below the fringes of her hoisted skirts, a Lilith-like "wild angel" (172) who leads Stephen into the much-discussed priesthood of the imagination, a true muse. She confirms Stephen in his decision not to join the priesthood; to enter Byron's public house, not Clontarf Chapel (164); Satanlike "to fall," but also (in an anticipation of *Finnegans Wake* with its natural cycles of life and death and life again) "to triumph . . . [and] to recreate life out of life" (172).

Joyce's most striking early development of the virgin/whore fantasy, however, and certainly his most important manifestation of this as a Beatrice/Eve fantasy, is to be found in the character of Emma. In *Stephen Hero*, Stephen identifies Emma as "the virgin" whom he will forsake for "the woman with the black straw hat" (192); she is the successor of Eileen and Mercedes whose unyielding "oracle" (his peculiar euphemism for "vagina") he will pass over for the more accessible charms of Fresh Nelly. As with all split imagoes, there is a tension here, and at moments Emma is more Eve than Beatrice. She is never desexualized, transfigured into insubstantiality like the beloved in *Giacomo Joyce*. Indeed, Stephen insists, she hotly lusts no less than he, though she resists (192). That resistance is the source of her torturous attractiveness. But it is also what keeps the virginal imago to the fore and links her more closely with Beatrice.

Already, in *Stephen Hero*, Emma is clearly imagined as Beatrice. Stephen thinks of Dante, and sees his own circumstances refitted in the frame of Dante's *Inferno*: his enemies frozen in painful gulfs of punitive ice and Emma "invok[ing] him" from the height of paradise (158–59). Even here, however, the negation of Beatricean purity intervenes, for the paradise is "Mohammadan" (159). Stephen has in mind the sort of paradise Joyce envisioned for James Clarence Mangan's beloved; in his essay on Mangan, written only the previous year, Joyce maintained that "[t]here is only one chivalrous idea, only one male devotion, that lights up the faces of Vittoria Colonna, Laura, and Beatrice. . . . But the world in which Mangan wishes his lady to dwell is different from the marble temple built by Buonarotti, and from the peaceful oriflamme of the Florentine theologian. It is a wild world, a world of night in the orient" (*CW* 183). Emma wearing the veil of Beatrice conceals the ministering houri of the camphor garden—and that, not in the mind of a devout Muslim, but of a European and a Christian apostate.

It is, of course, in *A Portrait* that Emma receives her fullest development as an ambiguous Beatrice. In *A Portrait*, Emma enters the story only insofar as she contributes to Stephen's development as an artist, only insofar as she inspires him as a muse or forces him to recognize the limitations of his art. She is a distant figure, a figure of literary imagination rather than real acquaintance, more akin to the Beatrice of the *Vita Nuova* than to the Emma

Clery of *Stephen Hero.* Indeed, in rewriting *Stephen Hero* into *A Portrait,* and thereby dramatically limiting the treatment and function of Emma, Joyce seems specifically to have had in mind Dante's representation of Beatrice in the *Vita Nuova.* In *Stephen Hero,* Stephen says that the *Vita Nuova* could serve as a model for "his scattered love-verses" (174); instead, Joyce seems to have made use of this model for his love-prose.

Specifically, Emma first appears in *A Portrait* as a young child, flirtatious on the steps of a tram, returning from a children's party (68), and she inspires Stephen to a Byronic effort, "To E___ C___" (70). She appears next as an absence, as someone who should have been waiting when Stephen emerges from the theater after his first efforts at the art of acting. Dante first met Beatrice in childhood also. Not as precocious as Stephen, he did not essay a poem then, but on their second meeting, nine years following, he wrote his sonnet, "To every heart"; after roughly the same interval, Stephen wrote Emma a second poem (222; see Reynolds 263).

Following the nonencounter at the theater, we next see Emma as imagined by Stephen in the anxious guilt of the retreat (roughly parallel to the next meeting between Dante and Beatrice, which takes place in a church). Here she is explicitly connected with both Beatrice and Eve. The fourth appearance of Emma is in the vilanelle, which functions primarily to link Emma with Eve; on the other hand, this nineteen-line poem in some degree parallels Dante's irregular twenty-line double sonnet, inspired by Beatrice at their next meeting. Subsequently, Emma passes Stephen and Cranly on the steps of the National Library. She greets Cranly, but willfully ignores Stephen (232). The next scene between Dante and Beatrice is strikingly parallel: "she who was the destroyer of all evil and the queen of all good [that is, Beatrice], coming where I was, denied me her most sweet salutation, in the which alone was my blessedness" (559). Beatrice's ill humor with regard to Dante was, it seems, due to malicious (and, he insists, unfounded) rumors that he engaged in fornication—rumors that we can imagine tainted the unsaintly image of Stephen as well. In any case, this slight once again closely links Emma with Beatrice.

The next and final meeting of Stephen and Emma makes explicit reference to Dante. Stephen and Emma are brought together by a crowd. After initial aggressiveness, Stephen "opened the spiritual-heroic refrigerating apparatus, invented and patented in all countries by Dante Alighieri" (252). During the subsequent conversation, Stephen manages to make a complete fool of himself. Emma departs quickly, with the perhaps mocking wish that Stephen would do what he had said. This is, at least in part, a straightforward allusion to the final meeting of Beatrice and Dante. Specifically, Dante is brought to a crowd of ladies in which Beatrice is present. A victim of his own refrigerating apparatus, he is paralyzed by fear and, like Stephen, quickly makes an ass of himself, earning the mockery of all the women present.

But, again, no transference is univocal and Emma is not Beatrice only; she is, at times, Eve as well. In this connection, Stephen is neither like Dante nor like Adam. He is, rather, the demonic rebel against divinity, leader of the fallen Seraphim, leader of the angels who, according to an apocryphal tale, were drawn into the gaping jaws of Hell by reason of their lust for seductive Eve (see Gifford for 217:28–30; there are similar stories in the Kabbalistic tradition, see Waite *Secret Doctrine* 85). In his villanelle, Stephen explicitly identifies Emma with that tantalizing Eve: "Lure of the fallen seraphim," he calls her (223). When Emma next appears, she (like Eve, like Lilith) is linked tacitly with the serpent and the Fall: "She had passed through the dusk. And therefore the air was silent save for one soft *hiss* that *fell*" (232; emphasis added).

The most important case of this ambivalence in Emma's character, or rather in Stephen's imagination of that character, occurs in the course of the retreat—a section thick with references to Milton. Father Arnall has just undertaken the Miltonic task of justifying the ways of God to man—"God's justice had still to be vindicated before men," he explains—through a harrowing sermon on death and judgment. Stephen leaves the church, suffering sharp-toothed agenbite. He is already tormented but, in crossing the square, he hears "the light laughter of a girl" (115). He is immediately smitten with shame and self-disgust over the fantasies of his "brutelike lust," and most particularly those to which he had subjected Emma. When his shame passes, he exalts Emma: "God and the Blessed Virgin were too far from him: God was too great and stern and the Blessed Virgin too pure and holy. But he imagined that he stood near Emma in a wide land and, humbly and in tears, bent and kissed the elbow of her sleeve" (116). As Gifford points out, "Emma is imagined as an intercessor for Stephen as Beatrice is for Dante in the 'wide land' of the Earthly Paradise at the end of the *Purgatorio*" (189). Suddenly, however, Stephen and Emma are placed together before the Blessed Virgin, as if transformed into Adam and Eve— and now they have *both* sinned. Mary addresses them, judging, "You have erred" (116). The now-lapsarian couple stands "hand in hand" (116), like Milton's Adam and Eve who, in the justly famous conclusion of *Paradise Lost*, "hand in hand with wand'ring steps and slow, / Through *Eden* took thir solitary way" (12.648–49). As if the connection between Stephen's fantasy and the sin of our first parents were not clear enough, the next sermon of the retreat, which is recounted almost directly afterward, deals with the fall of Adam and Eve and all its consequences. In this passage, we witness a particularly noteworthy instance of the Beatrice-Eve complex. Stephen suffers guilt over his own transgressions. At first he imagines Emma to be entirely pure, the object of worship whose image has been desecrated by the sacrilege of his lust. But then, without transition, he transforms her into Eve, who requires forgiveness, and is thus, implicitly, the temptress who is responsible for the Fall.

Father Arnall begins his directly following sermon with reference to Adam and Eve, but he turns quickly to Satan who was "hurled . . . into hell" (117), or as Milton has it, "Hurl'd . . . to bottomless perdition" (*PL* 1.45, 47), for the sin of pride—the sin of greatest importance to both Milton and Stephen. Father Arnall continues, explaining that "there fell with [Satan] a third part of the host of heaven" (117)—a statistic derived directly from Milton, through the words of Death in *Paradise Lost* 2 (692) and those of Raphael in *Paradise Lost* 5 (710). Moreover, Arnall maintains that "Adam and Eve . . . [were] created by God in order that the seats in heaven left vacant by the fall of Lucifer and his rebellious angels might be filled again" (117). As Gifford points out, this was not the standard view at the time. It derived ultimately from St. Anselm of Canterbury, but Joyce very likely took the idea from Milton, who followed Anselm on this point. In the words of God, quoted to Adam by Raphael:

> But lest his heart exalt him in the harm
> Already done, to have dispeopl'd Heav'n,
> My damage fondly deem'd, I can repair
> That detriment, if such it be to lose
> Self-lost, and in a moment will create
> Another World, out of one man a Race
> Of men innumerable, there to dwell,
> Not here, till by degrees of merit rais'd
> They open to themselves at length the way
> Up hither. (*PL* 7.150–59)

Subsequently, Arnall's description of the Fall agrees closely with that of Milton, though there is little to distinguish either from the account in Genesis and those in popular traditions. On the other hand, the misogyny of Milton's and Arnall's versions—including the emphasis on Eve's role as temptress of Adam and on Adam's uxoriousness—is worthy of note; it is not biblical, though it is by no means confined to Milton. More narrowly, his statement of the serpent's temptation "they could become as gods" perhaps echoes Milton's "ye should be as Gods" (9.710), though a biblical source is adequate. And his assertion that the seduction of Adam and Eve "brought death and suffering into the world" (134) recalls the opening sentence of *Paradise Lost*, where Milton makes the same (commonplace) claim in similar words, "brought death into the world and all our woe" (1.3).

Turning to Hell, Arnall emphasizes the "exterior darkness" of the place—"For, remember, the fire of hell gives forth no light. As, at the command of God, the fire of the Babylonian furnace lost its heat but not its light so, at the command of God, the fire of hell, while retaining the intensity of its heat, burns eternally in darkness" (120). This recalls Milton's well-known description of Hell: "A Dungeon horrible . . . / As one great Furnace flam'd, yet from those flames / No light, but rather darkness visible" (1.61–63). Similarly, "the sulphurous brimstone" described by Arnall as "specially designed to burn for ever and ever" while it "preserves that which it burns" (121) is a wordy version of Milton's "ever-burning Sulphur" that leaves its victims "unconsum'd" (1.69). Though Joyce could have had another primary source in mind for Arnall (for example, Pinamonti or St. Thomas), Milton's expression of this view was no doubt at least associatively relevant. Arnall's references to "the lake of fire" and "the burning ocean" (121) almost certainly allude to Milton's "burning Lake" (1.210) and "fiery Gulf" (1.52). Finally, Arnall's insistence that "each lost soul will be a hell unto itself" (121), while to a degree commonplace, is a view most famously found in *Paradise Lost*, as when Satan says, "Which way I fly is Hell; myself am Hell" (4.75).

When Stephen leaves the chapel after Arnall's terrorizing depiction of Hell, he ironically, even comically recapitulates Satan's exit from Hell. Just after departing, Stephen, thinking of death, encounters the "overcoats and waterproofs," which are "shapeless" (124) like Milton's Death "that shape had none" (2.667). More strikingly, he immediately feels that he cannot "grip the floor with his feet" and is "plunging headlong through space" (124). Similarly, in *Paradise Lost*, when Satan leaves Hell, passes Death, and enters Chaos, he too feels solidity dissolve into space beneath his feet: "that seat soon failing meets / A vast vacuity: all unawares . . . plumb down he drops / Ten thousand fadom deep" (2.931–34).

Stephen's headlong plunge suggests other Miltonic connections as well. Indeed, the closer verbal echo to Joyce's lines is God's expulsion of Satan, alluded to earlier in the sermon: "Him the Almighty Power / Hurl'd headlong flaming from th'Ethereal Sky" (*PL* 1.44–45). Milton's lines have frequently found revisers, at least two of which were important for Joyce. Most obviously, Byron rewrote this passage, emphasizing the sin of pride, when developing the Byronic hero, of whom Stephen is of course a late avatar: "Like Lucifer when hurl'd from Heaven for sinning; / Our sin the same, and hard as his to mend, / Being pride" (*Don Juan* 4.1). No less significantly, still earlier Pope had remade these lines in his translation of the *Iliad*, where Vulcan, in punishment for the Satanic act of defying Jove Thunderer, is "Hurl'd headlong downward from th'etherial height" (1.761). Stephen's Satanism ultimately incorporates not only the Byronic hero, but Vulcan as well: his Daedalian and Satanic flight at the end of the novel has a blacksmith's purpose: "to forge in the smithy of my soul the uncreated conscience of my race" (253). His prototype of the unserving poet was hammered out in the fires of both Satan and Satanic Vulcan (as well, of course, as Blake's Satanic and anti-Satanic Los, demiurgos).

After the retreat, Stephen makes his confession, like Adam and Eve before their expulsion from the Garden (*PL* 10.1100—through the agency of Michael, according to Arnall, as well as Milton), but also like Dante when he meets Beatrice in *Purgatorio* 30. Indeed, Stephen's confessor urges him to address himself to the Blessed Virgin, and Stephen sees his "purified heart" as "a heart of white rose" (145), an image Joyce derived, here as elsewhere, from Dante's vision of heaven in *Paradiso* 30.

The chapter ends with a final, comic reference to *Paradise Lost*. Stephen—having wept, like Adam and Eve, for his sins—exits the church, returns home, and contemplates "pudding and eggs" with the bliss of one whose soul has been purified. "How simple and beautiful was life after all," he thinks—"And life lay all before him" (146). This last sentence alludes to the lines of *Paradise Lost* that precede those quoted at the beginning of this passage, when Stephen and Emma stood "hand in hand." Specifically, Adam and Eve have just been expelled from the garden, and Milton writes:

> Some natural tears they dropp'd, but wip'd them soon;
> The World was all before them, where to choose
> Thir place of rest, and Providence thir guide:
> They hand in hand with wand'ring steps and slow,
> Through Eden took thir solitary way. (12.645–49)

By invoking these lines, Joyce implicitly compares Stephen's conversion to the expulsion from the garden of Eden, perhaps thereby indicating that it is a loss rather than a gain. In any case, he implicitly contrasts Stephen's asinine glee in "pudding and eggs" with the hopeful grief of Adam and Eve. Indeed, he continues the satiric use of Milton by describing, in the very next sentence, Stephen's *reaction* to the life that "lay all before him": "he fell asleep" (146). Thus Stephen shows ready success in the task of Adam and Eve in the world that "was all before them"—for recall that their aim was "to choose / Thir place of rest" (12.646–47).

But, of course, Joyce does not use precisely Milton's phrase here. He substitutes "life" for "World," "lay" for "was," and "him" for "them." The first is interesting because the world, for Milton, crucially involves *death*, and the punishment of death—something Stephen may feel he has superseded with his conversion, or may simply have forgotten in his spiritual ecstasy. The substitution of "him" for "them" is more suggestive. The passage began with Stephen joined with Emma—two souls seeking forgiveness, in imitation of their Edenic originals. But here, at the end of the passage, Stephen is entirely alone. His conversion, like any conversion to a repressive religion, has not brought him from lechery and promiscuity into a more profound relation with another human being. Rather, it has isolated him entirely and filled him with a short-lived and pathetically superficial sense of universal love and beauty.

Moreover, like all elements of influence, this quote is further altered and recontextualized by intervening revisions. Kenner has isolated the two most crucial: Wordsworth and Dickens (*Dublin's Joyce* 89). The transmutation of the line from a representation of sorrowful exile (in Milton) to an expression of individual liberation or pseudoliberation (in Joyce) recalls Wordsworth's introduction to *The Prelude*. Tritely declaring himself "free, / Free as a bird," released from the spiritual and aesthetic prison of the city, Wordsworth gazes upon nature and declares: "The earth is all before me" (1.8–9, 14). The doubled allusion is fitting, and furthers Joyce's irony. Wordsworth sought to celebrate the divinity of nature. Joyce, we might say, fixing Stephen's gaze on sausages, sees nature through the abattoir, ironizing not only Stephen, but Wordsworth—for nature is, after all, slaughter and food as well as gentle breeze and murmuring streams; the killing floor does not so much negate as extend nature. Perhaps even more important, Stephen's newfound devotion recalls, in a sort of identity of opposites, the aged Wordsworth, no more a horrible example of free thought, now ossified into pious orthodoxy and political reaction, defender of the established church, railing against Catholic emancipation and concessions to "the discontents prevalent in Ireland" ("Second Address" 169; see also Batho 149–52).

The revision by Dickens, in *Great Expectations,* is the stronger presence, and it moves in the opposite direction from *The Prelude,* which it also revises (Milton reverberating through Wordsworth reverberating through Dickens reverberating through Joyce [Hush! Caution! Echoland!]). "Opposite direction" here is both literal and figurative: Whereas Wordsworth escapes from the city, Pip enters. Whereas Wordsworth's revelation of a new world is utopian, Pip's, though hopeful, is disturbed by a nagging sense that hope is misguided. Pip has left on his journey to become a gentleman. The news of his benefactor and of his coming social elevation had filled him with the same delight that fills Stephen. And shortly before his Miltonic revelation, he wept, as did Stephen, as did Adam (Dickens 162). But like Adam, and unlike Stephen, Pip's tears are tears of remorse and of loss, the loss of home. And it is only when he realizes that it is "now too late and too far to go back" that the veil of romantic (and literal) mists is lifted momentarily and "the world lay spread before me." Dickens continues: "THIS IS THE END OF THE FIRST STAGE OF PIP'S EXPECTATION" (162). A structural division, but also an authorial comment. At the beginning of the following chapter, Pip enters a city that is "ugly, crooked, narrow, and dirty" (163), like the serpentine streets of the brothel district where Stephen falls into the dark swoon of sin. Yet Pip initially fails to recognize the lapsarian nature of his new habitat; in a passage that must have pleased Joyce, the older Pip attributes this blindness to English ethnocentrism (163).

Pip's misperception of the city is not his only lingering romantic delusion. More important, both in the novel and for the present study, is his imaginary betrothal with the proud Estella. Estella is another model for Emma, and is herself derived in part from Milton's Eve. The connection of Estella with Eve (and Pip with Adam) is strongest at the very end of the novel. Estella has, like Eve, repented of her pride. Pip takes her hand and the two of them—hand in hand, like Adam and Eve or Stephen and Emma—go "out of the ruined place." Here Dickens refers us back to Pip's earlier revelation: "and, as the morning mists had risen long ago when I first left the forge, so, the evening mists were rising now" (493). Both Pip and Stephen discover the world lying before them in a moment of isolation; and in a parallel scene both enter a world hand in hand with their beloved. But in the case of *Great Expectations,* the isolation precedes the union, and the union is real; the light at the end of book casts "no shadow of another parting" (493). In *A Portrait*, the isolation follows the union, growing only deeper with the end of the book, and the union is imaginary anyway.

The contrast is sharpened in the concluding paragraphs. Stephen has taken his final leave of Emma and calls on his mythical father, the "old artificer," to aid him in his work, "to forge in the smithy of my soul" (253); at the end of *Great Expectations*, when he takes Estella's hand and wanders forward into the tranquil light, Pip has just left the home of his foster-father, to whom he was formerly apprenticed in a forge. Much like the use of Wordsworth, the irony here cuts both ways: Stephen is alone, but remains a rebel against convention, devoted to forging in his soul a national and anticolonial art; Pip is a petit bourgeois, in effect forging coin for empire, and his union with Estella will be a petit bourgeois marriage. (Dickens recognized this in part, but his readers did not. In the first version of the book, there was no final union.) That Stephen is alone we may take to be bad, but not entirely blameworthy.

Certainly it comes as no surprise that Joyce criticizes repressive religion in *A Portrait* and parodies conversion wrought by way of psychological terrorism. But what is important in the present context is that Joyce depicts this religion in largely Miltonic terms and concludes his parodic critique with an ironic revision of one of Milton's most famous and most beautiful lines, filtered through Wordsworth and Dickens. Moreover, this line and those that surround it poignantly depict a profound conjugal love, a personal union Joyce no doubt found inconsistent with Milton's Puritanism (and, indeed, Milton's life) as well as the Milton-influenced teachings of Father Arnall. In "The Dead," Milton stood hazily in the background as an advocate of political and cultural imperialism. In *A Portrait* he is more visible—first, in providing a crucial exemplum for Joyce's transferential prototype of female sexuality; second, as a representative of what was, for Joyce, a related but even greater danger than imperialism—religious terror and sexual repression. Yet it is also in *A Portrait* that Joyce first begins to see in *Paradise Lost* a paradigm of conjugal love and devotion, which its Puritanism and misogyny would seem to preclude.

Finally, in part due to an ambivalence in Milton himself and in part due to the romantic reading and rewriting of Milton, these critical and transferential borrowings are not the only aspect of Miltonic influence on *A Portrait*. By the end of the novel, Stephen has taken on the role of Satan. He seeks, like Satan chained upon the burning lake (or like Prometheus), to break all manacles and achieve "unfettered freedom" for his life and art

(246). To Cranly and to himself he articulates defiance: "I will not serve that in which I no longer believe whether it call itself my home, my fatherland or my church" (247). Each refusal is expressed concretely in the novel. In choosing Byron's public house over the priesthood, Stephen overflew Urizen's Net of Religion. In separating himself from the rabblement who cry down Yeats's altruistic countess—a Promethean figure who sacrifices herself for her people—Stephen evaded the trap of reactionary parochialism, a master called The Irish Nation. In denying his mother's pleas to fulfill the Easter obligation, he struggles against the hardest of the three. (Joyce himself needed Nora to pull free at last from familial snares. Mother love, the one true thing in life, is stronger than God or nation.)

But there were two political nets. Joyce had to evade not only Eire, but Albion. And he did this in a youthful and courageous act of defiance, a Satanic act, but one closely modeled on the lives of the martyrs. All readers of Joyce recall young Stephen's brave defense of Byron in the face of Heron's accusations of heresy, his celebration of Tennyson, and the lash. And all recognize this as an instance of Stephen's proto-Satanic refusal to serve. However, most fail to see the politics that underlie this scene, politics that implicitly link the Irish once again with Milton's routed angels. It is worth drawing out some of the political suggestions of this scene. Tennyson, lauded by Heron, was the political contrary of Byron: a reactionary and vicious opponent of Irish Home Rule (see Martin *Tennyson* 574–76). And Heron drew his name not from Stephen's schoolmates (see Bradley 98–99), but from a notorious figure in Cork politics, a puppet candidate put up by the clergy against the Fenians O'Donovan Rossa and Charles Kickham (see Lee 62; Marx 402; see also *FW* 208.31 on the latter). Recall that Stephen's antagonists here stress Byron's apostasy and immorality, and recall also that the Irish ecclesiastical hierarchy had repeatedly served the interests of colonialism, as Mr. Casey recounts so poignantly the Christmas after Parnell's death. Indeed, to prepare us for this connection, Joyce had already introduced a relative of Charles Kickham as another of Stephen's schoolmates, one quite different from Heron: Rody Kickham, "a decent fellow" (8; on Rody's relation to Charles, see Bradley 20). And later, developing the same complex of associations, Joyce identifies Stephen as the "hawklike man" (169), thus tying him not only with Daidalos Artificer but with a third Fenian, James Stephens, who, for his work with O'Donovan Rossa, was christened *an seabhac siulach* [the wandering hawk] (see Lee 57). Stephen's Satanic defense of Byron is, then, not merely poetic. It is deeply, if tacitly, political as well. The first net Stephen evaded was the net of empire. This escape is the least obvious, but the most fundamental. Without this first refusal, he could not have struggled subsequently against nation, religion, and home. (From this seed all other deadly sins sprang forth.)

Thus, in *A Portrait*, Joyce is criticizing Milton. But at the same time he is, both consciously and unconsciously, drawing on Milton's work as a model for sexual womanhood, repressive religion, and artistic rebellion. The Milton of *A Portrait* exists both outside Joyce and inside him, both as the object of critical scrutiny and as a series of affective and cognitive principles bearing on Joyce's aesthetic production and aesthetic response. It is the internal principles that will come to the fore in Joyce's later works.

The Transition of Exiles

In *Exiles*, as in *A Portrait*, there are limited but significant Miltonic influences. And even more than in the later works, the links to Milton here remain entwined with references to Dante. Indeed, *Exiles* has, in effect, two plots. The first, developed plot line concerns Robert's attempted seduction of Bertha. The second, undeveloped line concerns Richard's obscure relationship with Beatrice. The first recapitulates the seduction of Eve by Satan and includes important elements that are specifically Miltonic. The second is, in contrast, Dantean in inspiration. Specifically, it concerns Richard's evidently unconsummated relationship with the distant and apparently chaste Beatrice. Turning away from his wife, Bertha, Richard, like Dante, devotes his poetic energies to Beatrice, the love of his youth. Indeed, in this, Richard is also like Joyce, for Joyce, in *A Portrait*, turned away from his wife and focused his poetic energies on a virginal love of his youth, Mary Cleary—whom, as we have seen, he implicitly compared with Dante's Beatrice.

But Joyce himself did not choose the Dantean fantasy, nor did he choose to develop the Dantean strand of *Exiles*. He married not Beatrice, but Bertha; in his Beatrice/Eve complex, he chose Eve, both in life and, ultimately, in art, through *Exiles* and *Ulysses*. As is well known, Joyce based his tales of attempted seduction and infidelity on experiences with his own wife: first, his unfounded suspicion, in 1909, that his son was fathered by another man; second, Roberto Prezioso's attempt to seduce Nora in 1911 (or 1913, see MacNicholas 12), an attempt that Nora reported immediately to James (see Ellmann *James Joyce* 316–17). In writing *Exiles*—and no doubt in life as well—Joyce partially understood and restructured both incidents by way of schemas, prototypes, and exempla of the Fall.

In keeping with this, the main plot of *Exiles* recapitulates that of the Fall in several respects, as MacNicholas has noted (19). The general theme of the seduction of a woman is clear enough. More important, Bertha refers to the entire situation as "[t]he work of the devil" (*Exiles* 63); when Bertha, like Eve, leaves her home, Robert/Satan waits for her "in the garden" (91); and when Richard, after Bertha's evening with Robert, enters the house "from the garden," he claims to hear many "demons" (128). In a more specific correlation with Milton, after the ambiguous seduction/Fall, Bertha sleeps badly. This is in part simple realism, but it might recall the Miltonic fact that Adam and Eve, after eating of the fruit and taking "largely" their "fill of Love and Love's disport," fell into a "grosser sleep / Bred of unkindly fumes" that provided nothing but "unrest" (9.1043, 1042, 1049–50, 1052). Moreover, in an early version of the play, Brigid conjectures that Bertha's restlessness is due to eating *plums* (see MacNicholas 26), and it is the plum that, in *Ulysses,* replaces the apple as the primary fruit of the Fall.

Probably the most Miltonic element in the story, however, is Richard's insistence that Bertha have "complete liberty" (65) and thus decide on her own how she will respond to Robert's advances, whether or not she will "fall." Clearly, Richard sees no value in compelled fidelity. His encouragement of the relation between Robert and Bertha (like Joyce's own encouragement of the relation between Roberto and Nora) has in part the function of a test. Here Richard's views directly recapitulate those of God who, in *Paradise Lost* 3, made Adam and Eve "Sufficient to have stood, though free to fall," because, "Not free, what proof could they have giv'n sincere / Of true allegiance, constant Faith or Love" (3.99, 103–4). Freedom, specifically the freedom to fall, is the most crucial element of both *Exiles* and *Paradise Lost*—it is the thematic focus of both stories.

Hugh Kenner was perhaps the first critic to explore the notion that Joyce's exiles "are exiled from Eden" (*Dublin's Joyce* 81), and in doing so he provided valuable commentary on the play. However, he tried too narrowly to identify Richard with God, or rather "the ape of God." Certainly, Richard's character suggests the Great Taskmaster. But it is crucial that Richard is human, that he is Adam, and that his quandary and his test are human. Joyce is here in part following Dryden, who suggested this shift from God/humanity to Adam/Eve when he had Eve ask Adam, moments prior to their separation and her seduction by Lucifer, "what pleasure hop'st thou in my stay / When I'm constrain'd, and wish my self away" (448). Yet Joyce's revision of Milton here as elsewhere goes well beyond Dryden, for Joyce eliminates divinity entirely and makes celestial dilemmas all earthly.

God's test of Adam and Eve seems a sham. He knew from the beginning that they would fall. Indeed, this is the thematic problem Milton set himself to solve in justifying the ways of God to man, in having the Almighty affirm that He made our first parents "Sufficient to have stood though free to fall" (*PL* 3.99). The proof of love sought by God appears meaningless, its results eternally foreknown with absolute certainty. In contrast, the proof of love sought by men and women is both meaningful and endlessly unknown, absolutely uncertain. Kenner cites Richard's assertion "I am what I am," commenting that the "parody of 'I AM WHO AM' is too close to be accidental" (*Dublin's Joyce* 83). But the point of the connection is, precisely, that Richard is not the divine subject. He is constrained, unfree, dubious. The phrases are connected by opposition, not (parodic) identity. "I AM WHO AM" is whole and all. "I am what I am" is only a fragment. Indeed, the full statement is: "I did not make myself. I am what I am" (134). Like *Paradise Lost*, *Exiles* is troubled by the paradox of free will and determinism. But in Joyce's drama, the trouble is all human. It is precisely because he is not divine and thus not omniscient that Richard needs to affirm freedom and to seek Bertha's free affirmation. Yet, in a paradox directly parallel to that treated by Milton, if Bertha is truly free, then Richard can never be certain of her love, for freedom allows duplicity as well as true affirmation. Without freedom, no love; with freedom, no knowledge of love.

Indeed, this ambiguity of freedom vitiates not only one's judgment of others, but one's self-judgment also. Thus Richard not only affirms freedom, but denies it, especially his own ("I did not make myself"). Through this denial, he tries to stem the swelling pain of remorse ("Richard: I tried to give her a new life. / Robert: And so you have. A new and rich life. / Richard: Is it worth what I have taken from her—her girlhood, her laughter, her young beauty, the hopes in her young heart?" [84]). Joyce drew from Byron's *Cain* the un-Godlike line we have been considering: "That which I am, I am. I did not seek / For life nor did I make myself" (3.509–10). This is Cain's statement of remorse over a second human Fall, the primal fratricide of Abel ("could I / With my own death redeem him from the dust. . . . Let him return today, / And I lie ghastly!" [3.510–12]). It is uttered by Cain before he and Adah wander into a second exile, repeating and intensifying the Fall and exile of their parents. Richard's statement not only is a lapsarian antithesis to divine self-assertion but also implies an endlessly repeating history of human guilt and suffering, born of being free to fall but, Joyce implies, insufficient to have stood.

Exiles ends differently from chapter 3 of *A Portrait*, but also differently from *Paradise Lost*. Richard is not alone; he and Bertha are together. Yet he is tortured by lapsarian uncertainty. Bertha softly calls for a return to the past, which, of course, will never come, and "holds [Richard's] hand" (147). Thus *Exiles* concludes with Richard and Bertha hand in hand like Adam and Eve embarking upon their irreversible exile, and the exile of all their descendants, all human kind. But unlike Adam and Eve, Richard and Bertha do not walk—they are still, and, more important, if they do walk, there is no Providence to be their guide. Like Leopold and Molly Bloom, Joyce's most fully developed and most fully Miltonic Adam and Eve, Richard and Bertha can only hope for a union that is at best partial, momentary, insecure in a Fallen world.

With *Exiles*, Joyce's relation to Milton becomes more fully personal. It is here that Milton comes to be centrally important for Joyce, crucial to the system or systems through which he organized and evaluated his own personal conflicts surrounding love, desire, fidelity, and personal freedom. The myth of the Fall and most particularly Milton's retelling of that myth provided Joyce—first, tentatively, in *Exiles* and then, far more fully, in *Ulysses*—with the literary schemas, prototypes, and exempla through which he could structure and transform into literature his own experiences of sexuality, marriage, parenting, and the uncertainties and insecurities of each. Indeed, it is the encoding and integration of his life in the forms provided by Milton (and his literary descendants) that ultimately allowed Joyce to develop in *Ulysses* far-reaching, structural connections with *Paradise Lost* and thereby to realize Stephen's youthful dream—and Joyce's youthful dream—of rewriting that poem. Only, in this new *Paradise Lost*, the Fall is neither despondent nor providential, and Eden is peopled with "those murderous Irish, the enemies of God and mankind."

Chapter 4

Ulysses: Remorse and the Epic

It is commonplace to observe that, in *Ulysses,* Joyce combines at least three important modernist techniques: stylistic experimentation, psychological realism, and structural parallelism with earlier work (what Eliot called "the mythic method" ["Ulysses" 27]). The first technique evidences a view of style as arbitrary. In the course of his novel, Joyce passes through a wide range of styles, developing, exaggerating, and abandoning each in turn. In contrast, Joyce's concern with psychological realism appears to manifest a belief in the accurate representability of human thought processes by way of such techniques as interior monologue and stream of consciousness. Finally, the mythic method is ambiguous between realism and conventionalism. Neither strictly representative nor merely arbitrary, it is probably best thought of as a sort of cognitive modeling, metaphorically constructive rather than literally mimetic or freely imaginative. Though Milton's presence in the style of *Ulysses* is slight, Joyce himself acknowledged some localized Miltonisms. For this reason, it is worth considering style briefly before going on to examine psychology and structure, the aspects of the novel to which Milton is centrally important.

Milton's Solemn Passage in "Oxen of the Sun"

In a letter to Frank Budgen dated 20 March 1920, Joyce outlined the history of English prose, which he sought to imitate and parody in "Oxen of the Sun." Following "the Elizabethan chronicle style" and preceding "a choppy Latin-gossipy bit," Joyce inserted "a passage solemn, as of Milton, Taylor,

Hooker" (*SL* 252). The passage, however, is extremely difficult to isolate (if it exists at all), as Robert Janusko, for example, has discussed (see *Sources* 64–65). The most obvious guide would be direct quotation, but there are few allusions to Milton in the course of the episode. In working through "Oxen," Joyce seems to have relied heavily on three anthologies of English prose: Peacock, Murison, and Barnett and Dale. According to Janusko, who has carefully compared these anthologies with Joyce's notesheets, Joyce did not draw any Milton from Peacock—perhaps the most central of the three—and he drew relatively little Milton from the other two. To make matters worse, what he did take is scattered through the chapter (lines 159, 200, 313, 322, 327, 1139, 1418). Three of the occurrences are, however, close, occurring within a single paragraph (14.313–33). Moreover, this paragraph does follow that of the Elizabethan chronicle style. As Joyce noted, the Elizabethan section begins with "[a]bout that present time young Stephen" (14.277). Assuming that this section runs only one lengthy paragraph, and that Milton does indeed begin the "Milton, Taylor, Hooker" section, we may have found our parody.

The paragraph does not begin solemnly, though it turns solemn almost at once, as Nurse Quigley chastises the rowdy medicals, insisting in stern tones that they quiet their revels. Moreover, Joyce's much-admired George Saintsbury (see *Letters* 1.195), repeatedly characterized Milton's prose style as involving excessively long and overqualified sentences (see *Short History* 448; *History* 169; both works were owned by Joyce in Trieste), a description that fits this passage reasonably well. On the other hand, Saintsbury also insists that Milton's style was crammed with quotation, overly latinate, and "unchecked by humor" (*Short History* 448; *History* 169). The passage here is not particularly latinate or full of quotes, and, despite the sad matron's gravity, is almost immediately checked by humor, when the revellers begin a Shakespearean torrent of abuse: "thou chuff, thou puny, thou got in peasestraw," and so on. Moreover, of the three allusions to Milton in the paragraph, only one could be identified as such without the notesheets, and thus the remaining two are of dubious value. Specifically, Joyce appears to have taken "dinged," "christian walking," and "puny" from Milton. But "puny" is clearly a common term. Although "dinged" is not common, Joyce does not use the term in the sense employed by Milton (see Janusko "Murrison's" 119); in addition, it occurs in the unsolemn opening of the paragraph, a percussive prelude to Punch Costello's bawdy catch, *Staboo Stabella* (14.313–14).

If there is a Miltonic imitation in "Oxen" it is probably the section we have been considering. (Atherton ["Oxen"] suggests 4.408–28 as the crucial passage, but this seems a particularly inappropriate choice; there are no allusions, the sentences are not particularly long, and so on). However, the connection remains unclear, and its meaning obscure. Perhaps Joyce initially intended a very Miltonic passage, but then changed his mind. Janusko's researches do show a fair number of quotations from Milton, copied out by Joyce onto the notesheets, but never included in "Oxen."

Thus the presence of Milton in Joyce's play of styles is both obscure and limited. What is perhaps more interesting, then, is that, although *Ulysses* is in many ways deeply indebted to Milton's poetry, Joyce admitted only an obscure and peripheral connection with Milton's prose style, in a narrowly circumscribed passage—but nonetheless a passage almost impossible to pinpoint. Perhaps Joyce's epistolary reference to Milton in this regard is simply another clever—and typical—denial, or displacement, of Milton's influence. He says, in effect: "Yes, there is some Milton in *Ulysses:* the phrase 'christian walking.'" This admission, needless to say, does not tell the whole story.

"Lycidas" and Mourning

> Weep no more, woeful Shepherds weep no more,
> For *Lycidas* your sorrow is not dead,
> Sunk though he be beneath the wat'ry floor,
> So sinks the day-star in the Ocean bed,
> And yet anon repairs his drooping head,
> And tricks his beams, and with new-spangled Ore,
> Flames in the forehead of the morning sky:
> So *Lycidas,* sunk low, but mounted high,
> Through the dear might of him that walk'd the waves,
> Where other groves, and other streams along,
> With *Nectar* pure his oozy Locks he laves,
> And hears the unexpressive nuptial Song,
> In the blest Kingdoms meek of joy and love.
> There entertain him all the Saints above,
> In solemn troops, and sweet Societies
> That sing, and singing in their glory move,
> And wipe the tears for ever from his eyes.
> Now *Lycidas,* the Shepherds weep no more;
> Henceforth thou art the Genius of the shore,
> In thy large recompense, and shalt be good

> To all that wander in that perilous flood.
> "Lycidas" ll. 165–85

The first area of *Ulysses* in which Milton's work shows genuine importance is that of psychological realism—primarily in the complexes of association that to a great extent define stream of consciousness and interior monologue. In writing *Ulysses,* Joyce sought in part to transcribe the patterns of thought that characterize any human mind. Often our thoughts are organized by explicit logical or narrative links. But often trains of personal association guide our thoughts more idiosyncratically. Indeed, even in the case of reasoning or narrative, something is always left out; when we listen to others or to ourselves, we are always filling in, completing tacitly. In successful interpersonal communication, we leave out only what is common and active (or primed) knowledge between ourselves and those with whom we are speaking. In private thought, we do the same thing. But in private thought, this leads to a far greater degree of ellipsis than in social speech. The trick of *Ulysses,* then, is a trick of communication: giving us what is necessary to understand the characters' thoughts, without rendering those thoughts inaccurately explicit. Many things guide personal association. It was Joyce's task to allow those to function, while at the same time allowing us to understand what they are.

An example may help to illustrate. M'Coy asks Bloom about Molly's concert tour: "Who's getting it up?" (5.153). It would hardly be plausible for Joyce to have Bloom think: "Since the expression has a sexual use as well as an entrepreneurial use, it reminds me of the affair between Molly and Boylan, which makes me think of the rude way in which Boylan addressed the letter this morning, as if I were dead or just out of the way." Rather, he merely has Bloom think "Mrs Marion Bloom" (5.154), and it is up to us to fill in the connections—relatively simply in this case.

There are many sorts of association that Joyce implies in the course of the novel. There are associations based on semantics, sound similarities (for example, time *ball* and Sir Robert Ball [8.109–10]), perception (as when Stephen looks at his flowing urine and, combining perception with a pun, thinks of Cock lake [3.453]), various sorts of empirical knowledge (for example, when Bloom thinks about Robert Ball and then about planets due to the fact that Ball wrote a book on astronomy), and so on. All of these are occasional. They are linked to momentary events—what happens in the street, what someone says, where Bloom or Stephen happens to glance. These events give rise to associations that we have to understand first of all contextually. Bloom need not have thought of Robert Ball, Stephen of Cock lake. It is purely accidental that they thought of these.

But there are other associations that are not accidental in this way. These associations are governed by what I will call "abiding concerns," which is to say, concerns that preoccupy the characters, consciously or unconsciously, for the entire novel. They may be called forth by accident, of course. Bloom might not have thought about Molly's affair at precisely that moment if M'Coy had not asked his ambiguous question. But whereas he might have gone the whole day without thinking about Sir Robert Ball, he could not have gone long without thinking of Molly's affair, for it is clearly one of his abiding concerns. He seeks to submerge the thought, but it resurfaces again and again, called forth on any possible occasion—even if immediately suppressed.

Associations determined by abiding concerns are, no doubt, the easiest to understand—witness the example with M'Coy. They are also the most important, for they tell us most about the character in general, not only at a particular time, in a contingent and temporary situation; they tell us what affects him or her deeply, what sorts of things he or she takes to heart. Predictably, Bloom has more such concerns than Stephen. He is more of an "all around" man. What Joyce said of Hamlet and Odysseus applies manifestly to their descendants, Stephen and Bloom; Stephen is "a son only," but Bloom is son, "father . . . husband . . . companion" (Budgen 15–16). Bloom is concerned about Molly's affair, about Milly's entrance into womanhood, about the deaths of his father and his son, and about the persecution of his race.

Unlike Bloom, Stephen has but a single abiding concern: his mother's death. All his thoughts, his actions, his associations, his errors, his lapses, turn about this center. Hugh Kenner and others have indicated that Stephen's mourning is a pose, "heady rhetoric" to justify the shirking of his duties, an excuse for profligacy (see Kenner *Ulysses* 60). As I hope to show, this view is hard to reconcile with the way Stephen's mourning structures his thought and determines his actions. The importance of this for our present study comes with Stephen's teaching of "Lycidas" in the Nestor episode. For when Stephen teaches "Lycidas," this poem becomes part of his mourning, it becomes enmeshed in the complex of associations that organize his thought around his mother's death, and it, in turn, reorganizes that complex. In short, it becomes for Stephen an exemplum linked with the schemas and prototypes that operate his remembrance and his grief.

Though rarely understood as such, *Ulysses* is in many ways a book of mourning. In describing *Ulysses* to Arthur Power, Joyce said "man's position in this world is fundamentally tragic" (Power 98). All of Leopold Bloom's abiding concerns surround loss—that of his wife, his daughter, his father, his son, his country. Molly too mourns: the death of Rudy, her estrangement from Leopold, and, long ago, the death of Lieutenant Gardner (see Hogan "Molly Bloom's"). And Stephen suffers the death of his mother. It is a book of loss, aptly linked to the great English epic of loss. It is a book about a lapsarian condition. But it is neither theological nor merely personal. It is also a portrait of a society in which only some 5 percent of children were educated past primary school (Lyons 93), and the entire university population was only thirty-two hundred—one thousand of whom were at the protestant Trinity College (97). Unemployment ran to 20 percent in Dublin, a city rotten with pollution and disease, and suffering one of the highest mortality rates in Europe (277–78), in a country with one of the lowest marriage rates (45). Stephen is clear about the causes of this condition: his two masters, one English, one Italian—the imperial British state and the Holy Roman Catholic and Apostolic Church.

And Joyce too was clear. In his essays on Ireland, he spoke bitterly of the economic devastation of colonial rule. And when, slightly over a year after the event, he wrote to Nora Barnacle concerning his mother's death, he connected it unequivocally with economy and religion: "When I looked on her face as she lay in her coffin—a face grey and wasted with cancer—I understood that I was looking on the face of a victim and I cursed the system which had made her a victim. We were seventeen in family" (*SL* 25). When Stephen, lingering by the "40 foot" bathing area, angrily denounces his two masters, Haines grants British unfairness, and blandly observes that "history is to blame" (1.648–49). Indeed, it is. But the effects of that history were still painfully evident in Dublin in 1904, as they are in Belfast (and even Dublin) today. That history is the terrible background to the loss and suffering that we encounter constantly in *Ulysses*. Stephen cannot be as nonchalant as Haines about the matter; his family has no food, his father is a drunken tyrant, and he is despondent and rotten in the mouth. History is, indeed, a nightmare from which Stephen is trying to awaken.

And once again Milton is deeply a part of that nightmare. Indeed, "Lycidas" is a poem that concerns the drowning of a young pastor in the Irish Sea, a pastor who, Milton hoped, would begin to educate the Irish and lead them from evil and barbarity into truth. It is an elegy perversely appropriate to this book of mourning, for it is an elegy written by a defender of the murderous Cromwellian campaigns, the devastating Cromwellian confiscations, the brutal Cromwellian persecutions, and it is an elegy that paternalistically mourns the loss of a man who might have helped civilize the Irish before those particular campaigns, confiscations, and persecutions became "necessary." It is a poem that takes up the themes of "The Reason of Church Government," already quoted in "The Dead." It explores the problems of Anglican hierarchy, on which Milton had earlier blamed the atavism of the Irish. It is exactly the sort of poem that must have perfectly called forth Joyce's ambivalence toward Milton, for it is a poem that opposes church hierarchy, and thus represents the best, the most libertarian strain in Milton. But at the same time, it is a poem that, implicitly but clearly, assumes English cultural and, indeed, human superiority over the Irish and calls for the destruction of Irish culture and its replacement by English culture. It is an antihierarchical poem that prefigures all the authoritarianism of Milton's later political career.

But "Lycidas" is, first of all, a poem of death and mourning. And Stephen's whole mental life on this day circles around his mother's death. May Goulding Dedalus was buried on 26 June 1903. Assuming the funeral took place three days after the death, as in the case of Dignam, this would place her death on 23 June 1903. If so, 16 June 1904 is precisely one week before the first anniversary of her death. Stephen is still in mourning—a slightly old-fashioned, but not at all absurd, practice, Gifford tells us (see Gifford and Seidman for 1.120). And in the final days before this year of mourning ends, it would be surprising if Stephen's grief did not intensify.

The topic of Stephen's mother is initially addressed, callously, by Mulligan. First he mentions the sea as "[o]ur mighty mother!" (1.85), a link that will be developed subsequently, in part by way of "Lycidas." He then comments, "The aunt thinks you killed your mother" (1.88). Stephen responds "gloomily" that "[s]omeone killed her" (1.90). The "someone" to whom Stephen refers is ambiguous. It is himself, of course; it is also his father; and it is the two masters whom he later names for Haines. Today, however, Stephen's first concern is his own contribution. And Mulligan completes the accusation, recalling Stephen's religious battles with his mother—battles that, we know from *A Portrait*, he fought for his freedom, freedom necessary to an artist. It is easy for us to scoff at this need as irresponsibility. But it is not irresponsibility. Stephen was raised in a tradition that held up as the highest ideal martyrs who would not deny their faith to save themselves or their families, who placed the honest affirmation of their beliefs above all concerns of well-being. It is the ideal to which

Stephen aspired when he bravely refused to denounce Byron in *A Portrait*. We may think of the moral system operating here as mistaken. Yet it is a venerable system. And it is the system that Stephen's mother professed, but herself refused to follow. Stephen does indeed have the "cursed Jesuit streak" in him, as Buck Mulligan avers (1.209). In fact, he is more Catholic than the Catholics, more Jesuit than the Jesuits. It is only "injected the wrong way" (1.209), for the principles he upholds are principles of freedom, not church doctrine—in many ways, the principles affirmed, but not practiced, by Milton.

Stephen stares at the fraying edge of his black coatsleeve: "Pain, that was not yet the pain of love, fretted his heart" (1.102), for now he feels the pain of remorse, and the pain of anger, and the further pain of another remorse, this because of his anger. He recalls a dream, from shortly after she had died. He smells the wax sealing her mouth and nostrils, the rosewood of the coffin. He looks to the sea and recalls the bowl of bile wretched up from her cancerous guts. Everything is a symbol or an image of her death. Brutally, Mulligan repeats the accusation a moment later, and then, when Stephen complains about Mulligan's callousness just after his mother's death, he repeats it yet again (1.207–8). Mulligan's words open wounds in Stephen's heart, and to shield himself Stephen claims (and it is clearly false) that he is concerned only with himself, not with his mother.

When Mulligan descends, he bellows three lines from "Who Goes with Fergus?" (1.239–41). This gives rise to one of the most moving recollections in the book. Stephen's mother was on her deathbed, and in another room Stephen, at the piano, sang at her request that very song, then entered her room where she lay weeping. "For those words, Stephen: love's bitter mystery" (1.252–53). Later, we find Stephen thinking of *amor matris*, mother love, and determining it as both objective and subjective genitive, both the love for the mother and the love from the mother. Stephen links them, makes them inseparable. Both are mysterious, and both are bitter.

And then, without self-indulgence, without melodrama, Stephen asks the question of all mourning: "Where now?"—where is his mother now, and where is that bitter, mysterious love, and where is all that life, the events, the moments he recalls, the singing, the entering into the room, the weeping. He recalls her room after her death, the flotsam of her life gathered like wood or shells or trinkets cast up on a seashore. Trivialities from her girlhood. He imagines her laughing as a child. Where now? "Folded away in the memory of nature with her toys" (1.265). An ambiguous response—does he accept a memory of nature, a vast mystic eternal repository, or is the memory of nature a void?

He recalls again the dream, but now it is more sinister. Her death functions like the adolescent retreat that exploited his guilt to make him conform. He feels her strangling him from the grave, and as he rebels internally, the sanguine voice of Buck Mulligan calls him below to breakfast.

Stephen's obsession with his mother's death, with his part in that death, recurs in every context. The mention of washing reminds him of Lady Macbeth's unwashable spot, an invisible stain from murdering a man so like her father (1.481–82). And when Haines asks him if he is religious, Stephen "with grim displeasure" replies, "You behold in me . . . a horrible example of free thought" (1.625–26)—horrible because of its consequences for his mother, and for himself. After this last comment, Stephen explains why his thought still cannot be free—for he still has masters, British and Italian. He recalls schools of heresies, mockery, the church militant, Michael's host, perhaps from *Paradise Lost,* and then he and Haines hear a boatman speaking of a man drowned nine days before. The image will stay with him when he audits the classroom recitation of "Lycidas."

The second chapter does not move to Milton immediately, but begins with Stephen asking a question about Pyrrhus. The question is doubly relevant here. First of all, it concerns the battle at Tarentum. At this battle, Livius Andronicus was captured; in Rome, he translated the *Odyssey* into Latin and thus introduced the Greek epic tradition into the mainstream of European culture, resulting in *Paradise Lost* and *Ulysses,* among other works. Secondly, it suggests that here too Stephen's concern about his mother is not far from the surface of his thoughts. Specifically, as the student hesitates, Stephen thinks again of memory, and then the end of time. While his thoughts superficially play on themes from William Blake, they focus on death, and associate death, through Pyrrhus, with "toppling masonry" (2.9). Later, Stephen explains the allusion: "Had Pyrrhus not fallen by a beldam's hand in Argos" (2.48). Pyrrhus was killed by a roof tile, a bit of masonry heaved by a mother protecting her son. Pyrrhus battled him in the street below her window, and she came to his rescue. It is important that Stephen recalls this story, that he links it with the end of time—and also that he fails to mention, even to himself, that it was a mother who killed Pyrrhus, not any beldam. He asks his students the question that is troubling him, "What was the end of Pyrrhus?" (2.18).

When Stephen returns to Pyrrhus a moment later, he considers time and necessity. He thinks of how each act ousts infinite possibilities and wonders about free will. He wonders, what would have happened if a mother had not killed Pyrrhus, if Julius Caesar had not been killed? But perhaps there was no choice, no possibility: "But can those have been possible seeing that they never were? Or was that only possible which came to pass?" (2.51–52). Though he does not here think explicitly of his mother, Stephen's thoughts are the thoughts of all remorse: could it have been otherwise? He has abstracted and intellectualized the same concern we all have when we suffer a pain of loss that is not yet the pain of love. And as if to signal this, the students interrupt Stephen's meditations and ask him—haunted by the ghost of his mother—to tell a ghost story (2.55). Stephen demurs, and turns to "Lycidas." But he is unable to avoid the implicit characterizations of the arranger. When Stephen asks the students "Where do you begin in this?" Comyn responds with a quote that could just as well have been advice: "Weep no more" (2.57).

Aptly, Stephen asks Talbot to recite. The Talbots had been hereditary admirals in the British navy since the time of Edward IV (as Gifford and Seidman point out at 10.156–58) and thus a Talbot is a particularly relevant choice to recite an imperialist sea lyric. He begins, and Stephen's thoughts drift immediately back to the issue of possibility, now transformed into an Aristotelian concern about movement. Talbot begins the poem at line 165, "Weep no more," and finds himself stuck on line 173, "Through the dear might of Him that walked the waves." He continues for a few lines, then closes his book.

It is difficult to determine precisely what portion of the poem Stephen's students were required to memorize. The time allowed for the second section appears too short for Talbot to have continued to the end of the poem—a further 21 lines. Moreover, Stephen's question, "Have I heard all?" (2.91) would be phenomenally obtuse if Talbot had recited the famous closing line of the poem, "Tomorrow to fresh Woods, and Pastures new," a line familiar even to Bloom, as we discover later (see 16.632–33). Sentences end on lines 177 and 181, but the entire concluding section of the poem runs only to line 185 (the last eight lines functioning as a sort of coda, as noted by A. W. Verity in one of Joyce's editions of the poem; see appendix). It seems most plausible to assume that the students were assigned the entire twenty-line concluding section, rather than a twelve- or sixteen-line portion of that section. This inference, moreover, allows us to discern a typically Joycean joke: the line that immediately follows Talbot's recitation, and that could be read as a comment on Talbot, is—"Thus sang the uncouth Swain." More important, the last sentence, announced by Talbot to Stephen, proclaims the addressee a sort of lifeguard, assigns to him the role of saving those who drown: "Henceforth thou art the Genius of the shore, /

In thy large recompense, and shalt be good / To all that wander in that perilous flood." In the following chapter, Stephen wonders about precisely this role; and in "Wandering Rocks," he sees himself as failing in it.

Before turning to this, however, it is worth considering more fully the presence of "Lycidas" in this passage and its relation to immediately subsequent events. Though Stephen is not listening to the poem directly, he hears it nonetheless and it in some degree subconsciously guides his thoughts. Specifically, when Talbot recites the first lines about mourning, Stephen thinks of possibility—again, the central concern of mourning. As Talbot turns to "the watery floor" (line 167) Stephen thinks in a watery image of words having "floated" (2.68) into the library. Talbot speaks of the setting of the sun (line 168) and Stephen recalls his time in the library "night by night" (2.70). As Talbot refers to the "drooping head" of the sun (line 169), Stephen imagines his companions in the library, their heads bent low over books: "feeding brains" with "beating feelers" (2.71, 72). Recurring to the image of Lycidas "beneath the watery floor" (line 167), Stephen thinks of the library as "the underworld" (2.73). When Talbot speaks of the "beams," the "new-spangled ore" or dawn (line 170), Stephen thinks of "brightness" (2.73); "Flames in the forehead" (line 171) elicit thoughts of the "brightness" of thought, the "candescent" form of the soul (2.74–76), before Talbot sputters to a halt. Without the Milton, an odd progression: from the darkness of the Paris library—whither he fled Ireland and his mother, and whence he was called home—to the light of the spirit. A distracted chain of associations, half his own, half derived subconsciously from the poem.

After Talbot begins again, Stephen continues for a moment to reflect on the preceding line: "Of him that walked the waves. Here also over these craven hearts his shadow lies and on the scoffer's heart and lips and on mine" (2.83–85). When Talbot comes to "Kingdoms" and, subsequently, "troops" (lines 177, 179), Stephen's thoughts turn to tribute and then to Caesar, the ruler he had already contemplated (2.85–86). As Talbot speaks of "glory" (line 180), Stephen thinks again of God (2.85–86), then of a "long look from dark eyes" (2.86–87) as Talbot reads "[a]nd wipe the tears for ever from his eyes" (line 181). When Talbot repeats the phrase "weep no more" (line 182), Stephen recollects a riddle (a form parodically related to the quandaries and paradoxes that have occupied his mind all morning), then thinks of weaving (2.87), an image already associated with remorse (2.52–53). Finally, at the end of the poem, Lycidas is assigned by God Allfather the task of sustaining life (lines 183–85) and simultaneously Stephen recalls a rhyme about a son who has been entrusted by his father with planting life-sustaining seeds (2.88–89). Again, the associations are in part Stephen's own, in part guided by the poem.

The students are to be let out early to play hockey—an English sport, brought with English cultural domination of a sort related to that which Edward King/"Lycidas" sought to carry across the channel. Stephen agrees to a conundrum. But what he tells makes no sense. It concerns death—the death of a fox's grandmother, Stephen asserts. P. W. Joyce claims that the usual answer concerns the fox's *mother* (see Gifford and Seidman for 2.102–7). In either case, the question tells us more about Stephen's mourning and guilt than about humor.

When the boys go out to hockey, Cyril Sargent stays behind for instruction in maths. He too provides Stephen with a reason to think about mothers, to return to Pyrrhus and to the riddle. Mothers, like the mother who killed Pyrrhus, are saviors, protectors, and their love is perhaps the only true thing in life: "someone had loved him, borne him in her arms and in her heart. But for her the race of the world would have trampled him underfoot.... She had loved his weak watery blood drained from her own. Was that then real? The only true thing in life?" (2.140–41). From here, Stephen's thoughts turn to St. Columbanus, who scorned his mother for what he believed—and was canonized and held up to young Stephen as an example to imitate. With breathtaking suddenness, he turns from thoughts of Sargent and of Columbanus, to thoughts of his own mother—indicating that in fact he had been thinking of her all along: "She was no more: the trembling skeleton of a twig burnt in the fire, an odour of rosewood and wetted ashes. She had saved him from being trampled underfoot and had gone, scarcely having been," her life not lived, but deferred by religion, family, and the economy of colonial rule, the brutality of three masters. Stephen then thinks of "[a] poor soul gone to heaven" (2.147), his mother and the "grandmother" of the fox. He imagines the animal, guilty of "rapine" (2.148), burying her. Later, in "Circe," he more straightforwardly links himself with the beast: "Burying his grandmother. Probably he killed her" (15.3610–11). As Sargent finishes, Joyce returns to the thought of mother love, linking inseparably the two loves between mother and child: "*Amor matris:* subjective and objective genitive" (2.165–66).

In "Proteus," Stephen wanders the strand, like the "Genius of the shore" he has been inadvertently christened by Talbot. In his remorse, he compares himself to Hamlet and thinks briefly of suicide: "If I fell over a cliff that beetles o'er his base, fell through the *Nebeneinander* ineluctably!" (3.15–

16). He returns to the topic later, "hearing Elsinore's tempting flood" (3.281). Here Stephen's Byronic character comes to the fore. His poetic soul, his brief exile to the continent, and most of all his sense of guilt recall Manfred (a revision of both Satan and Hamlet, as well as Byron himself): "My injuries came down on those who loved me— / On those whom I best loved" (2.1.84–85). And Manfred too considers ending his sorrows by plunging from a cliff. Stephen is Alastor as well (from Shelley's poem that in part revises "Lycidas" and *Paradise Lost*), the youthful poet who, "When early youth had passed, he left / His cold fireside and alienated home / To seek strange truths in undiscovered lands" (lines 75–78). A woman comes to him in a dream like Stephen's mother; he follows her to the seashore, and the water, violent and destructive, leads him to the precipice where he dies.

Indeed, the associations with Byron and with Shelley extend further. The lines from Yeats, sung by Stephen for his mother, themselves revise lines from *Manfred* and from "Alastor." "And no more turn aside and brood / Upon love's bitter mystery" takes up Manuel's account of Manfred who, in melancholic prelude to an unhouseled death, did "turn aside / From men and their delights" (3.4.24–25) to brood upon the shared love that destroyed his sister. And "the white breast of the dim sea" more obviously combines "the white ridges of the chafed sea" and "[t]hat snowy breast . . . The dim and horned moon" from "Alastor" (lines 322, 601–2). The first line from the latter poem describes the water that will carry Alastor to his death; the second and third lines sketch the scene of that death. In each case, the lines from Yeats echo with threat; in their sources—well known to Joyce and Stephen—they at once conceal and suggest a malevolent reality. For Stephen, that threat, that reality, is the woman who bore him. (Yeats transforms the hard, thanatic "ridge" to the maternal "breast"; Stephen recalls both.) Remorse threatens to ensnare more thoroughly than the nets of any master.

As he continues along the strand, Stephen's thoughts circle still around his mother's death, held in the orbit of that event even when it is not explicit. He thinks of alibis for murder; the night when a man murders his wife, Stephen sees himself in the felon: "Other fellow did it: other me. . . . *Lui, c'est moi*" [Him, it's me] (3.182–83). Even when he writes his poem, he moves with a woman "beyond the veil" (3.425). He wonders, "She, she, she. What she?" (3.426). He thinks that it is a fantasy, an imaginary love, but "[t]he virgin at Hodges Figgis' window on Monday" (3.427–28) is not beyond the veil. Only his mother is beyond the veil. He calls to her, "Touch me. Soft eyes. Soft soft soft hand. I am lonely here. O, touch me soon, now.

What is that word known to all men? I am quiet here alone. Sad too. Touch, touch me" (3.434–36). In "Scylla and Charybdis," Stephen tells us the word: "Love, yes. Word known to all men" (9.429–30). And later we learn that the love is amor matris. In "Circe," Stephen repeats his cry, calling to his mother, now explicitly the "she": "Tell me the word, mother, if you know now. The word known to all men" (15.4192–93).

This scene too draws on Byron and on Shelley. Manfred's sister rises from the grave and he asks of her "One word for mercy!"; one word to answer the question: "am I forgiven?" (2.4.155, 153). Stephen's question too, though unuttered. And Prometheus begs of his mother the words of a curse "which all remember" (1.210). She will not answer, but a Phantasm explains that the curse is agony "like remorse" (1.287–89). An answer to Manfred's question as well, and Stephen's. Later, Shelley celebrates Love as God of all, but still, it is remorse, not love, that all remember. Had Stephen's mother answered—or produced another Phantasm to answer in her place—Stephen might have discovered what he already felt, that what every man and woman knows is, of all things, not love, but unforgiven guilt (what Christians call original sin).

So now Stephen cannot write a love poem, unless it is a poem about mother love. Though even he does not recognize it, his every thought is determined by this one fact: his mother is dead, and by this one feeling: he is responsible. Even when he thinks "Mouth to her mouth's kiss" (3.400), the beloved's mouth is transformed into the dead mother: "mouth to her moomb. Oomb, allwombing tomb" (3.401–2). Finished, and departing, he thinks, "Welcome as the flowers in May" (3.440–41), a line from a lyric that is doubly fitting. First, it contains the name of Stephen's mother, "May." Second, it is a line sung by the mother in the poem. From here, Stephen, his thoughts already guided unconsciously or subconsciously by the recollection of his mother, remembers the verse from Yeats, "And no more turn aside and brood," but he stops just short of recalling "love's bitter mystery," the theme that has haunted him.

Later, Haines explains to Mulligan that he is certain Stephen suffers from an idée fixe (10.1068), a single idea that determines his thoughts. Haines is not far off. Some of the most moving cases of this, and certainly the cases most relevant to the study of Joyce and Milton, surround the images of drowning, images linked in Stephen's mind to the death of his mother both through the case of the drowned man and through "Lycidas." The first passage of this sort occurs near the end of "Proteus." Stephen thinks of Mulligan, "He saved men from drowning" (3.317), and contrasts his own cowardice. He recalls an image of the House of Death, but he stops short, can only think, "House of . . ." (3.319). Yet he cannot avoid the death. He wonders if he too could save a drowning man. He thinks of the man drowned nine days ago. "I would want to. I would try. I am not a strong swimmer" (3.323–24). But he is thinking of something else. His mother had saved him, but he cannot save her, he cannot "be good / To all that wander in that perilous flood." His eyesight is weak, he cannot see. He imagines himself lost in the water. To save, what would he have to sacrifice? "I want his life still to be his, mine to me mine. A drowning man. His human eyes scream to me out of horror of his death I . . . With him together down." Then suddenly the pronoun changes, revealing what had been the real topic of this self-questioning and self-justification from the beginning: "I could not save her. Waters: bitter death: lost" (3.327–30). To give his mother what she asked, would be to sacrifice himself. He pleads: I had no choice.

Later in the chapter, Stephen hints at a repetition of this sequence. He looks out at the sea and, projecting his own grief onto the world, he thinks that creation groans day and night over wrongs (3.466). He denies teleology. "To no end gathered; vainly then released"—tides by the pull of the moon, lives too. He imagines the corpse of the drowned man washed ashore and recalls Lycidas, "Sunk though he be beneath the watery floor" (3.474). Seemingly thinking of this man's decayed corpse, Stephen again shifts to his mother, thinking "Dead breaths I living breathe" (3.479), recalling her breath of wetted ashes.

This image of drowning and saving, drawn from "Lycidas," recurs again in "Wandering Rocks." Stephen is at a bookstand, his attention caught by a book on "How to win a woman's love" (10.847), repeating the ambiguity of his earlier poem: is this woman beloved or mother? While leafing through the book, he encounters his sister Dilly. The family has little to eat. Stephen has money, coins jingling in his pocket. But he does nothing. Hugh Kenner indicates that here Stephen shirks his duty, and his morning resolve to aid the drowning (*Ulysses* 60). But this resolve was already qualified, even denied—for he too would drown. Whether Stephen will ultimately become a poet is irrelevant. He cannot become the Genius of the shore if he is even to aspire "to soar / Above th'*Aonian* Mount" (*PL* 1.14–15).

Stephen looks at Dilly's face and sees "[a] Stuart face of nonesuch Charles" (10.858). She recalls for him Charles I, allied with the Irish and executed by the same revolutionaries who devastated Ireland and led to its present immiseration. Dilly is like Charles in that she has been condemned by the same nightmarish history that condemned him, a distant but real casualty of those violent acts so vigorously defended by John Milton.

Dilly has just bought a French primer. It is a symbol of escape from the history of nonesuch Charles and all that followed. It is linked with Stephen and his escape, or attempted escape, which Dilly would wish to emulate—though, as a woman, and as a younger child, she has even less opportunity than Stephen. It is linked also with the failed French alliances against the English, vain attempts, damned from the outset. Like the hopes it represents, it too will no doubt be lost in the struggle for mere subsistence ("I suppose all my books are gone. / —Some, Dilly said. We had to" [10.872–74]).

Stephen returns to the image of drowning, and his assigned task as Genius of the shore: "She is drowning. Agenbite. Save her." He suffers sharp-toothed remorse, "Agenbite," but he cannot save her any more than he could accede to his mother's demands: "She will drown me with her" (10.875–76). History is to blame. "We. / Agenbite of inwit. Inwit's agenbite," he exclaims: "Misery! Misery!" (10.878–80). Here, Stephen is surely referring to suffering, but his cry is more specific, more historical, and less melodramatic. As he and Dilly speak of learning French and as his thoughts stretch out in chains of association relating to the expropriation of Irish wealth, he diagnoses the illness that drowns Dilly and will drown him too, the illness brought by colonialism and religion: misery, or French *misere*, the suffering of poverty. (Joyce himself used the French word in this way when discussing a suicide with Arthur Power: "that seemed to everybody to be the complete and explanatory answer, *la misere*, a word for which there seems to be no adequate equivalent in English" [Power 82].) This is not a self-indulgent and insincere pose, mere "heady rhetoric" (Kenner *Ulysses* 60), but an acute observation. And although it only hints at Milton, it implies all of Joyce's ambivalence toward this libertarian and imperialist, and toward his libertarian and imperialist poem of drowning, "Lycidas."

Though it has relatively little relation to Milton, we should turn, in conclusion, to the appearance of Stephen's mother in "Circe." Stephen, drunken, famished, and exhausted, dances in the brothel. He stops at the vision of his mother, her body rotten and leprous, amidst a chorus of virgins. Mulligan too, he sees, mocking, weeping tears of butter. Stephen "choking with fright, remorse and horror" pleads that he did not kill her, that it was cancer and destiny (15.4186–87)—destiny, one might assume, both personal and social. Recounting the events of the day, his mother mentions "Love's Bitter Mystery," to which Stephen replies with his query about "[t]he word known to all men" (15.4192–93). Aptly, she then recalls Stephen's meditations about amor matris and protection: "Who saved you the night you jumped into the train at Dalkey with Paddy Lee? Who had pity for you when you were sad among the strangers?" (15.4195–96), and a moment later she recalls Stephen's thoughts of the womb, while writing his poem on the beach, when she tells him "Years and years I loved you, O, my son, my first born, when you lay in my womb" (15.4203–4).

But the specter is misusing Stephen, calling for his repentance, his conversion, his orthodoxy. Like Father Arnall at the retreat in *A Portrait*, she invokes the fires of Hell. And he must again refuse submission. It is like a scenario from the lives of the saints, whom howling demons threaten and tempt. But the strain is injected the wrong way and Stephen shouts out his Satanic cry, "Non serviam!" He raises his ashplant and strikes out against the light, crying "Nothung!" (15.4242), saying that his mother and the light (both literal and figurative, visible and Christian) are nothing, and (alluding to Wagner) that his is the "Needful" weapon (German *Nothung*) that will bring about the twilight of the gods. He links the smashing of the light with the end of time, and sees a vision of "toppling masonry" (15.4245)—an image of the mother as protector but also as destroyer, ripping a roof tile from the ledge to smash a man's skull.

It is no accident that Stephen leaves the brothel, having rejected his mother and her church, only to encounter the brutal stupidity of his third master, the British Imperial Army, manifest in the persons of Privates Carr and Compton. As he asserts universal humanity (15.4426–27), the privates contemplate beating him to a pulp. He explains that it is in his mind that he "must kill the priest and the king" (15.4437). He is quickly reminded that both, especially the king, command powerful forces outside of his mind as well, forces that quickly leave him knocked senseless on the pavement.

Clearly, Stephen cannot free himself from his three masters by crushing the purple chimney of a whorehouse lamp, however much that act might manifest a sincere effort to stifle his inner Furies. Everywhere he turns, the representatives of church and state and family face him still with pleas and manacles. Even in his mind, he continues to be haunted. In "Eumaeus," he cannot bear the sight of a knife because it reminds him of Roman history: Julius Caesar, whose death, and that of Pyrrhus, he contemplated earlier, considering the possibility of all that did not come to pass. This disquiet too has its roots in remorse. In the end, it is difficult to imagine Stephen now or later overcoming his adversaries, even partially, tentatively, and, like his more fortunate creator, forging the conscience of his race by rewriting *Paradise Lost*—under the title of *Ulysses* or any other.

Ulysses and *Paradise Lost*

Joyce's first model for *Ulysses* was, of course, the *Odyssey*. However, Joyce could hardly have undertaken to write an epic in English without setting himself up against Milton, considering the popularity and unparalleled stature of *Paradise Lost* in the eighteenth and early nineteenth centuries. It was not only widely published, widely read, widely reedited and rewritten, it was widely imitated (see Havens 109). It became, in effect, the model for all epics in English—including the classical epics as rendered into English. First Virgil, then Homer were translated on the model of Milton (see Havens 104–7). In keeping with this, in the postscript to his translation of the *Odyssey*, Alexander Pope advocated "use . . . of the style of *Milton*" to overcome the difficulties of rendering Homer into English (390; see also his preface to the *Iliad*, 43). In the course of the century after Pope's comment, it became difficult to look at an English Homer except through the lens of Milton—another reason Joyce could not evade *Paradise Lost*, even in rewriting the *Odyssey*.

But it was equally inevitable that Joyce would strive to substitute other poets for Milton, other epics for *Paradise Lost*. The contrast with Homer was there already, awaiting Joyce's use. Milton and Homer were frequently compared and, as Havens documents, a range of critics insisted upon Milton's superiority to Homer (20–22), primarily for religious reasons. In this regard, elevating Homer and concealing Milton was, for Joyce, a refusal of Christian dogma. At the same time it was also a refusal of English empire and English cultural imperialism. For Milton had assumed a special significance in the cultural self-representation of England, here too linked with and opposed to Homer. Specifically, he provided a definitive English "classic," a work of Homeric stature that placed English literature in a small elite group with the literatures of Greece and Rome. Samuel Johnson's estimation is representative: to "lessen the reputation of Milton," he tells us, is to "diminish in some degree the honour of our country" (181).

Even more important, *Ulysses* was an attempt to create for Eire a national epic. The project is announced clearly at the end of *A Portrait*: "to forge in the smithy of my soul the uncreated conscience of my race" (253). As Northrop Frye explains, the "function of the epic" is "primarily to teach the nation . . . its own traditions"—or, more exactly, to teach it what it is, to forge its self-understanding. He continues, "As the epic mode of thought ... is most typical of a culture in the first flush of its vigor, the major epic tends to come rather early in the nation's history" (316). Though Joyce could not have planned this, it is no accident that *Ulysses* was born with the Irish Free State. The nature of the epic, then, and Joyce's national circumstances situated his work in such a way that encountering Milton was not only an aesthetic, but also a political necessity.

Indeed, the date of the novel's action may provide a hint of the political conflict implicit in Joyce's attempt to forge a second and greater epic in English. The standard explanation for the date of 16 June is that it memorializes Joyce's first appointment with Nora. This is valid and relevant (for reasons we have touched on, concerning the difference between Joyce and Stephen). But there may be a further reason as well. As Samuel Johnson notes, 16 June was the day on which the House of Commons ordered the arrest of John Milton and the burning of his tracts in support of regicide (127). It is, perhaps, not mere coincidence that the date of the new Irish epic was the date of Milton's fall, and the legislated destruction of his Cromwellian writings.

There is, of course, more explicit indication of the link between these epics in *Ulysses* itself. Indeed, there is as much textual warrant for a connection with *Paradise Lost* as with the *Odyssey* (a tie signaled only in the title, though much advertised by Joyce in extratextual material). Specifically, in the library, amidst some of Dublin's guiding literary figures, Stephen—who, Satan-like, rebels against the dominant aesthetics and philosophy of the Celtic revival—is mocked by John Eglinton: "Have you found those six brave medicals, John Eglinton asked with elder's gall, to write *Paradise Lost* at your dictation? *The Sorrows of Satan* he calls it" (9.18–20). Thomas Lyster has been discussing Wilhelm Meister's (fictional) translation of *Hamlet*. Eglinton's comment, presumably a reference to a past claim of Stephen's, identifies Stephen's future work as a sort of translation of Milton, specifically, a translation that follows the romantics in conceiving of Satan as a suffering hero. Through the allusion to Marie Corelli, it also, and more obviously, expresses a dim evaluation of Stephen's capacity for undertaking such a project. Here Joyce was no doubt seeking to expose and criticize the underestimation of his own youthful talents. But stripped of its mockery and misperception, this is not an inapt description of *Ulysses*. For Joyce's epic is the story of the Fall of humankind translated to Dublin in 1904. And it is in part structured by Milton's telling of the Fall, and the tellings of his revisers.

In general outline, the connections between *Ulysses* and the stories of the Fall are the following: Stephen is clearly and straightforwardly linked with Satan. From his black clothing to his motto of "Non serviam," Stephen remains the fallen angel he has been since *A Portrait*. As in *Paradise Lost*, the opening of Joyce's epic concerns Stephen/Satan and his cohorts. Malachi Mulligan is linked with Moloch, primarily by his name. Indeed, in *Finnegans Wake*, Joyce several times puns on the names "Moloch" and "Malachi," in effect confirming the verbal connection suggested in *Ulysses*. Most strikingly, he writes of a time "ere Molochy wars bring the devil era" (*FW* 473.7–8), referring to the stretch of Irish history between King Malachi and Eamon de Valera (both involved with civil wars), as well as the angelic civil war prosecuted in part by "horrid" Moloch, "besmear'd with blood" (*PL* 1.392). This sort of consonantal repetition ("Malachi" for "Moloch") is recurrent in both novels. It was in part derived from Joyce's Kabbalistic sources, such as Mathers.

Moloch is first in the demonic procession from the lake of fire in *Paradise Lost* 1, and he is associated with Chemos. While Moloch becomes a god of homicide and is a personification of "hate" (*PL* 1.417), Chemos becomes a fertility god, a personification of "lust" (*PL* 1.417). Mulligan, with his plans for instituting a charitable institution where he will provide sexual services for frustrated ladies, is more clearly a figure of lust. His companion Haines, however, is associated with hate. He has a propensity for shooting (1.57–62) and, more important, in French his name means "hates"—indeed, Joyce puns on this meaning in "Circe," where he introduces "Mr Haines Love" (15.4700). The pairing is not exact, but the link is one of dhvani, not of allegory. The conjunction of these figures of lust and hate, and the connection between Mulligan's given name and the name "Moloch," do not refer to but rather associatively suggest Moloch and Chemos in *Paradise Lost* 1. If we turn to the demonic congress of book 2, we find another possible link of suggestion in the third speaker, avaricious Mammon (*PL* 1.679ff.); he provides a nicely parallel figure for the third major character with whom Stephen interacts: parsimonious Deasy, with his monetary obsession, his financial wisdom, and the light on his back flickering like gold coins (2.448–49).

It certainly makes sense that the first two figures of the demonic procession in *Paradise Lost* should make their way into the opening scenes of *Ulysses*, along with Satan. However, a major figure from *Paradise Lost* 1 is missing here: Satan's companion, Beelzebub. He appears to be linked, rather, with the demonic seducer, Blazes Boylan. In general terms, the huge blazes of Hugh Blazes' name can hardly help but evoke the fires of Hell. More specifically, Blazes' name recalls Beelzebub in its consonantal structure, as Malachi's recalls Moloch. Indeed, the connection is even closer than may at first appear. In the eleventh edition of the *Encyclopaedia Britannica*, one of Joyce's sources on the Kabbalah (see Atherton *Books* 169), the article on "Beelzebub" emphasizes that the name is probably a variant of "Beelzebul" or "B'L 'ZBL"—closer still to BLaZes BoyLan. Moreover, in *Finnegans Wake*, Joyce refers to Beelzebub as "blzb" (194.17); though there is no direct connection with Blazes here, this indicates at least that Joyce was thinking of "Beelzebub" consonantally. Elsewhere in the *Wake*, Joyce refers to the "House of Blazes," the "Parrot in Hell," and "Belzey Babble" (clearly a version of "Beelzebub/l") in the same paragraph (63–64), linking them at least implicitly; and later he refers to "Blaublaze devilbobs" connecting the name "blaze" with a demon, and strongly hinting at Beelzebub.

At the same time, Blazes is a Kabbalistic figure, a seducer who brings about Eve's fall by enticing her sexually (on the seduction of Eve, see Waite *Doctrine and Literature* 301; Waite *Secret Doctrine* 101; *Jewish Encyclopedia* articles on "Eve" and "Fall of Man"; all three sources were available to Joyce and he certainly used at least the Waite volumes—see Cope 79). Thus he is linked with both Samael (the Kabbalistic seducer of Eve) and Satan. Perhaps it is worth noting in this connection that several Kabbalistic sources connect Samael with Asmodeus; for example, Scholem points out that the tradition often views Lilith as the spouse of Asmodeus rather than Samael (358); Waite and Blavatsky both name Samael as the angel of death (see Waite *Secret Doctrine* 86; Blavatsky 35, 286), and Blavatsky identifies both Asmodeus and Samael as the angel of death (35). This is relevant because the Talmud identifies Asmodeus with Beelzebub, as Blavatsky points out in her *Theosophical Glossary* of 1892, which allows us to see a very possible, if somewhat removed, identification between Beelzebub and Samael. (Similar links may be traced in Rappoport [see 55, 79, 91], and elsewhere.) It is worth noting that the characterization of Beelzebub as seducer of Eve is not entirely un-Miltonic, for in *Paradise Lost* it is Beelzebub who proposes the seduction of humankind (see *PL* 2.368), though of course he does not carry out the act himself. Moreover, the larger, sexual construal of the Fall is not unrelated to the Miltonic paradigm, and its revision by Dryden and others.

As this connection between Blazes and Beelzebub/Samael/Satan indicates, Molly Bloom is linked with Eve, Leopold is matched with Adam, and 16 June 1904 is the day of the Fall. Molly/Eve falls to the seductive Blazes/Beelzebub/Samael. Bloom also follows the Kabbalistic pattern. Just as

Adam is seduced into spilling his seed by Lilith (see Waite *Secret Doctrine*, 103–4, 108–9)—and much as Alastor loses paradise when seduced in sleep by a phantom modeled on Lilith (lines 140–91)—Bloom is seduced into masturbation by Gerty. The Fall is explicitly represented in these Kabbalistic terms in *Finnegans Wake*. There the (doubled) seductresses are directly identified with Lilith (see, for example, *FW* 75, "those lililiths undeveiled which had undone him"—see also 205, 366) and one is even linked implicitly with Gerty (see *FW* 143ff.). There may be a consonantal/Hebraic connection here as well. One of Lilith's few companions, and one with whom she is often paired, is Ogeret. Indeed, as Waite points out, in some versions, Adam is seduced by Lilith and a companion (*Secret Doctrine* 103). Besides Ogeret, the other possible companions are Naamah and Machalath (104n.1). The *Jewish Encyclopedia* article on "Lilith," appropriately authored by a certain "L.B.," links two of these as "Agrat bat Mahlat [or Machlat]" (88). This demon, then, shares with Gerty MacDowell the GRT consonantal structure of the first name, even the *geret* in Hiberno-English pronunciation, as well as the first syllable of the family name.

Some of the broader connections have been noted before. S. Foster Damon has remarked that "[p]robably Milton suggested the first part" of *Ulysses* (482). Mary Reynolds has linked 7 Eccles Street with the Earthly Paradise of Dante (39). Cope stressed the Kabbalistic significance of Bloom's masturbation (85), though not in connection with Adam. Stuart Gilbert was probably the first to link Molly directly with Eve (401), and Virginia Moseley has linked Bloom with Adam as well. Most important, in his "Scribbledehobble" notebook, Joyce unequivocally connected Bloom with Adam, and the Fall with Molly's seduction, when he wrote "Adam 1st cocu [French cuckold]: LB [= Leopold Bloom]" (Scholes and Kain 119). Thus most of the major connections, Stephen/Satan, Bloom/Adam, Molly/Eve, adultery/the Fall, were drawn explicitly by Joyce himself.

In the course of *Ulysses*, the parallels between the story of the Fall, and most particularly its Miltonic version, are sometimes clear and sometimes obscure, sometimes centrally important and sometimes peripheral. At times they amount to little more than possibilities. In the following pages, I try to distinguish between what I take to be fairly well-established connections, and what I intend as conjecture. While wild speculation is always undesirable, in my view it is better to suggest a possible connection, which readers can reject, than to suppress a possible connection, which readers may miss. This seems especially true for a writer such as Joyce whose own claims of connection between *Ulysses* and the *Odyssey* would not infrequently strain credibility if put forth by anyone other than the author himself.

In the first chapter of the book, we find, again, a scene comparable to that at the outset of *Paradise Lost*. In Milton's poem, Satan and his cohorts awaken floating upon a "fiery gulf" (*PL* 1.52), somewhat like Stephen/ Satan and his companions who awaken on Dublin bay, which is "radiant" "in sunlight" (1.131). In *Paradise Lost*, the angels have been defeated by the angelic hosts led by Michael. In connection with this, Stephen thinks of Mulligan as a mocker who will be defeated by "those embattled angels of the church, Michael's host" (1.663). And just after this, Stephen hears about the man who has been floating in the bay for nine days, precisely the period—"Nine times the Space that measures Day and Night"—that Satan and "his horrid crew / Lay vanquisht, rolling in the fiery Gulf," after their defeat by the angelic host (*PL* 1.50–52).

The second book of *Paradise Lost* moves to the interior of a debating hall. In a not dissimilar manner, the scene of *Ulysses* changes in the second chapter to a schoolroom. The demons discuss their military defeat, just as Stephen and his students discuss the military defeats of others, and then recite Milton. In both cases, the discussion ends with a loud sound that signals the beginning of sporting contests and other diversions for all but the central figure, Satan/Stephen, who sets off alone on a long journey through chaos (a narrative element repeated and emphasized by the romantics, in, for example, the journeys of Manfred and Alastor). Specifically, a bang at the door announces to Stephen and his students that it is time for hockey (2.18–19), while in Pandemonium:

> Then of thir Session ended they bid cry
> With Trumpet's regal sound the great result. . . .
> Thence . . . the ranged powers
> Disband . . .
> Part on the Plain, or in the Air sublime
> Upon the wing, or in swift Race contend,
> As at th'*Olympian* games or *Pythian* fields. (*PL* 2.514–15, 521–23, 528–30)

Indeed, the very problems of predestination and determinism that bother Stephen in the course of this episode, provide the topic of a Daedalian, mazelike discussion for those fallen angels more intellectually or less sportively inclined:

> Others apart sat on a Hill retir'd,
> In thoughts more elevate, and reason'd high
> Of Providence, Foreknowledge, Will, and Fate,

Fixt Fate, Free will, Foreknowledge absolute,
And found no end, in wand'ring mazes lost. (*PL* 2.557–61)

In the second half of book 2, Satan exits through the gate of Hell and passes through Chaos on his way to Eden. The "Proteus" chapter of *Ulysses* presents us with a closely related scenario. Having "passed out through the gate" by "lions couchant on the pillars" (2.429)—less threatening adversaries than Sin and Death, admittedly—Stephen finds himself (following a brief, unreported train ride) wandering through an indistinct landscape, hazy due to Stephen's weak eyesight. Stephen asks himself, "Am I walking into eternity along Sandymount strand?" (3.18–19). As Gifford points out, Stephen here alludes to Blake's *Milton,* at the moment when Blake is possessed by the spirit of Milton, implying that he too—or perhaps his Original, the author—has been possessed by Milton. In a more concrete connection, the question indicates the spatial and temporal illimitability of the ocean by which Stephen walks, an ocean as unbounded as the oceanic Chaos of *Paradise Lost*: "a dark / Illimitable Ocean without bound, / Without dimension, where length, breadth, and highth, / And time and place are lost" (2.891–94). (The scene was a favorite one of the romantics, contributing, for example, to waters of "Alastor.") Eyes closed, he wonders, "If I fell over a cliff that beetles o'er his base, fell through the *nebeneinander* ineluctably" (3.14–15), calling to mind (beyond Manfred's near suicide and Alastor's death) an image of endless descent, such as that into which Satan almost fell upon entering Chaos:

> Into this wild Abyss the wary fiend
> Stood on the brink of Hell and look'd a while,
> Pondering his Voyage . . .
> . . . but that seat soon failing, meets
> A vast vacuity: all unawares
> Flutt'ring his pennons van plumb down he drops
> Ten thousand fadom deep. (*PL* 2.917–19, 931–34)

In a typically inverted fashion, Stephen meets Death and canine-wombed Sin, gatekeepers of Hell, not at the beginning of his trip through Chaos, but at its conclusion. As he sits, he spies a man, a woman, and a dog, which, he fears, threatens to attack him. The dog, he conjectures, was "got in spousebreach" (3.363), much like the canines snarling from the womb of Sin, fathered by their mother's own son, Death (see *PL* 2.781–800). (In the nineteenth century a wide range of threatening and hellish hounds—from *Prometheus Unbound* to *Wuthering Heights*—strengthened this associative link with the brood of Sin and Death, making such suggestive priming almost automatic.)

Finally, Stephen indicates the divine geography of the environs—or, rather, the divine geography through which he, and Joyce, structure the surround—when, following a brief reflection on "crucified shirts," he "crossed the firmer sand towards the Pigeonhouse." The pigeon is immediately identified with the Spirit of God (3.156ff.). Thus Stephen indicates that, parallel to the geography of *Paradise Lost*, here too the solid ground where Chaos ends leads to the house of God (see *PL* 3.418–21). Furthermore, Stephen makes an imaginary telephone call, telling the operator, "Put me on to Edenville" (3.39), which is to say, telling the operator to connect him with precisely the spot where Satan's chaotic trajectory tends—thereby indicating the telos of his own journey as well. Indeed, Stephen does eventually arrive at Eden, in the form of 7 Eccles Street, though he leaves without engaging in any Satanic seduction, that job having already been handled, and "damn well" handled, as Molly puts it (18.1511), by another demon. (In putting Satan on the horn, Joyce updates the technology by which Byron modeled demonic communications. In "The Vision of Judgement," Byron had stressed that Satan's messages are transmitted by means swifter than the telegraph [lines 441–48].)

In a different sort of connection, Stephen links the man and woman on the beach with Adam and Eve, referring to them with a passage from Shelley's *Hellas* (see Gifford and Seidman at 3.391–92). This connection may seem not to cohere with that linking the dog with the beasts of Sin. But, again, the point of drawing these connections is not to claim that Joyce is developing an allegory. At certain points he is, I believe, self-consciously establishing a structural parallel between *Ulysses* and *Paradise Lost*. At other points, however, elements of *Paradise Lost* and other retellings of the Fall insinuate themselves into *Ulysses* in a less systematic manner—in a manner that fits associatively, that is effective with respect to the rasadhvani of the work. In this way, the seemingly contradictory connection actually increases the suggestiveness of the passage, reenforcing the tacit links with the Fall and with Milton.

Less narrowly connected to images of Chaos, Stephen also thinks thoughts of Satanic seduction: "Will you be as gods?" (3.38), and wonders over the issue of consubstantiality of father and son, an important issue in the debate between Satan and Abdiel concerning rebellion (see *PL* 5.803–55).

Finally, as he leaves the strand, he recalls the fall of Satan (3.486–87), implicitly linking himself again with the angelic rebel.

Already in these first three chapters, Joyce has drawn numerous connections between sexuality and the Fall. The theme, which will become prevalent only with the introduction of Leopold/Adam and Molly/Eve, is first broached by Stephen. Most strikingly, in the first chapter, Stephen views "woman's unclean loins" as "the serpent's prey" (1.421–22), identifying the Fall as a sexual seduction. In "Proteus," Stephen links Adam's Fall with sexuality as well, thinking, "Unfallen Adam rode and not rutted" (3.386)—a view well illustrated by Milton in his portrayal of the lascivious postlapsarian intercourse of Adam and Eve (*PL* 9.1027–45).

Unsurprisingly (given his religious and political views), Joyce deletes divinity entirely from his story of the Fall. Thus the scenes of *Paradise Lost* that take place in Heaven have no parallel in *Ulysses*. If, however, we disregard the congress in Heaven of book 3, the action of *Paradise Lost* switches from Satan to Adam and Eve just after Satan finishes his journey through chaos. Likewise, after Stephen has finished his walk along the strand, the action of *Ulysses* switches to Leopold and Molly Bloom. "Calypso," then, parallels book 4 of *Paradise Lost*, in which Satan seeks to seduce Eve during her sleep, and she awakens disconcerted. Specifically, Adam awakens "to find unwak'n'd *Eve* / With Tresses discomposed" (*PL* 5.9–10). Eve's sleep was troubled because Satan whispered "close at the ear of [sleeping] *Eve*, / Assaying by his Devilish art to reach / The Organs of her Fancy" (*PL* 4.800–802). In the case of *Ulysses*, the tempter does not arrive in person, but in the form of a letter, addressed in a "bold hand" to "Mrs Marion Bloom" (4.244; it is worth recalling that in *The Sorrows of Satan*, this sort of penmanship is linked with Satan when Rimanez—the incarnation of Satan—introduces himself by a letter that he has written in "characteristic bold handwriting" [20]). Molly slides this letter—which assays by its devilish art to allow Boylan to reach the organs of his fancy—beneath her pillow, thereby placing the seductive voice of the devil close by her ear. Following this, Leopold "walk[s] through the warm yellow twilight towards her tousled head" (4.247–48), her tresses discomposed.

There are other, more humorous connections between this episode and *Paradise Lost* as well. "Calypso" is a chapter much concerned with food and digestion, from its very first words—"Mr Leopold Bloom ate with relish the inner organs of beasts and fowls"—to the defecation with which it ends. The parallel book of *Paradise Lost* is comparably gastric in nature. The visit of Raphael to the first couple provides occasion for an extensive discussion of Angelic diet, touching especially on the delicate topic of Seraphic waste. In fact, frutarian Adam himself awakens from a sleep "Aery light, from pure digestion bred, / And temperate vapors bland" (*PL* 5.4–5), whereas Leopold Bloom, no Edenic vegetarian, consumes pigmeat for breakfast and at the close of the chapter savors the unbland scent of his unseraphic and lapsarian excrement (4.513).

Another example of Joyce's satiric relation to his Miltonic Original comes when Bloom implicitly assimilates John Milton to Mr. Philip Beaufoy of the Playgoers' Club, and *Paradise Lost* to Beaufoy's prize tidbit, "Matcham's Masterstroke." Surveying the story, Bloom thinks: "Begins and ends morally. *Hand in hand*" (4.514–15; emphasis in original). The most famous literary work that ends morally with the phrase "hand in hand" is undoubtedly *Paradise Lost,* the final sentence of which reads: "The World was all before them, where to choose / Thir place of rest, and Providence thir guide: / They hand in hand with wand'ring steps and slow, / Through Eden took thir solitary way" (*PL* 12.646–49). In a vulgar but amusing touch, Joyce has Bloom use this Miltonian, and cathartic, story to wipe himself clean after completing his motions. This particular satire of Milton as popular author in the newspaper age of mass readership and disposable literature is developed and varied subsequently when Eglinton links *Paradise Lost* with *The Sorrows of Satan*. It is also, perhaps, implicit (as a sort of in-joke) in a scene of "Aeolus," where Joyce has a newspaper editor quote (or misquote) Milton's Beaufoyan words, addressing Bloom as Adam: "Begone! he said. The world is before you" (7.435). In *The Sorrows of Satan,* Geoffrey Tempest, addressing himself as Adam, identically misquotes Milton's famous line as "the world is before you" (44).

In the following chapter, parallels with the visit of Raphael are further developed. Most significantly, at the end of the chapter, Bloom enters a church where he hears the priest speak of how the "prince of the heavenly host, by the power of God thrust Satan down to hell and with him those other wicked spirits who wander through the world for the ruin of souls" (5.445–47). This functions as a sort of warning to Bloom about Blazes, and thus is relevant to the parallel in general terms. More specifically, however, it relates to Raphael's story of the vanquishing of Satan and his legions, a story told to Adam, also as an implicit warning, at the end of book 6 of *Paradise Lost*.

A more comic parallel may perhaps be found in Molly and Blazes' planned singing tour, an enterprise closely linked to the adulterous Fall. In this chapter, we learn that the engagements will take place in the north

(5.151–52). Similarly, in his history of the angelic rebellion, Raphael recounts Satan's original "journey to the North" (*PL* 5.688), an early act of wilfulness that drew in its train the Angelic Fall, thereby the Fall of humankind, and all our woe. Specifically, "Orchestral Satan" (as Stephen terms him, before quoting Milton [9.32]) exhorts his fellow insurgents in terms that could equally characterize Blazes' operatic venture: "haste [to] . . . / The Quarters of the North, there to prepare / Fit entertainment" (5.686, 688–90).

More important, it is in this chapter that the plum is introduced as the fruit of the Fall, a fruit of both illicit sexuality and death. M'Coy asks after Molly. Leopold answers perfunctorily and reads idly an advertisement for canned meat: "What is home without / Plumtree's Potted Meat? / Incomplete. / With it an abode of bliss" (5.144–47). Knowing that "to pot your meat" was an expression meaning "to have sexual relations," we may translate the advertisement easily and see its relevance to Bloom's situation: "What is home without sex? Incomplete. With it an abode of bliss." (Recall that Leopold and Molly have not had normal sexual relations since 27 November 1893 [17.2280]—a point that has further significance in this context, for, as Waite points out, in the Kabbalistic tradition Adam had no desire for Eve after he was seduced by Lilith [*Secret Doctrine* 103].) Just after this, Bloom mentions to M'Coy the concert tour, and M'Coy responds with the unintentional pun, "Who's getting it up?" (4.153).

Here the connection between plums (or Plumtree's, at least) and Molly's adultery is clear enough. The equally important, and closely related, connection between plums and death becomes clear subsequently. It first appears in the following chapter, "Hades," the chapter of death, when Bloom comes upon a vendor selling plum cakes outside of the cemetery; "cakes for the dead" (6.501), he calls them. It is repeated and reenforced when we discover that the Plumtree's advertisement appears with the obituaries (see 8.139). Here the potted meat is not only the male meat in the female pot, but the dead meat in the funereal pot. The two are connected as poles in the cycle of regeneration, the womb and the tomb remembered and fused by Stephen. Indeed, recalling that "abode of bliss" was sometimes used to refer to Heaven (as in *A Portrait* 113), one can almost taste a Satanic seduction. Lucifer, in his modern form as an advertisement, lisps into your ear that if you only eat from Plumtree's, you will be as Gods, while the obituary context provides a modern substitute for God's dire warning that to eat of the forbidden (Plum)tree (or, equivalently, to pot one's meat) means certain death.

"Hades" functions primarily to develop this major consequence of the Fall—death—just as "Oxen of the Sun" focuses on that part of God's judgment according to which all women will bring forth in pain. (Both motifs are present in Milton, but more obviously available from the Bible.) In connection with this, "Hades" presents a possible connection with a later section of *Paradise Lost*. Specifically, Sin and Death build a causeway to the gates of Hell, making "a passage broad, / Smooth, easy, inoffensive" for the dead (*PL* 10.304–5). This may appear in *Ulysses* transformed into Bloom's funerary tramline for transporting the dead to the cemetery gates (6.406–7). The reasons for Bloom's proposal are identical. It would avoid the bumps and turns that sometimes upset the coffin (6.415–16, 421); in other words, it would be *smooth*. It would be *easier* than making one's way through the traffic-congested city (6.383–404; this is the topic that prompts Bloom's suggestion). And it would be "more decent than galloping two abreast" (6.412–13), which is to say, it would be *inoffensive*.

The episode also includes some comic references to the larger Judeo-Christian mythology—as when Dignam is noted to have waited three days for burial (6.869; unfortunately it was not for resurrection) and is attended by thirteen mourners (6.825). But none seems to have any specific reference to Milton or great importance for the development of the theme of the Fall.

"Aeolus" further develops the connection of the Fall with adultery, on the one hand, and with plums on the other. Stephen, who as Satan is a sort of inverse Christ figure, tells a parable about "Wise virgins" (7.937), which inverts Jesus' parable on the same topic. In the canonical version, the wise virgins are those who are ready for death whenever it comes; for this reason, they will enter heaven. Stephen's parable, in contrast, concerns two virgins who, he indicates, will never reach their goal. Stephen calls his parable "A Pisgah Sight of Palestine" (7.1057), a pisgah sight being, of course, a sight of that which one will never attain, specifically, the promised land. Moreover, Stephen contrasts this title with that proposed by Professor MacHugh: "Deus nobis haec otia fecit" [God has made this peace for us] (7.1056), thereby stressing that the virgins have been denied the divine peace implied in reaching the promised land.

More exactly, the story Stephen tells concerns two spinsters who sit atop the Nelson monument, eat brawn and plums, and spit plum stones out between the railings. Stephen is careful to emphasize that Nelson was an adulterer (7.1018). One can imagine several possible interpretations of this story. At one level, it addresses once again the paralysis of Dublin life, the hopelessness and insignificance of daily existence for Irish women such as

Stephen's two virgins. But there is clearly more to the story than this. Perhaps the virgins, never having experienced carnal union, can only glimpse from afar the "abode of bliss" for which potted meat is a necessary condition. Or perhaps they have been exiled from this heavenly abode because, like Jimmy Carter, they hotly lusted in their hearts and in that moment fell. In any case, Joyce again links plums with illicit sexuality, and with adultery in particular, by conjoining a visit to the "onehandled adulterer" with the eating of plums. As Gifford and Seidman point out, the plum was used in Christian writings as a symbol of fidelity (7.1057–58). Thus Stephen inverts this Christian symbolism too, just as he inverts the situation of the virgins. Finally, it is worth mentioning that the title of Stephen's parable may have been taken from a work by Samuel Fuller (published in 1650); today Fuller's book is probably used most frequently as a guide to the geography of *Paradise Lost* (particularly 1.331ff.).

Plums recur in "Lestrygonians," in connection with both death and illicit sexuality. Early on, Bloom links prostitution to a peculiar error involving plums: "Mayonnaise I poured on the plums thinking it was custard. Her ears ought to have tingled . . . . Want to be a bull for her. Born courtesan" (8.354–56). Later, he thinks how "Molly looks out of plumb" (8.618–19), homophonously associating plums with her condition on the day of her adultery. Subsequently, Bloom remembers that the Plumtree's ad appeared "[u]nder the obituary notices," recalls the idiom "[a]ll up a plumtree" (meaning "done for"—see Gifford and Seidman), and connects Dignam's corpse with "potted meat" (8.744–45).

Perhaps more important for our present concerns, Joyce comically links Molly's adultery with the Fall by way of a contingent feature of Dublin geography. Specifically, Bloom, while passing an Edenic location, recalls Boylan's successful attempt at propositioning Molly: "He other side of her. Elbow, arm. He. . . . Touch. Fingers. Asking. Answer. Yes. Stop. Stop. If it was it was. Must. Mr Bloom, quickbreathing, slowlier walking passed Adam court" (8.589–93). It is almost as if Bloom were not passing a real street named "Adam court," but rather experiencing, passing through the judgment or lawcourt that condemned Adam and all his descendants to lustful and obscene lapsarian sexuality, so unlike the unashamed and blissful union that preceded the Fall (compare *PL* 4.736–75, 9.1011–16).

"Scylla and Charybdis" has a number of more specific links with *Paradise Lost*. Though primarily a statement of a simple biological fact, Stephen's argument about the uncertainty of paternity (see 9.828–45) in many ways recalls Satan's argument that none can know he was begotten by God (*PL*

5.853ff.). Indeed, when Stephen speaks of "only begetter to only begotten" (9.838–39), he refers to the relation between God the Father and God the Son—one particular crux of uncertainty on which Satan focuses in rallying his rebellious troops. This chapter also includes several direct references to Milton. It is at the outset of "Scylla and Charybdis" that Eglinton asks Stephen if he has yet begun his rewriting of *Paradise Lost*. Later on, Stephen recalls other of Eglinton's thoughts about the need for a national epic of Ireland, perhaps to be written by George Moore (see 9.309–10). The irony is clear: it is the very book we are holding that is the Irish national epic, the work to rival the English *Paradise Lost*, and it was not written by Moore, but by a fellow who bore a certain resemblance to Stephen Dedalus.

Directly following Eglinton's question about *Paradise Lost*, Stephen recalls two lines from this poem, along with one line from, unsurprisingly, the *Inferno*: "Orchestral Satan, weeping many a rood / Tears such as angels weep. / Ed egli avea del cul fatto trombetta" (9.32–34). The first line concerns Satan's bulk as he lay on the burning lake, and is thus appropriate to the opening scene of *Ulysses*, though one imagines that Stephen is considerably less imposing a figure. A further connection with the scene on the fiery gulf may perhaps be glimpsed when Stephen thinks of himself as "fallen, weltering" (9.954). As Gifford and Seidman suggest, this may allude to Satan's first discovery of fallen Beelzebub "welt'ring by his side" (*PL* 1.78). The second quote from *Paradise Lost* concerns Satan's suffering, remorse, and self-pity. This line, which recurs significantly in *Finnegans Wake*, is particularly important, for it links Stephen's misery directly to Satan's misery. Insofar as it concerns Stephen, *Ulysses* is indeed relevantly conceived of as a book about "the sorrows of Satan."

There are other, briefer connections as well. Stephen's reference to "an androgynous angel" calls to mind Milton's angels, who are male or female at will ("For Spirits when they please / Can either Sex assume, or both" [1.423–24]). And elsewhere, Stephen recalls a line from "L'Allegro" (9.873), and another from "Lycidas" (9.1124).

In addition to these direct references, elements of the chapter restate some of the main connections between the central action of the book and the events of the Fall. Most important, in his discussion of Shakespeare as (Bloomian) "bawd and cuckold" (9.1021), Stephen directly links Ann Shakespeare's (putative) adultery to "original sin," specifically, "original sin, committed by another in whose sin he too has sinned . . . original sin that darkened his understanding and weakened his will and left in him a strong inclination to evil" (9.1008–9, 9.1006–7). When Stephen interprets

Shakespeare's works in these terms, it is difficult not to read this as an authorial instruction to understand *Ulysses* as dealing in part with the same sort of original sin.

"Wandering Rocks" develops these themes in a limited way by repeating the link between Molly and an Eve-like sin that is related to eating; when Leopold is browsing at a bookseller's table, he thinks, apropos of Molly, "*Sweets of Sin*. More in her line" (10.606). Though the first meaning here is merely that Molly likes to read that type of fiction, the authorial implication is that eating the sweet fruits of sin is Molly's role in *Ulysses*. This connection is reenforced by the fact that during this chapter we discover that Boylan sends Molly a basket of fruit prior to his seduction. Though the basket does not contain plums, it seems clear that this adultery-linked fruit and the fruit of original sin are closely related.

"Sirens" is the episode that leads up to Blazes' meeting with Molly, and it contains a number of relevant references. Some of these surround a song sung by Miss Douce. This song concerns a woman named "Idolores" who is the "Fair one of Eden" (quoted in Gifford and Seidman for 11.9); her connection with Eve is, thus, straightforward. Later in the chapter, Leopold identifies Molly with Idolores (11.734), which would seem to constitute an unequivocal connection with Eve. This is not a connection made by Bloom—who misquotes the relevant line as "Fair one of Egypt" (11.383). However, it is, presumably, a connection made by Joyce.

More important, in this chapter Joyce further associates Molly's adultery with the Fall, and most particularly with Milton's version. Specifically, Bloom thinks of his past life with Molly, their early days together, their visit to the Furry Glen, and, implicitly, his proposal (11.582). He then repeats the words of a song being sung in the other room: "All lost now" and, "Mournful," reflects, "Fall, surrender, lost" (11.635, 636). And later: "Woman. As easy stop the sea. Yes: all is lost. / —A beautiful air, said Bloom lost Leopold. I know it well" (11.641–42). Cope connects these thoughts not only with Molly's adultery, but directly with the Fall (93). Indeed, this connection seems to be as explicit as Joyce could effect without surrendering subtlety and verisimilitude. The adultery is explicitly a "Fall" that finalizes the progressive alienation that has rendered their earlier Edenic relation "lost." Indeed, it is difficult to imagine an English-language writer treating a Fall and using the word "lost" without specific reference to *Paradise Lost*. Moreover, the moment to which Bloom alludes, the moment of the Fall itself, is described by Milton in words quite similar to those of the song that Simon Dedalus happens to be singing, and that Bloom echoes:

> So saying, her rash hand in evil hour
> Forth reaching to the Fruit, she pluck'd, she eat:
> Earth felt the wound, and Nature from her seat
> Sighing through all her Works gave signs of woe,
> That all was lost. (*PL* 9.780–84)

These lines are among the most famous in Milton's poem. Bloom's line, "All lost now," not only echoes Milton's line, "all was lost," but occurs in the immediate context of references to a Fall and to a past that is lost, and in the larger context of an unequivocal link between adultery and original sin. Moreover, the line in *Ulysses* first arises from an unseen source almost as if it arose, as in *Paradise Lost*, from Nature herself. (Stephen has already told us that creation groans day and night over wrongs [3.466; see Gifford and Seidman for translation].) Given all this, it seems unlikely that Joyce did not self-consciously intend an allusion to Milton's lines; at the very least, it seems highly improbable that Milton's lines were not associatively relevant to his unselfconscious aesthetical intent.

"Cyclops" appears to present little of relevance beyond a further connection between adultery—in this case, the adultery of Devorgilla—with the Fall, implicit in the statement: "A dishonoured wife, says the citizen, that's what's the cause of all our misfortune" (122.1163–64). "Nausicaa," however, leads us to the Fall of Adam. Joyce's understanding of this Fall is derived primarily from the Kabbalah, though there are elements of *Paradise Lost* as well. Again, in one Kabbalistic retelling, Adam falls when Lilith seduces him to spill his seed. As Leopold has been rather clearly linked with Adam, and as Molly's preceding adultery has been equally clearly linked with Eve's Fall, it seems almost impossible not to connect Leopold's masturbation before Gerty with Adam's ejaculation before Lilith. And, once again, a similar scene is played out in *Finnegans Wake*.

Gerty is certainly demonic for Bloom. She has "raised the devil in him" (13.517–18) and was herself a "Hot little devil" (13.776) and "little limping devil" (13.851–52). Her limp—due to a deformed foot—is reminiscent of Satan's cleft foot or more generally the view of the *Zohar* that the feet of demons are crooked (see Scholem 323). In keeping with Gerty's oceanic location, it also recalls a mermaid's inability to walk—a relevant point for, as Waite notes, Lilith was of the "mermaid type" (*Secret Doctrine* 104n.1). In addition, Gerty is indirectly associated with Boylan/Beelzebub/Samael—as well as mermaids or "seagirls"—when Bloom sees her as a "lovely seaside girl," which is to say a girl fitting the description in Boylan's "theme song," "Seaside Girls." Thus Leopold thinks, "Those girls, those girls, those lovely seaside girls. Fine eyes she had" (13.906) and "When she leaned back. . . . Your head it simply swirls. He's right" (13.941–42). Furthermore, Gerty is associated with apples: "I begin to like them at that age. Green apples. Grab at all that offer" (13.1085–86). On the other hand, Bloom recognizes that, like Adam, he has only gotten the leftovers of the fruit; as he reflects, concerning the other fruit of seduction and in reference to Boylan, "He gets the plums, and I the plumstones" (13.1098–99).

Finally, it is in this episode that Bloom discovers his Waterbury has stopped. Just before thinking of Gerty as a "little limping devil," he recalls the watch: "Funny my watch stopped at half past four. . . . Was that just when he, she? O, he did. Into her. She did. Done" (13.846–47, 849). Leopold's connection between the stopping of his watch—a sort of metaphorical stopping of time—and the act of adultery (see 13.983–86) could perhaps mirror, and invert, the traditional association between the Fall and the *beginning* of time, the end of Edenic timelessness.

Given that the preceding chapters present the Falls of both Leopold/Adam and Molly/Eve, it is not surprising that the next chapter, "Oxen of the Sun," should focus on one of the main results of the Fall—suffering in childbirth. Indeed, this connection with the Fall is explicitly drawn when Stephen and the six brave medicals he needs to rewrite *Paradise Lost* point out toward the beginning of the chapter that "in the beginning, they said, the woman should bring forth in pain" (14.208–9). This is the result of the judgment of God, His punishment of Eve for eating of the forbidden fruit—though a more relevant punishment for a sexual, than a gustatory sin, it would seem. This condemnation is paired with a promise, however: that salvation shall come to all from a woman's giving birth. This part of the judgment is equally implied in "Oxen," if parodically. First of all, Mrs. Purefoy has been in labor for three days; thus the time of her son's birth is the time of the savior's rebirth. Moreover, her name presents us with an implicit characterization of her chastity; the opposite of Spenser's faithless Sans Foy, as well as Molly Bloom, she is—like her prototype, the Blessed Mother—"pure faith." Indeed, her husband's name is "Theodore," and he is thereby linked with theos, God. As Stephen extrapolates, "Thou art all their daddies, Theodore" (14.1415–16).

There are other lapsarian connections in this chapter as well. Most important, there is yet another explicit connection between the Fall and illicit sexuality when the Burkean narrator observes that "mettlesome youth . . . is ever (as the chaste fancy of the Holy Writer expresses it) for eating of the tree forbid" (14.871–73). And there are direct references to both Lilith (14.242) and Eve (14.299–301).

"Circe" is perhaps the only episode of *Ulysses* that has been linked with *Paradise Lost* virtually since publication. As Stuart Gilbert points out, "This scene . . . is usually described as the Walpurgisnight or Pandemonium of *Ulysses*" (7). More important, late in the episode Joyce himself refers to the scene as "Pandemonium" (15.4662). Elsewhere, Gilbert links the episode to Milton's masque, "Comus" (see 327–28n.), which is of considerable importance to *Finnegans Wake*. Not surprisingly, this chapter has multiple points of contact with both Milton and the myth of the Fall more generally.

"Pandemonium" is Milton's name for the palace of devils in *Paradise Lost*, and it is one of the crucial terms Joyce uses in "Circe" to describe Nighttown (see 15.4662). More exactly, "Circe" parallels the scene in which Satan returns to Pandemonium after having seduced Eve. He celebrates his victory, but he and his companions are transformed into serpents who must climb illusory trees heavy with illusory fruits that, when bitten, turn to ashes in the mouth—perversely recalling the ghost of Stephen's mother, with "her breath of wetted ashes" (15.4182). As in both the *Odyssey* and *Paradise Lost*, "Circe" is the episode of transformation. But it is in many ways more demonic than Circean. It is not only referred to as "Pandemonium," it is a place where "Brimstone fires spring up" (15.4661), a place in which Father Malachi O'Flynn announces that he will ascend the devil's altar *[Introibo ad altare diaboli]* (15.4699).

Indeed, the narrative and geography of this scene parallel those of *Paradise Lost* in surprising ways. To arrive at Pandemonium, according to *Paradise Lost*, one must pass through the "Paradise of Fools," whose inhabitants prominently include "the builders . . . of Babel" who "Still with vain design / New *Babels* . . . would build" (*PL* 3.466–68). It is precisely such a Babel-like scenario with which we are presented in the jumbling and decomposition of dialect that closes "Oxen of the Sun," where Stephen begins the trip that will lead him, in the immediately following chapter, to Pandemonium. Moreover, this trip of Stephen and his associates is immediately preceded by a storm. This too directly parallels events in *Paradise Lost*, for a storm follows close after the Fall and narratively precedes the return to Pandemonium. Subsequently, Bloom enters Nighttown by walking through "hellsgates" (15.578) and the centrally important "Street of harlots" is identified as "Serpentine avenue" (15.3930). Furthermore, in the course of the chapter, Bloom envisions "Figures [which] wind serpenting in slow woodland pattern around the treestems, cooeeing" (15.3408–9), figures very reminiscent of the transformed demons of *Paradise Lost* 10; indeed Bloom is himself similarly transformed and "crawls jellily forward under the boughs" (15.3242).

Beyond these connections, it is only in "Circe" that Stephen follows the order of statement and response in the Catholic mass and at last responds to Buck Mulligan's initial *Introibo*. But in this case, it is clearly a black mass, a Satanic mass, and Stephen perverts the meaning of the response by changing "God" to "goddess": "ad deam qui laetificat juventutem meam" [to the goddess who gave joy to my youth] (15.122–23). This ties "Circe" to the initial episode by the sea, just as Satan's return to Pandemonium is linked with, and in a sense replies to, the initial scene by the burning lake.

Another possible Miltonic connection may be found in Stephen's reference to the "Uropoetic" (15.4388). Stephen is speaking with two British soldiers and some others. He refers to himself as poetic and those around him as uropoetic. First of all, "uropoetic" merely means "making water" and thus is a joke at the expense of his auditors. However, there are in addition two possible links with Milton. First, Stephen has implicitly linked urination with Milton by way of the similarity between the Latin verb for "urinate," *mingo, minxi, mictum, mingere* and the like-sounding phrase from (watery) "Lycidas," "smoothsliding Mincius" (see 9.762, 9.1124). Second, and more important, Milton's muse in *Paradise Lost* was Uranus, and the "Uro" of "Uropoetic" may hint at a connection with Milton's Uranus-poetry. If there is a connection here, it is not at all irrelevant that Joyce connects Milton with the British soldiers—all Uropoets—once again emphasizing Milton's imperialist position.

Beyond some incidental links—including a brief reference to the Miltonic demon Belial (15.1907), and another to Lilith (15.1899)—there are more general connections to the Fall as well. It is in this episode that Stephen reaffirms his identification with Satan by crying out "Non serviam!" (15.4228). And when Bloom is phantasmically enthroned we find that it is "year 1 of the Paradisiacal Era" (15.1632), another suggestion of Bloom as Adam, ruler of Paradise. On the other hand, it is typical of this chapter that identities become uncertain, that Stephen and Bloom are fused into Stoom and Blephen (see 17.549, 551). Thus it is not surprising to find that Stephen is briefly linked with Adam, when Beelzebub tries to seduce him with "a fubsy widow" in "Serpentine avenue" (15.3930–31; note that the seduction here is sexual and the agent of this seduction is Beelzebub, not Satan—an explicit connection that adds weight to the preceding analyses). Similarly, Bloom is spoken of as coming "from the roots of hell" (15.1754) and as crawling like a serpent. More directly, he is called "Satan" by the Nymph (15.3459) and, when Stephen takes a match from Bloom, Stephen says, "Lucifer. Thanks" (15.3599); Stephen is, of course, referring to the match, but the phrase is ambiguous and hints that Bloom is, at that transformed moment, Lucifer as well.

Other relevant themes are touched on briefly. The link between the Fall and illicit sexuality is restated when Virag refers to an act of fornication as the "Fall of man" (15.2545). Bloom at one point gives the name "Copula Felix" to an imaginary horse (15.1504). This is a pun on "copulation" and *felix culpa,* Augustine's term for the Fall (a "happy fault" because it brought our savior)—again indicating that the Fall was a sexual act. Interestingly, this linking of the Fall and sexuality to a horse recontextualizes something from "Oxen of the Sun." There, Lenehan, or the arranger, had associated the phrase "[a]ll is lost now" with a horse race (14.1134). Earlier, this phrase was linked directly with Molly's adultery and indirectly with *Paradise Lost.* Moreover, this peculiar complex of associations is taken up, in a sort of culminating moment, when Boylan, at his tryst with Molly, becomes "a perfect devil" and swears "blazes" precisely at the moment when he loses the horse race (18.423–24). (This rather idiosyncratic connection between the Fall and losing a horse race recurs significantly in *Finnegans Wake.*)

Connections between the Fall and forbidden fruit are also taken up in this chapter, as when Molly is offered a mango in a "cloven hoof" (15.321). The animal here is a camel, but the connection with the cloven hoof of Satan and the fruit of the Fall seems clear. Similarly, Stephen thinks of two "Frauenzimmer" who are "plumstained" (15.4145). The stain appears to be both physical and spiritual, for it evidently accounts for the derogatory term *Frauenzimmer,* often used to mean "wench" (see Gifford and Seidman for 3.30)—thus no longer the virgins of the original parable. It is obviously relevant that the stain—the macula that, like the stain of original sin, prevents these Frauenzimmer from being immaculate—is the stain of a plum.

Moving on to "Eumaeus," we find what may be a rough parallel with book 11 of *Paradise Lost.* There Michael speaks to Adam, foretelling the history of the world up to and including the Flood, while Eve lies sleeping in her bower. In what is perhaps a related manner, D. B. Murphy tells Bloom about his adventures on the ocean, while Molly lies at home asleep. Beyond this possible connection, there are only matters of incidental relevance. For example, Bloom links Molly's impetuous character with Satan (16.873–74, 876–77). And later he implies a link between adultery and apples when he refers to the adulterous fall of Parnell: "it was just the wellknown case of hot passion . . . upsetting the applecart" (16.1046–47).

In *Paradise Lost*, Michael's instruction of Adam, which follows Satan's return to Pandemonium, is in turn followed by the expulsion of Adam and Eve from the Garden. There is a sort of inverse parallel to this scene in "Ithaca." It is now Friday, the day on which Adam and Eve were evicted. Bloom returns to his home with Stephen. Having forgotten his key, he jumps over the railings—somewhat reminiscent of the wall around Paradise, which Satan must leap at his first entrance (*PL* 4.178–83)—and crouches "in preparation for the impact of the fall" (17.88–89), a passage that is difficult to read as anything other than a pun. Ultimately, Bloom and Stephen leave the house in a procession distantly reminiscent of Michael's expulsion of Adam and Eve, but, again, in this case Adam and Eve stay, and they stay in what is explicitly a "house of bondage" (17.1022). As they exit, Bloom and Stephen encounter a mythical tree of fruit blue like plums: "What spectacle confronted them when they . . . emerged silently, doubly dark, from obscurity by a passage from the rere of the house into the penumbra of the garden?" the catechist demands, and is answered, "The heaventree of stars hung with humid nightblue fruit" (17.1036–39). But Bloom reflects "that it was not a heaven tree" (17.1139), implying that, like the forbidden Tree of Knowledge, "whose mortal taste / Brought Death into the World, and all our woe" (*PL* 1.2–3), one only realizes after the Fall that it is more akin to a tree from Hell.

Bloom reenters and wistfully recalls his former, now poignant, dreams of residence in "Flowerville," living an Edenic existence. (According to some Kabbalistic sources, Adam spent his time in Eden cultivating roses; see Waite *Secret Doctrine* 72 n. 2.) He wonders too about his marriage; he puts aside the possibility of divorce, but only for the moment (see 1.2202). As this is not the Fall itself, merely the repetition of a Fall that has always already occurred, Bloom cannot lose Eden; he can only remain trapped in a house of bondage, from which Eden is always already inaccessible. Indeed, this is completely consistent with Kabbalistic writings on the Fall itself, for according to the *Zohar*, Adam and Eve were not expelled from the Garden but trapped in the Garden from which God had departed, a garden that was no longer Paradise (see Waite *Secret Doctrine* 105 n. 3).

Having dreamt and put away his dreams of paradise, Leopold returns to Molly, and the bed in which the adulterous Fall has taken place. Images of the Fall are ubiquitous and unmistakable. Bloom sees the commode with a cover of printed apples (17.2102–3). He enters the bed, which now has "snakespiral springs" and "pendent viper radii" (17.2116, 2117). He recalls having met Boylan in Mesias's (compare Messiah's) shop on "Eden Quay" (17.2171).

"Penelope" restates and reenforces the themes we have been examining.

Indeed, it parallels Eve's speech ending the pseudepigraphic "Life of Adam and Eve," a major source of beliefs about the postlapsarian life of our first parents. In the Greek version, Eve delivers a lengthy address on the Fall near the end of the book. In the Latin version, the speech is briefer; however, excepting a brief coda, it—like Molly's monologue—ends the book (see Charles 252–54). Joyce seems to have drawn on both versions.

Paralleling Leopold's statements about Gerty, Molly directly refers to Blazes as "a perfect devil" (18.423). In addition, by an amusing ambiguity, she connects herself with Eve, saying "Id have to introduce myself not knowing me from Adam very funny wouldnt it Im his wife" (18.1484–85). Molly has Stephen in mind, but syntactically the "his" could refer just as readily to "Adam," thus making Molly into Adam's wife, Eve. In keeping with the more general imagery, she refers to (lapsarian) women as "such a mixture of plum and apple" (18.1535). Similarly, she remembers that, before their tryst, Boylan sent her a basket of "port and peaches" (18.341)—which is especially relevant when one recalls that, etymologically, a "peach" is a "persian apple." Moreover, this prefaces the concupiscence of the Fall with the proffering of a sort of apple and wine, exactly as in *Paradise Lost*, where the fruit had the effect of wine (see 9.793), or certain Kabbalistic writings, where the "fruit" was wine (see, for example, Waite *Secret Doctrine* 77). She recalls her work at winning Leopold in terms of Eve's seduction, reflecting that she "had the devils own job" in getting him to propose (18.196). And, toward the end of the episode, Molly menstruates, a further link with Eve and with the Fall for, at least since the seventeenth century, one Judaic view has been that Eve was menstruating at the time of the Fall (see Patai 456, referring to Naftali Herz Bacharach).

Beyond these various connections with the broader tradition, Molly recalls her day with Boylan in such a way as to connect it more narrowly with *Paradise Lost*. In Milton's epic, Adam and Eve eat of the apple, the sky thunders, they engage in lascivious sexual relations, fall asleep, and wake up guilty and fearful. Molly and Blazes begin with the sexual relations, then take their fill of "port and potted meat" (18.132), then fall asleep, and are awakened by thunder, which Molly interprets as a prelude to divine retribution: "I thought the heavens were coming down about us to punish us" (18.134–35). The altered order of events is due not only to the internal logic of the episode, but also in part to Dryden, who restructured the sequence of the Fall in a parallel fashion. In *The State of Innocence,* fallen Adam and Eve are frightened by the thunderclaps that follow their wanton intercourse (454–55).

In this context, it is difficult to say whether Molly's final "Yes" is a "paean of affirmation" (Gilbert 403), as is frequently believed, or a mere repetition of the Fall. It is, of course, a Yes to Leopold's proposal of marriage, and thus perhaps a recapitulation of Adam and Eve's loving and hopeful passage through Eden at the end of *Paradise Lost*. But at the same time it echoes her adulterous Yes to Boylan, recalled by Bloom as he passed Adam court: "He other side of her. Elbow, arm. He. . . . Touch. Fingers. Asking. Answer. Yes" (8.589–91). Moreover, even as a Yes to Leopold, it is the seductive culmination of "the devils own job." "[T]hen he asked me would I yes to say yes my mountain flower and first I put my arms around him yes and drew him down to me so he could feel my breasts all perfume yes and his heart was going like mad and yes I said yes I will Yes"—perhaps this should be followed by "[t]he World was all before them, / where to choose / Thir place of rest, and Providence thir guide: / They hand in hand with wand'ring steps and slow, / Through *Eden* took thir solitary way." But perhaps the more appropriate sequel would be: "So saying, her rash hand in evil hour / Forth reaching to the Fruit, she pluck'd, she eat: / Earth felt the wound, and Nature from her seat / Sighing through all her Works gave signs of woe, / That all was lost" (9.780–84).

In light of the preceding references and parallels, it appears that Joyce sought self-consciously to pattern *Ulysses* in part on *Paradise Lost*. However, even if he did not—and he certainly never set out to publicize the connection, as he did with the *Odyssey*, for example—*Paradise Lost* is still an important presence in Joyce's unselfconscious aesthetical intent; it is still important to the rasadhvani of the work—both for Joyce in its creation and for us in its reception. Once again, the very way in which Joyce conceived of death, sexuality, mourning, hope, and loss was significantly organized and directed by principles abstracted from Miltonic themes, characters, events, and phrases. Once again, this is precisely what influence is: cognitively modeling the artistic rebel on Satan, the fallible man on Adam, the act of adultery on the Fall, the moment of narrative resolution on the loss of Paradise—subconsciously conceiving of each through these schemas, subconsciously organizing traits and properties by reference to these prototypes, evaluating each stage of production by subconscious comparison with these exempla. It is not that Milton was Joyce's primary influence. He was not. He was one of many influences, many authors who went to define Joyce's sense of character, event, language, and so on. But Milton's influence is nonetheless extensive. Moreover, it is both various and highly conflicted. Indeed, in its diversity and complexity, it is almost an ideal case for the study of influence.

All of this is even more true for *Finnegans Wake,* for this novel, to use a contemporary idiom, is almost nothing but "the play of influences." By severing his ties with realism, and by fashioning a multiply overdetermined language, Joyce created a situation in which a variety of lexical models could surface and combine in both characters and events, mingling almost freely, forming a work that is tightly structured, but tightly structured by an expansive aesthetical intent, unbounded by many of the conventions that ordinarily limit and constrain the freedom of such intent, the breadth of its dhvani. The presence of Eden in *Ulysses* is limited by Dublin, by human psychology, by the nightmare of history. In *Finnegans Wake,* this is far less true. And thus the presence of Milton in Joyce's aesthetic intent is most fully manifest in this culminating work.

Chapter 5

Dreaming of Eden: The Paladays Last of *Finnegans Wake*

> But God . . . in derision sets
> Upon thir tongues a various Spirit to rase
> Quite out thir Native Language, and instead
> To sow a jangling noise of words unknown.
> *Paradise Lost* (12.48, 52–55)

> . . . Nature rests
> . . . in her absence mimic Fancy wakes
> To imitate her; but misjoining shapes,
> Wild work produces oft, and most in dreams,
> Ill matching words and deeds long past or late.
> *Paradise Lost* (5.109–13)

The presence of Milton in *Finnegans Wake* has been acknowledged more fully, and for a longer time, than has his presence in any other of Joyce's works. Beyond the references cited earlier, many Miltonic allusions are noted in McHugh (on whom I rely heavily in the following pages) and further connections have been drawn by Atherton, Glasheen (see 174–75), Hart (117), and others. More important, Joyce himself in effect acknowledges the influence of Milton within the text of *Finnegans Wake* itself. Specifically, the Joyce character, Shem the Penman, is frequently referred to as a plagiarist. The primary occasion for this accusation is to be found in Shaun's description of Shem: "what do you think Vulgariano [Shem] did but study with stolen fruit how cutely to copy all their various styles of signature so as one day to utter an epical forged cheque on the public" (181.14–16). The first point to make here is that Shem's putative plagiarism is also a form of parody. He learns "how cutely [or cleverly] to copy" the styles of other writers. This is, again, an important aspect of Joyce's response to influence. More directly relevant to our Miltonic concerns, however, is the way in which this plagiarism is linked with the Fall of humankind—perhaps the main concern of the entire book—through mention of the "stolen fruit." Finally, by referring all of this to an epic, Shaun (or Joyce) strongly suggests that this literary fruit is stolen or plagiarized from *Paradise Lost* and has been used in both the present work and the multistyled, epical *Ulysses*.

This likely link with Milton is reenforced by the physical description of Shem in the act of plagiaristic writing. In the following paragraph, leaving aside an interpolated personal ad from an unemployed writer named "Jymes" (as if the connection between James and Shem were obscure), Shem is again accused of being a literary sham and a word thief. "Who can say," Shaun asks indignantly, "how many pseudostylic shamiana, how few or how many of the most venerated public impostures, how very many piously forged palimpsests slipped in the first place . . . from his pelagiarist pen?" (181.36–182.3). This is immediately followed by an account of alcoholic Shem's knowledgeable, lantern-nosed writing process: "but for that light phantastic of his gnose's glow as it slid luciferously within an inch of its page . . . Nibs never would have quilled a seriph to sheepskin" (182.4–5, 10–11).

The most obvious connection with Milton is the expected one—the reference to Shem as Lucifer and the implication of his quelling a seraph in Satanic rebellion. The most unequivocal connection, however, is the reworked quotation from "L'Allegro," perhaps a sort of illustration of Shem's/ Jymes's pelagiaristic practices: "Come, and trip it as ye go / On the *light fantastic toe*" (33–34; emphasis added). By way of these references, Shaun— or Joyce—indicates that Milton is at the source of Shem's Satanic ability to write. The implication is not without irony, but neither is it frivolous. For Joyce certainly believed that he could never have set pen to paper, or killed the Seraph within, had he not engaged in Satanic rebellion, had he not fallen into the light of knowledge (the gnosis glow) of good and evil, his soul "awakened to spiritual life by sinning" (as Stanislaus put it [*My Brother's Keeper* 160]). And both this rebellion and this Fall were structured and exemplified for Joyce by the works of Milton and the works of Milton's progeny.

Significantly, this passage again conjoins Milton with Dante, for later in the sentence, Shaun associates Shem with Paolo, presumably of Paolo and Francesca—but here, for the first time, it is Milton who is emphasized while Dante is partially occluded. This new emphasis on Milton is neither accidental nor inappropriate. For to a considerable extent, Joyce's project in *Finnegans Wake* was, paradoxical as it may sound, Milton's project but without God: a justification, not of God's allowing the Fall, but of the fallen condition itself and of a very ordinary human capacity "of our evil . . . to bring forth good" (*PL* 1.163).

Pelagiarist Puns Slipped from Stylic Schemata

The clearest influences of Milton on *Finnegans Wake* are, as one would expect, in characterization, theme, and, in a more limited way, narrative structure. More surprisingly, even the style of *Finnegans Wake* is significantly Miltonic. The basis of Wakean style is obviously a form of punning. As John Shawcross has noted (in another context), Milton too puns, and he does so "by methods not dissimilar to Joyce's" ("They that dwell" 207). Moreover, Milton's use of wordplay is not merely occasional or stylistically peripheral. Merritt Hughes points out that Milton follows "the theory that poets should pun and ought to make their puns out of the differences between the meanings of their words in everyday life and the meanings . . . from which they were . . . derived" (Milton *John Milton* 203). Indeed, Hughes understates the breadth of Miltonic wordplay. For Milton not only puns through etymologies; he also fuses features of other languages into English. Thus Samuel Johnson writes: "One source of [Milton's] peculiarity was his familiarity with the Tuscan poets: the disposition of his words is, I think, frequently Italian; perhaps sometimes combined with other tongues." Thus "he wrote no language" but "a Babylonish Dialect," Johnson continues, quoting Butler (190–91). The fundamental stylistic technique of *Finnegans Wake* is precisely this "Babylonish," interlingual synthesis—including the "Connection of Epithetes, or the conjunction of two words in one," which Dryden decries (without specific reference to Milton) in his prefatory apology to *The State of Innocence* (424). Though Joyce extended the technique far beyond Milton's use, he almost certainly drew it in part from Milton or, at least, found his own independent inclination confirmed by Milton's practice.

Indeed, Joyce at times repeats puns used by Milton. For instance, Milton was fond of the words "empyreal" and "empyrean," using them some seventeen times in *Paradise Lost* (for comparison, Shakespeare never used either word), thereby making them at least mildly marked as Miltonic for many readers. Despite their archaic flavor (or perhaps because of it), in *Finnegans Wake* Joyce too used these words a number of times, each time with a possible suggestion of Milton. In book 5 of *Paradise Lost*, Milton puns on empyreal/imperial in the lines: "The empyreal host / Of angels by imperial summons called" (5.583–84). Joyce employs the same pun during the dialogue of Butt and Taff, referring to "empyreal Raum" (353.29; imperial Rome/empyreal space [German *Raum*]). Both use the pun to connect political structure with spiritual structure—angels as royal subjects and angels as celestial beings for Milton, the Roman empire and the Kingdom of Heaven for Joyce.

More exactly, in *Finnegans Wake*, Taff fumes about the degradation of the Russian general as the latter, HCE-like, defecates in full view. He expresses his outrage in terms of angelic conflict, and indeed in such a way as to make it unclear whether he is siding with God or Satan. Specifically, Taff "asbestas can, wiz the healps of gosh and his bluzzit maikar, has been sulphuring to himsalves all the pungataries of sin praktice in failing to furrow theogonies of the dommed" (352.35–353.1). Taff is doing the best he can—as if protected by asbestos—but he is still quietly (to himself) suffering purgatorial fires, because he has failed to further the agonies of the damned and has equally failed to follow the theogonies of those dwelling in the celestial dome. In narrative context, he is pretty burnt up about this Russian general business and is suffering because he has not done anything about it. The purgatory in which he suffers is a place of battle (Italian *punga*, "fight"), like the scene with the general and like heaven during the Satanic rebellion. Under this construal, Taff seems to be on the side of heaven against the damned defecator. But there is a good deal of heresy and blasphemy here as well. God is reduced to an expletive—and distinguished from the maker (or from Michael) who is perhaps not so much blessed as a buzzard.

Along the same lines, Taff exclaims of the general, "Trisseme, the mangoat! And the name of the Most Marsiful, the Aweghost, the Gragious One!" (353.2–3). Thus he calls out against the man/goat—recalling goat-footed Satan—in the name of the Most Merciful, the Holy Ghost (and St. Augustine), the Gracious One. But at the same time he calls out against the man/God (that is, Jesus) in the name of the most Mars-like (thus the most belligerent), the awesome ghost (and Augustus Caesar), the egregious one—all suggestive of Satan. Despite Taff's angelic/Satanic fulminations, Butt continues to hold back from shooting the general. But when the general picks a "sob of tunf . . . for to wollpimsolff" (353.16–17; a sod of turf to wipe himself), Butt, infuriated by "that intsullt to Igorladns" (353.18–19; insult to Ireland), blows the general to bits. The narrator remarks that "Similar scenatas are projectilised from . . . empyreal Raum" (353.28–29)—

similar scenes are projected (using projectiles—for example, arrows or bullets) from imperial Rome (human war) and empyreal space (heavenly battle).

In *Paradise Lost*, Raphael makes this pun when beginning the story of Satan's rebellion (that is, the heavenly battle). Thus, not only is the pun the same, the contexts are related, at least in this general way. There may also be a narrower, contextual link. In *Paradise Lost*, the "imperial summons" prefaces God's decree concerning His only son. Satan finds this decree an insult to all the rest of heaven and in response he takes up arms. Finally, it is worth noting that when Joyce told the story to Ottocaro Weiss, he seems to have used the phrase "grassy turf," rather than "sod of turf" (see Ellmann *James Joyce* 398; the latter phrase fits the subsequently added Irish theme better because of the pun on the phrase "old sod" for Eire). If so, this may indicate a further, genetic connection with Milton, who used the phrase "grassy turf" twice in *Paradise Lost* (5.391—close to the passage we have been discussing—and 11.324) and once in "Comus" (line 280).

Another example of a pun taken by Joyce from Milton may be found in two passages connecting Satan and Ophiuchus. In *Paradise Lost* 2, during his encounter with Death, "Incensed with indignation Satan stood / Unterrified, and like a comet burned, / That fires the length of Ophiuchus huge / In the arctic sky" (2.707–10). Ophiuchus is a constellation, but the word itself means "serpent bearer." While he does not explicitly bring out the etymological meaning of the term, Milton clearly intended to play upon it in connection with Satan, who brought death into the world when borne by a serpent.

In the parallel passage of *Finnegans Wake*, the evangelists are interrogating Yawn, whose body has been usurped by ALP in order that she might defend HCE against accusations of impropriety. Shortly following a reference to *Paradise Lost* ("parroteyes list," 493.5), the four dismiss ALP's defense, then begin to discuss astronomy, using heavenly bodies as analogies for bodies involved in the park incident of HCE's fall. "Ophiuchus being visible above thorizon, muliercula occluded by Satarn's serpent ring system, the pisciolinnies Nova Ardonis and Prisca Parthenopea, are a bonnies feature in the northern sky . . . Apep and Uachet! Holy snakes, chase me charley, Eva's got barley under her fluencies! The Ural Mount he's on the move and he'll quivy her with his strombolo!" (494.9–12, 15–17). Here we have the same pun as found in Milton, in this case signaled by the name "Ophiuchus" along with the combination of Satan, serpent, and Saturn in "Satarn's serpent ring system."

Indeed, in Joyce's version, the connection with the Fall—both that of HCE and ALP and its prototype, that of Adam and Eve—is explicit as well. Eve/ALP, the little woman (Latin *muliercula;* see Schork 70) is occluded by Satan and the serpent, both in the sense that she has fallen and in the sense that Adam's/HCE's attention has been drawn away from her to other seductive objects in his Fall. The pisciolinnies are not only stars in the Pisces constellation and little fishes (Italian *pesciolini*), but also the two pissing Lily's/Liliths. HCE looks on at the "bonnies feature in the northern sky" (elsewhere referred to as a night with two moons [502.11–14], because the two temptresses have bared their rumps). He gets moving, quivering, and his strombolo will soon erupt like the volcano Stromboli in an orgasmic scenario comparable to Bloom's fireworks-linked ejaculation in *Ulysses* and related to the fire image of Ophiuchus in *Paradise Lost*. Though HCE usually falls by masturbating behind the two Liliths, here he appears to engage rather in lustful copulation with Eva, who is perhaps also urinating ("Eva's got barley under her fluencies!"), thus reminding him of the Liliths and thereby arousing him. The connection of Satan, the serpents, and Ophiuchus, then, is straightforward. The pun is shared by Milton and Joyce, and the contexts are related, at least in that both bear on the Fall. (For a treatment of some other points of connection here, see Schork 70.)

Beyond taking over some of Milton's puns, Joyce at times made new puns out of Milton. There are points in *Paradise Lost* where Milton appears to suggest, but not make a pun. Because the apple was eaten first by the serpent, Adam refers to it as "foretasted fruit" (9.929), just before he agrees to eat, and suffer the resultant fate. Joyce takes this idea of a "foretasted fruit" and turns it into a joke, relating the brothers' conflict to "that Jacoby feeling again for forebitten fruit" (303.16–17). Here he refers to a feeling, relevant to the conflict between Jacob and Esau—a clearly lapsarian conflict—which is the result of the earlier eating/forebiting (by Adam and Eve or by HCE and ALP) of the forbidden fruit.

In sum, the most basic stylistic principles Joyce followed in composing *Finnegans Wake* were an extreme version of the principles employed by Milton. Joyce generalized from Milton (and others) a "procedural schema" of lexical synthesis or punning that Milton followed only in more highly constrained and localized contexts. (A procedural schema is a schema for production, rather than reception, understanding, and so on). Moreover, he incorporated into his own text a number of exempla of this schema drawn from Milton.

Even more important, however, a wide range of nonstylistic elements and structures of the *Wake* were pelagiarized from Milton also. *Paradise Lost* is the most significant work in this context. However, other of Milton's writings, most particularly "Comus," furnished Joyce with productive schemas, prototypes, and exempla as well. Thus, before examining the (nonstylistic) presence of *Paradise Lost* in *Finnegans Wake*, it is important to consider the extensive connections that link Joyce's final work with Milton's early masque as well.

Here Comus Everybody

Finnegans Wake includes a broad range of debts to Milton. Some are only indirect hints. For example, HCE's underwater burial and his association with Jesus in this context (see 76ff.) may in part derive from Milton's drowned Lycidas, who figures so importantly in *Ulysses* and who is also linked with Jesus. Perhaps the most unexpected of these miscellaneous connections are the several allusions to Milton's sonnet 7, "How soon hath Time." In this sonnet, Milton bemoans the passage of his youth. He has reached the ripe age of twenty-three and has yet to produce a major work. However, he expresses confidence in providence and concludes by affirming, "All is, if I have grace to use it so, / As ever in my great task-Master's eye." Joyce several times employs the phrase "great task-Master's eye," though with little reference to the sonnet. He uses it primarily to allude to a harsh deity judging HCE's Fall—in other words, the God of *Paradise Lost*, who would be inadequately signalled by the common, undifferentiated name, "God."

One clear allusion of this sort occurs early in the book. HCE is, as usual, swearing his innocence and loyalty. He is, he insists, willing to take an oath "upon the Open Bible and before the Great Taskmaster's (I lift my hat!) and in the presence of the Deity Itself andwell of Bishop and Mrs Michan of High Church of England" (36.26–29). In this context, the phrase—"Great Taskmaster's I" / great task-Master's eye—is clearly Milton's and also clearly associated with a judging and punishing deity. We find much the same situation in the third chapter, when HCE, speaking to the cad with the pipe, insists that "my guesthouse and cowhaendel credits will immediately stand ohoh open as straight as that neighbouring monument's fabrication before the hygienic glllll . . . lobe before the Great Schoolmaster's. (I tell you no story.) Smile." (54.27–29, 55.1–2). The gist of this is that HCE has kept honest accounts, so honest that they would stand inspection by all, even the Great Schoolmaster, who would look at them with his Great Schoolmaster's I/eye and smile.

A less unexpected and more extensive connection is that between *Finnegans Wake* and "Comus." Stuart Gilbert claimed that this masque was a model for the "Circe" episode of *Ulysses,* and though I do not find this particular connection convincing, it may indicate that Gilbert knew "Comus" to be a work on Joyce's mind. Indeed, as the child of Circe and Bacchus, one would expect Comus to make an appearance in Joyce's book of the night. But the degree to which "Comus" is present in *Finnegans Wake* is still surprising. "Comus" appears, in fact, to have provided Joyce with some of the most basic structural principles for his final work.

Milton's masque concerns a young girl; her two continuously arguing brothers; a deity disguised as a servant, Thyrsis; a water nymph, Sabrina, who is at once the river Severn; and a lecherous man, Comus, who has designs on the young girl. One can immediately see parallels with the Earwicker family—the young girl, Issy, and her two battling brothers; the servant Sackerson; ALP who is identified with the river Liffey; and the lecherous HCE. The connection between Sackerson and Thyrsis is made more plausible by the fact that in "Comus," Thyrsis has the function of assuring that good is done and evil vanquished, while Sackerson is both a servant and, it seems, a police officer—"patrolman Seekersenn" (586.28), charged with protecting morals in County Dublin (see 583.24–25). The connection with HCE is more strikingly reenforced by the fact that Comus has two sources of power: a "luscious liquor" that he administers to everyone who enters his hall and a magic "wand" that he always carries (lines 652–53). HCE is a publican who, of course, makes his living by serving liquor to those who enter his hall, and who, mysteriously, always carries a stick of some sort. Indeed, this is related to his masturbatory function—he has his pole in his hand at all times—which further links him with Comus as in both cases the wand is associated with lust. Moreover, Comus's wand is a trident given him by Neptune (lines 18–27) and, at one point, HCE refers to his stick precisely in these terms, saying "there . . . did I upreized my magicianer's puntpole, the tridont sired a tritan stock" (547.21, 23–24).

As to plot, we find the following in "Comus": the embattled brothers join with Thyrsis to rescue their sister from Comus. Thus we have three men stopping one man from committing sexual improprieties with a young girl. Comus flees and the three men call upon Sabrina to free the young girl from a spell—Sabrina having become the deity of the Severn when she drowned herself (lines 826–42). *Finnegans Wake* also involves three men coming upon HCE when the latter is engaged in sexual improprieties, in this case involving two girls. Moreover, there are hints in *Finnegans Wake* that the battling brothers and the servant Sackerson are HCE's three antagonists (just as the two brothers and the servant Thyrsis are Comus's three antagonists) and that the boys' sister Issy or Isolde is one or both of the urinating girls (just as the boys' sister is the girl abducted by Comus). Thus, in one recounting of the events in the park, the "Grenadiers" who spy HCE are the trinity, "Three in one, one and three. / Shem and Shaun and the shame that sunders em" (526.13–14), which is to say, Shem and Shaun and the sham, that Sackerson. (Sackerson is a sham because he is a patrolman in the guise of a servant; Thyrsis could be called a sham for similar reasons.) As to the identification of Issy with the temptresses, there is one particularly striking passage where the two temptresses are named Lizzy and Lissy (538.22), their names combining the two short forms of "Isolde" ("Issy" and "Izzy") with "Lilith."

There are also several looser connections. For example, one of the temptresses commits suicide (67.33–35). Though she does not drown herself in this particular version, she is elsewhere linked with Parthenopea (see 542.21), a siren who did drown herself (see McHugh). Moreover, at one point there is an indication that Issy has drowned herself (see 159.6–18). Beyond again identifying Issy with the temptresses, these images of drowning (along with punning references to the two girls as water nymphs) link all three with Sabrina as well. This is an association one would expect in *Finnegans Wake*, given the repeated identification of mother and daughter and given the clear parallel between ALP/the river Liffey and Sabrina/the river Severn. It is also an association one would expect from the broader relation between the two works, for Sabrina and the abducted girl form a pair roughly parallel to the two girls in the park.

Finally, in typical Joycean manner, there are a few more purely comic links between these works as well. For example, Iris, introduced at the end of the masque, is perhaps connected not only with the rainbow girls, but with the temptresses also—given that she enters and then "[w]aters the odorous banks" (line 993). Though it is unlikely that Milton had a urinary pun in mind here, it is less unlikely that such a pun would have occurred to Joyce. Along the same lines, the young girl at the end of the masque dances in a way reminiscent of "the mincing Dryades / On the lawns" (lines 964–65; recall Stephen's pun on Milton's "smoothsliding Mincius").

Thus it appears very likely that the characters and plot of "Comus" significantly guided Joyce in structuring *Finnegans Wake*, while occasionally suggesting more local and humorous elements as well. Certainly, Joyce was not merely rewriting "Comus," taking Milton's characters and revising them into HCE, Issy, and so on. But it seems that Milton's masque contributed importantly to Joyce's understanding and development of this work, and to his subconscious, evaluative sense that it was "right," aesthetically complete. "Comus," then, provides an important set of cognitive structures—narrative, structural, characterological—and furnishes an important aspect of the suggestion or dhvani of *Finnegans Wake*. Indeed, this seems to be as clear a case of nonderivative influence as we are likely to come upon. On the other hand, the thematic significance of *Finnegans Wake* does not appear to be significantly engaged in its relation to "Comus." That is reserved for the relation between *Finnegans Wake* and *Paradise Lost*.

Past Eve and Adam's: A Pisgah Sight of Lost Paradise

For Joyce, the fallen condition of humankind is twofold. It is erotic and it is thanatic. It involves lust and perversion, on the one hand; hatred, war, and, above all, death, on the other. It also involves the uncertainty of ordinary life—the wheel of fortune, which is a function of both. But the Fall, in Joyce's mythic, untheological conception, is still fortunate. For it is because of lust and death that love and new life are brought forth—wife and husband, our parents in us, we in our children, generation by generation. It is an old philosophy—that Spring is the child of Winter—and a simple one. And *Finnegans Wake* retells an old story, an old tragedy, an old comedy of death in life and life in death. In rewriting this tragicomedy, Joyce draws on as many previous tellings of that story as he can: Hindu, Buddhist, Muslim, Jewish, and of course Christian. *Paradise Lost* was one of the most important of these. John Shawcross calls this recurrent tale of "generation and continuance," "the myth of life itself" ("They that dwell" 208). He stresses that it was a myth redeveloped by Joyce on the basis of Milton and others. Redeveloped but, we must add, also changed, for Milton's notions of life, of birth, and of rebirth were spiritual and sublime, whereas Joyce's were, once again, solid, fleshly, mundane.

There are many points at which the presence of *Paradise Lost* can be felt in *Finnegans Wake*. Indeed, the entire book, like *Paradise Lost*, deals with the Fall. It begins "riverrun, past Eve and Adam's" (3.1); thus, we are introduced immediately to the river of Eden and our "Originals." Dublin here is also Paradise—before Sir Tristram ("passencore"), before America ("nor yet"), before the conversion of Eire ("nor"), before even the conflict of Isaac and Esau ("not yet, though [because biblical] venissoon after"). When?—the second paragraph tells us. "The fall" marked by a thunderclap. The time of the novel is the eternally recurring time of the Fall.

"Eve and Adam's" is not the name of the Dublin church to which Joyce is presumably referring in the geographical aspect of the opening sentence.

That church is "Adam and Eve's." Why, then, does Joyce reverse the names? There are two obvious reasons, and a third less obvious. The first is that the Fall was initially Eve's, and only subsequently Adam's. It was only after, indeed through, Eve that Adam fell. The second reason is that it is only through the second Eve, Mary, that Adam and others may be redeemed. This is true in the Catholic and Miltonic view of the virgin birth; Milton repeatedly emphasizes that it is through the "woman's seed" that mankind will receive a savior (see, for example, *PL* 11.116). But it is also true in any natural birth—the truly happy consequence of the Fall for Joyce. (Joyce once remarked that the "most important thing that can happen to a man is the birth of a child," and "I can't understand households without children. I see some with dogs, gimcracks. Why are they alive? To leave nothing behind, not to survive yourself—how sad!" [quoted in Ellmann *James Joyce* 204, 204n].) Eve is first, then, because it is only Eve who gives birth—female generativity propagating life. Finally, Eve is first because, it is she, in the form of ALP, dying, giving birth, being born, daughter/wife/mother, Anna in a riverlike cycle of generation, who dreams the dream of *Finnegans Wake*, a dream that ends as she dies, a death-dream, repeated over and over in the cycles of life, which are her cycles.

From the very first page, Joyce's conception of the Fall is linked with that of Milton. His reference to "the stream Oconee" alludes not only to the Oconee River in Georgia, but echoes of the "ocean stream" (of "Norway foam," *PL* 1.202, 203) mentioned by Milton in relation to Satan as he "lay floating many a rood" in the burning lake (a line quoted by Stephen in *Ulysses*). Later in the same paragraph, Joyce refers to the postdeluge rainbow whereby God promised never to destroy the earth again: "the regginbrow was to be seen ringsome on the aquaface" (3.14). In this line, Joyce imagines the rainbow as a sort of brow on a face. In book 11 of *Paradise Lost*, when Michael tells Adam about the Flood and the rainbow, Adam sees the "colored streaks in Heaven, / Distended as the brow of God appeased" (11.879–80), employing the same image. The Fall too is presented in a Miltonic fashion due to its conjunction with a thunderclap. While thunder in *Finnegans Wake* is certainly a Viconian device, it is Miltonic also, for both the angelic and human Falls in *Paradise Lost* are associated with divine thunder. Thus Satan recalls the thunder that followed them as they fell "from the precipice / Of Heaven" into "[t]he fiery surge" (1.172–73). And when Adam ate of the apple, "Nature gave a second groan; / Sky low'r'd, and, muttering thunder, some sad drops / Wept at completing of mortal Sin / Original" (9.1001–4).

Of course, these allusions are typically parodic—Milton's awesome Ocean stream turned into an obscure river by Dublin, Georgia; the divine rainbow reduced to the happy flushed face of a drinker of home brew; the thunder of the human Fall metamorphosed into the clatter of a drunken hod carrier's tumbling wheelbarrow. But however comic each treatment, Joyce's theme is perfectly serious, as is the importance of Milton to the development of this theme. Hugh Kenner noted regarding *Ulysses* and Homer that "detailed correspondences are largely comic," but "larger correspondences are more usually serious" (*Dublin's Joyce* 182). The point can be generalized across Joyce's works and precursors.

For the most part, Joyce's use of *Paradise Lost* is of the sort we would expect from our discussion of *Ulysses*, only it is more extensive. The Fall is sexualized in a Miltonic/Kabbalistic manner. HCE/Adam is seduced to spill his seed by a pair of urinating Liliths, though there are only a few hints of impropriety between ALP/Eve and Father Michael (the interloper figure). The Fall brings "death into the world, and all our woe" (*PL* 1.3), prominently including war, the dire result of Angelic battle. However, there is good drawn out of evil by natural design (see *FW* 297.5, 621.29)—a sort of secular (and Aristotelian) version of the Divine Providence that it is Milton's purpose to "assert" in *Paradise Lost* (1.25).

Finally, Joyce has not abandoned his romantic identification with Milton's freedom-seeking rebel, Satan. Shem is as Satanic as Stephen, perhaps more so. And Hell is a palpable presence in *Finnegans Wake*—along with its peculiarly Miltonic ambiance (for example, flute music)—in a way that Heaven never is. But Shem is even more ironized than Stephen. Joyce's concerns in *Finnegans Wake* continue his development away from earlier celebrations of the heroic artist/rebel disdaining the masses, and manifest, instead, a deep care and admiration for the strength and beauty of soul to be found in ordinary people, especially ordinary women. Biographically, Joyce has turned from an obsession with himself to love and care for his suffering, distracted daughter and for the suffering, emotionally brutalized mother whose death and life he never ceased to mourn. What is most important for our purposes is that in each case, Milton provided Joyce with some of the most important models for his artistic understanding of these deeply personal concerns.

Hubbub in Edenborough: The Sexual Fall

The scene of *Finnegans Wake* is, again, not only Dublin (Howth Castle and Environs), but Eden. HCE/Adam, Joyce informs us at the end of the first chapter, is "he who will be ultimendly respunchable for the hubbub caused in Edenborough" (29.34–36); here the *h*ubbub *c*aused in *E*denborough as fully identifies HCE with Eden as with *H*owth *C*astle and *E*nvirons. Elsewhere, noting the particular sexual nature of the Fall, ALP (here "*A Laughable Party*"—it is a fortunate Fall, after all) addresses a letter to HCE at "*Hy*de and *C*heek, *E*denberry, *D*ubblenn [due to the two "ends" of the girls, with their hide and cheeks unhidden], WC [due to their micturition]" (66.16–18), thereby repeating and reenforcing this identification. More interestingly, Shem describes HCE as "between youlasses and yeladst glimpse of Even" (130.3)—between the temptresses (lasses) and the soldiers (lads) glimpsing Heaven/Eden or paradise (that is, the bared lasses), but also between *Ulysses* and Eden in the sense that he is Everyman, Here Comes Everybody (32.18–19), thus all who have lived between the present (or at least 1922) and the dawn of time. Finally, HCE is between *Ulysses* and *the last glimpse of Eden,* which is to say, *Paradise Lost,* the last glimpse of Eden in the English literary tradition; he is situated between these two great retellings of the Fall. Here the relation is not so much temporal as conceptual, for HCE is not so completely realistic as Leopold Bloom, yet not so completely mythic as Milton's Adam.

More important, the incident in the park, alluded to by ALP and Shem, is, like Bloom's masturbation, a straightforward recapitulation of the Kabbalistic Fall of Adam. Indeed, the two temptresses are directly connected with Lilith. We have seen one instance of this already in the case of the names Lissy (Lilith + Issy) and Lizzy (Lilith + Izzy). But these "two quitewhite villagettes who hear show of themselves so gigglesomes minxt the follyages" (83–84; who here show themselves/hear that they have shown themselves giggling [a felix culpa] and urinating [minxing] in the foliage/across all ages of folly, thus recurrently), are more clearly connected with Lilith and the Fall elsewhere. At one point, the girls appear as two plays (also on show to HCE): "The Bo' Girl and The Lily" (32.35)—elsewhere, he gives the long form of "Lily" as "Lilyth" (34.33), clarifying the connection. At another point they are reduced to one woman who makes cunning use of her hams: "It was the first woman, they said, souped him, that fatal wellesday, Lili Coninghams" (58.28–30). In both cases, the temptresses are tacitly linked with Lilith, by name and, in the second case, by her being "the first woman"—for Lilith did indeed precede Eve.

There are several explicit connections. Defending HCE, Glugg refers to the two as "lilithe maidinettes" (241.4). And later, HCE defends (and implicitly incriminates) himself with regard to accusations concerning "the lilliths oft I feldt" (366.25; the lilies of the field/the Liliths I often felt). Perhaps the most interesting of these references comes at the beginning of chapter 4, when we are informed that HCE "bedreamt him stil and solely of those lililiths undeveiled which had undone him" (75.5–6). This is a significant passage for several reasons. For one thing, it explicitly links the nudity of the temptresses with satanic seduction—their *unveiling* being the work of the *devil*. Beyond this, the doubled initial syllable of Lilith serves several functions. First of all, it mimics HCE's characteristic stutter—a stutter no doubt worsened during periods of excitement, as when thinking of the "undeveiled lililiths." More important, it recalls the doubling of the temptresses, and links this doubling with the Kabbalah, for as Waite points out, in some versions of the story, it is not one, but two demons who seduce Adam (*Secret Doctrine* 103).

Finally, this doubling recalls the fact that in Kabbalistic tradition there are two distinct Liliths or two distinct conceptions of Lilith (see Scholem 357). One of these is the seductress, the other a murderer of infants ("Lilith, patron of abortions," Joyce calls her in *Ulysses* [14.242]). These Liliths conjointly represent the prime woes of the Fall for Joyce: distorted sexuality and death. Indeed, the wakean lililiths manifest the same division of lapsarian functions, for one becomes a prostitute (see 67.35–68.18) and the other kills herself (see 67.33–35). Moreover, Issy, with whom they are identified, combines these strains, as when she is condemned to "eurn bitter bed by the sweet of her face" (291.6). This echoes God's condemnation of human kind to struggle for sustenance: "In the sweat of thy face shalt thou eat bread" (*PL* 10.205). Joyce's revision of this judgment indicates that Issy will have to earn her sustenance in bed by using her sweet face (that is, through prostitution), but she will ultimately die anyway, her bitter life reduced to ashes in a funerary urn.

This doubled Kabbalistic Lilith is also one of the reasons for the inclusion in *Finnegans Wake* of another Lily parallel to the seductive Lili Coninghams: Lily Kinsella, "child of Mammon" (205.10–11). This Lily is associated with the sinister MacGrath, sometimes identified with the "cad with the pope" (618.3–4) who is responsible for the final fall of HCE. The pairing of these two is particularly relevant for it is strongly reminiscent of the pairing of Lilith and Samael. Indeed, Lily Kinsella is elsewhere referred to as "the wife of Mr Sneakers" (618.4–5), a significant connection when one recalls that "sneak" is a frequent pun for "snake" in *Finnegans Wake* (see, for example, "sworming in sneaks" [19.13]), the two being homophonous in Hiberno-English. Moreover, this reference occurs just after MacGrath has been metamorphosed, Satan-like, into "MacCrawls" in a malicious deceit (or pose) that gives rise to the fortunate Fall, "O, felicious coolpose!" (618.1). Indeed, in the final title of ALP's "untitled mamafesta," the Cad is referred to as "the Snake" responsible for the (near) "Fall" of HCE (107.3, 5). Lily Kinsella is, then, like Lilith, wed to the Prince of Darkness.

The masturbatory nature of this Fall is also clear. It is indicated, for example, at the very outset of the work when Finnegan's fall is described in the following terms: "(There was a wall of course in erection) Dimb? He stottered from the latter. Damb! he was dud. Dumb! Mastabatoom, mastabadtomm, when a mon merries his lute is all long. For whole the world to see" (6.9–12). Certainly this refers to Finnegan's physical fall from the ladder to his death, the clattering sound of the crash recalling the name of the Mastaba tombs in Egypt. But it is also a masturbatory fall of HCE's sort, a fall of the "erection" ("Phall if you but will, rise you must" 4.15–16), a Mastabatom Mastabadtomm, a fall where a man is making merry with his own long lute for the whole world to see, and for the world to see his hole (as he has dropped his pants for the act and is visible from the rear).

Another early example is to be found when HCE appears in the darkness of the park and the narrator exclaims, "But look what you have in your handself!" (20.20–21). This is in part a statement to the reader—"look at this book!" (see Rose and O'Hanlon 20). But it appears also to be a statement to/about the "busy eerie whig" who has "a bit of a torytale to tell": "One's upon a thyme [Once upon a time, one—HCE—was on the grass or herbs, the thyme] and two's behind their lettice leap [and two—the temptresses—are in the lettuce at Leixlip with their behinds visible] and three's among the strubblely beds [and three—the soldiers—are in the stubblebeds outside the garden]" (20.23–25). The exclamation seems to imply that the one, HCE, has taken himself in hand when viewing the two behinds. (Note also that the three soldiers—sometimes identified with the three S's, Shem, Shaun, and Sackerson, as we have seen—may also have a Kabbalistic parallel in the three angels or saints sent by God to chastise Lilith, also named by three S's: Snwy, Snsnwy, and Smnglf, or Sines, Sisinnios, and Synodoros [see Scholem 357]. The difference is, of course, that in this retelling, the soldiers chastise Adam, not Lilith.)

A late instance may be found when Dave the Dancekerl refers to "my old faher's onkel that was garotted, Caius Cocoa Codinhand" (467.12–13). Though HCE is presumably Dave's/Shem's father and his initials are not CCC, the persecution described in this passage most obviously applies to him. Indeed, it is HCE who is garotted early in the book (see 78.36). If so,

"Codinhand" is probably another reference to his masturbation. This is so for several reasons. First of all, "cod" here recalls "codpiece" and thus the male organ. Secondly, fish are identified elsewhere as sexually perverse creatures who engage in HCE-like behavior quite regularly (see 524–25). Finally, the name puns on the commonplace "A bird in the hand is better than two in the bush." As is well known, "bird" is vulgar for "penis." Understood in this sense, this commonplace is particularly appropriate to HCE, for he takes his bird (or his fish) in his handself precisely because he sees two in a bush.

There are other Kabbalistic connections as well, which eventually feed into *Paradise Lost*. Most significantly, whereas the temptresses are, like Gerty, sometimes linked with apples (for example, at one point they are named "Lotta Crabtree" and "Pomona Evlyn" [62.34], the latter associated with Eve, obviously), they are also connected with figs. Figs are in general an important fruit of the Fall in *Finnegans Wake*. Joyce apparently chose the fig for three reasons. The first is lexical. "Fig" is phonetically close to "fuck"—a name for the degraded form of sexual congress that characterizes the fallen state. The second is that, in this state of degraded sexuality, the fallen Adam and Eve first noticed their nakedness and clothed themselves in fig leaves. The third, and perhaps most important, is that in the Kabbalistic tradition, the fig was seen as the fruit of the Fall (see Waite *Secret Doctrine* 96 and the pseudepigraphic "Life of Adam and Eve" [Charles 146]).

As to the fig/fuck similarity, Joyce directly puns on these words—for example, in Willingdone's belligerent correspondence with the jinnies, a martial version of HCE's encounter with the temptresses. The jinnies have sent a "dispatch for to irrigate the Willingdone" (9.3)—they have sent a letter to irritate him, but at the same time they have issued some liquid that will irrigate the garden in which he, like HCE, is standing. Willingdone's riposte is: "Figtreeyou!" (9.13). Perhaps his name—"Willingdone" rather than "Wellington"—is explained here in that his signature, immediately following "Figtreeyou!" indicates that he would be happy to take upon himself the task of figtreeing the irrigating jinnies. In any case, this exchange is followed by the firing of canons (compare, again, Bloom and the fireworks) described as "Tonnerre!"—thunder, the Miltonic sign of the Fall. And while Willingdone cries, thunderlike, "Brum! Brum! Cumbrum!" the jinnies cry, "Underwetter!" punning on the German for "storm" and the "wetting under" of the urinary pair.

Elsewhere, the temptresses are themselves directly related to figs (as they are directly related to apples). After a "Tea for Two"-like melody about fearsome fruit ("furchte fruchte"; 94.14) and the woe associated with "ana mala" (94.16; an apple/bad Anna = ALP = Eve), we find the following scenario: "A pair of sycopanties with amygdaleine eyes, one old obster lumpky pumpkin and three meddlars on their slies" (94.16–18). Clearly, this refers to the two girls, HCE, and the three soldiers. The meddling soldiers are amusingly assimilated to meddlar fruits, both sly and sliced. HCE is an old, lumpy Humpty Dumpty, shaped like a pumpkin and about to fall. The two girls are the most interesting. They have the almond eyes of prostitutes (Greek *amygdalon* = almond + Mary Magdalene), luring HCE. They themselves are, as objects of sexual desire, figs (Greek *sykos* = fig), or fig-showers (Greek *phaino* = show), because they have dropped their panties and revealed their genitalia. Finally, they are sycophants who seduce by flattery.

The fallen sexual relation between ALP/Eve and HCE/Adam is fig-infested as well. During their lovemaking late in the book, "the park's police peels peering by for to weight down morrals from county bubblin'" (583.24–25; as the police/soldiers from the park pass by the Earwickers' in their effort to weigh the morals of County Dublin, but also to keep the morals low [weigh them down] in relation to the bubbling [urinating?] out in the county). HCE/ALP are "fucking," going "a gallop a gallop"—recalling Bloom's steed, Copula Felix. Unfortunately, their image is visible against the Persian blinds and thus their felicitous copulation will be known to everyone soon, throughout the entire universe. But for HCE/ALP it is, it seems, an anniversary and thus an act repeated "From the fall of the fig to doom's last post" (583.22–23). Their sexual intercourse is like a horse race run from the fall of the flag to the finishing post. But it is also the generative act, repeated from the sexual Fall ("of the fig") to the end of time. Finally, it is the very particular relation of the Earwickers, the relation between his fall and her continuing efforts to support and defend him through her letters (the post)—up until her last plea, which immediately precedes her death (or doom) at the end of the novel.

The anniversary theme is taken up and clarified elsewhere, this time in connection with Milton. Speaking of HCE, ALP explains:

> he never battered one eagle's before paying me his duty on my annaversary to the parroteyes list in my nil ensemble, in his lazychair but he hidded up my hemifaces in all my mayarannies and he locked plum into my mirrymouth like Ysamasy morning in the end of time . . . he simply showed me his propendiculous loadpoker, Seaserpents

hisses sissastones, which was as then is produced in his mansway . . .
with the remere remind remure remark . . . this is for Snooker, bort!
(493.4–15)

While parts of the passage are obscure, the general drift is clear enough. HCE never failed in his sexual duties on their anniversary—itself perhaps the anniversary of *paradise* being *lost* ("parroteyes list"), at least in the sense that that loss allowed for sexual generation (in Joyce's version of the Fall). HCE kept his eagle eye on ALP when she was in her altogether ("nil ensemble"), he held up her buttocks ("hidded up my hemifaces") and locked onto her mouth in a kiss that seemed to last an eternity ("like Ysamasy morning in the end of time") and that was at the same time a taste of the merry or felicitous forbidden fruit, the plum ("he locked plum into my mirrymouth"). It is important to point out that Christmas here—or, rather, Christmas and the birth of Issy, hence "Ysamasy"—brings in the theme of salvation through *physical* birth, regeneration, rather than through death and resurrection. In this way, it is important that this is Ysamasy at the end of time and not, say, Easter at the end of time. Following the kiss, HCE reels out his prodigious, serpentine, hissing organ ("his propendiculous loadpoker"), another snake to ALP's Eve, and says, "This is for Snooker"— a comment that hardly requires explanation.

Evidently, the anniversary copulation is a sort of commemoration of the happy Fall. But why is *Paradise Lost* changed to "Parroteyes list"? The problem is illuminated by other references to parrots in *Finnegans Wake*. The first concerns a pub named "the Parrot in Hell" (63.23). This connects parrots further with the Fall and with Satan, but obscurely. Later in the chapter we have been discussing, we find a fuller and more helpful reference. HCE speaks of the cad as "Snakeeye! Strangler of soffiacated green parrots" (534.27–28). The cad is, as we have seen, demonic. "Snakeeye" supports this identification, as does the phrase "to strangle a parakeet," (French) slang for "drink absinthe," a Joycean, Shemian, and thus Satanic characteristic. Moreover, the parrot is not merely suffocated, but *soffia*cated, harmed somehow by *sophos*, knowledge—in other words, harmed by precisely that which caused the Fall, eating from the tree of knowledge now equated with drinking intoxicating beverages (in accordance with some Kabbalistic and even Miltonic views; see *PL* 9.793, where the fruit has an intoxicating effect, and Waite *Secret Doctrine* 77).

Thus parroteyes are, at least, the eyes of the fallen, of those who are intoxicated with the knowledge of good and evil, who are subject to death due to this disequilibrating sophos, into which they were tempted by old Snakeeye. As a result of this, they are perhaps also lustful eyes, eyes that "dart contageous fire," in Milton's words (9.1036), or even weak eyes, if we follow Milton in thinking that the Fall harmed the "visual nerve" (9.12–16)—a concern that touched Joyce in much the same way it touched Milton. As to "list," Joyce no doubt chose this because it is cognate with "lust" and thus means "desire"—fitting well with the preceding interpretation of "parroteyes." In addition, the sense of "list" meaning "to prepare for planting" fits well into the theme of generation and connects nicely with lust in the general thematics of *Finnegans Wake*.

Returning to the paradigmatic copulation of the Earwickers "From the fall of the fig to doom's last post," we find that both figs and, bizarrely, horse races have Miltonic connections as well. Interestingly, there is another passage in *Finnegans Wake* in which the two are conjoined, though it is somewhat obscure. Kersse the tailor has returned from the racetrack and is asked how things went. He describes the race and indicates that something happened to his nemesis the captain ("Same capman no nothing") "gig for gag." One of his auditors responds, "That's fag for fig, metinkus, confessed, mhos for mhos" (322.30). Assuming that Joyce is using Irish orthographical conventions here, the *h* of "mhos" functions to change the *m* from a bilabial nasal stop to a bilabial glide, *w*. This makes the response mean something like "I think that's tit for tat, woes for woes." How "fag" fits here, I don't know. "Fig" does fit with woes, with the horse race, and once again with illicit sexuality, here emphasized by its relation to a "knockingshop" or brothel (see 322.27). "Woes" are clearly the result of the Fall. Elsewhere, Joyce speaks of "the lilipath ways to Woeman's Land" (22.8), the seductions of Lilith that pave the way out of Paradise to a no man's land of woe. Moreover, *woe* is a word Milton used frequently in connection with the results of the Fall. For example, at the very outset of the poem—in lines echoed in *Finnegans Wake*—Milton tells us that his topic will be "man's first disobedience, and the fruit / Of that forbidden tree, whose mortal taste / Brought death into the world, and all our woe" (1.1–3). And, in other lines to which Joyce alludes, when Eve eats of the apple, Milton writes, "Earth felt the wound, and Nature from her seat / Sighing through all her Works gave signs of woe / That all was lost" (9.782–84). In fact, Milton uses some version of the word *woe* almost forty times in *Paradise Lost*, all of which gives the term a Miltonic resonance, at least in the context of the Fall.

This somewhat distant connection is strengthened by looking at two other instances of horse races in *Finnegans Wake*. The first is a television broadcast in which some horses repeat the scene in the park (342.19–28):

Emancipator, the Creman hunter (Major Hermyn C. Entwhistle) with dramatic effect reproducing the form of famous sires on the scene of the formers triumphs, is showing the eagle's way to Mr Whaytehayte's three buy geldings Homo Made Ink, Bailey Beacon and Ratatuohy while Furstin II and The Other Girl (Mrs "Boss" Waters, Leavybrink) too early spring dabbles, are showing a clean pairofhids to Immensipater. Sinkathinks to oppen here! To this virgin's tuft, on this golden of evens! I never sought of sinkathink.

Emancipator, the Creman *h*unter and its owner *H*ermyn C. Entwhistle are clearly two versions of HCE (one equine, one human). He is observed by three males—one of whom, "Homo Made Ink," is clearly a Shemhorse. In addition, he is himself observing the clean pair of hinds of Princess II/ Burst-in-two and another filly who is passing water at the edge of the Liffy. When he is viewing them, he is changed into "Immensipater," immense pater or big daddy, indicating the connection of the fillies with Issy. The commentator is shocked that such a thing as the opening of a sink (for the passing of water) could happen here ("Sinkathinks to oppen here!"/Such a thing to happen here!). Especially as the turf is clean, and the evening is so golden, and those showing their tufts are virgins, and this is the Garden of Eden ("To this virgin's tuft, on this golden of evens!").

This broadcast interrupts a discussion between Butt and Taff. When these disputants return, now as Muta and Juva, they discuss a colloquy between St. Patrick and Balkelly. Their encounter too is compared to a horse race. The odds, Juva explains, are "Tempt to wom Outsider!" (610.18). The ultimate result, we discover, is "Peredos Last in the Grand Natural" (610.34–35). The phrases go together under two interpretations. The first relates to the colloquy. Patrick is the outsider/foreigner and is favored to win, ten to one, over his native, presumably Druid, competitor. As we all know, Christianity did indeed win out over paganism in Eire and thus *Peredos*, the seat of the (Greek) pagan deities, lost. In contrast "Velivision" is "victor"—meaning either that Rome won (Velivision = veni, vidi, vici, Caesar's statement in *The Callico Belly* about his conquests of the Celtic Gauls), or that even St. Patrick has lost out to television—certainly true now, but in 1939 an extremely prescient claim. As to the race, it is the Grand National. Thus the Druids lost out to the Christians—and the Christians lost out to mass media—in the race for the nation. (Under a related interpretation, Patrick's competition is Bishop Berkeley. In this case, Catholicism won out over protestantism in conflict over the nation.)

Further suggestions connect the horse race more directly with the Fall and associate betting with the Miltonic problem of whether those who fall are, as Milton's God insists, truly "Sufficient to have stood" (*PL* 3.99). One suggestion of these lines is that the Outsider is Satan, who has a ten to one chance of tempting the woman ("Tempt to wom Outsider"), which is to say, Eve or her descendant. Another is that there is a ten to one chance that immigrant/outsider HCE will be tempted by the two girls (that is, temptation by two women to one outsider) in a recapitulation of Adam's Fall. The implication in both cases is that the original Fall and all its repetitions are virtually inevitable. Ultimately, for Joyce, Paradise *is* Lost in the Grand Natural—in the normal course of fallible human life, itself both determined and redeemed by the ordinary, natural processes of conception, birth, and death.

Returning to figs, there is one final passage to which it is worth turning in this connection. It does not refer directly to figs, but hints at the presence of fig leaves. During *The Mime of Mick, Nick, and the Maggies,* Shem/Nick/Satan, beloved of Issy, has been defeated. Issy is sad for a moment, but "among the shades that Eve's now wearing she'll meet anew fiancy" (226.13–14). Certainly this means that she will meet a new beau in the now gathering shadows of evening. But Joyce capitalizes the first letter of "Eve" and thereby indicates that *Eve,* our ancestor, is wearing shades as clothing and, in that clothing, she will meet a new fiance/fancy. This makes of Issy a lapsarian Eve going off, apple in hand, to find Adam for lustful purposes. In this context, the shade is appropriately understood as the fig leaf. Certainly Issy, though most often linked with Lilith, is not infrequently identified with Eve as well. And if we follow *Paradise Lost,* "shade" is a perfectly reasonable metonymy for the fig leaf. According to Milton, the fig tree that provided clothing for Eve and Adam following their Fall and consequent lascivious intercourse was "not that kind for Fruit renown'd," but rather the sort that yields "a Pillar's shade / High overarch't and echoing Walks between" (*PL* 9.1106–7). The connection extends our preceding analysis. For the fig leaf is a metonymy for lapsarian, sexual shame, just as the fig itself is a symbol of lapsarian, sexual lust.

From the Garden of Erin: Characters and Prototypes

The link between Issy and Eve is worth considering at greater length, before continuing on to explore the other character correspondences. There is a hint of this connection in the chapter of Shem's questions when Issy speaks to a lover (perhaps imaginary—a fiancé of fancy), telling him "you may go through me!" then exclaiming, "ever for bitter be the frucht of this hour!" (148.29). Perhaps Issy is playing her more usual role as the temptress/seductive Lilith here, rather than Eve. (She does earlier tell her lover: "Liss, liss! I must whiss" = I must know / I must urinate.) But in this case she seduces to sexual congress, not masturbation, and when she speaks of "the fruit of this hour," she has an Eve-like ambivalence about whether it is *bitter* or *better*.

Indeed, in the course of the Parable of the Mookse and the Gripes later in this chapter, it becomes clear that the bitter fruit of Issy's exclamation is certainly the fruit of the Fall (once again associated with illicit sexuality). Specifically, the Shaunian Mookse addresses the Shemian Gripes—now evidently "subsquashed" and on their way to becoming wine. (This alcohol-producing transformation being what makes grapes another Kabbalistic fruit of the Fall; see, for example, Waite *Secret Doctrine* 77.) He concludes, saying, "there I must leave you subject for pressing . . . but 'tis bitter to compote my knowledge's fructos of" (155.18, 21–22). He thus links bitter fruit to the fruit of the tree of knowledge (in this case nicely arranged in a compote—perhaps necessary, given the number of forbidden fruits in the book).

Moreover, bitterness at the hour of the Fall ("ever for bitter be the frucht of this hour!") at least hints at Miltonic connections. Specifically, the bitterness of this fruit suggests *Paradise Lost* due to Milton's use of the term "bitter" in connection with Sin—a "bitter morsel," he tells us (2.808)—or with "bitter ashes" (10.566) chewed by the serpent-metamorphosed demons when they bite imaginary apples, thus making these apples bitter fruit. On the other hand, the bitterness of sin is a common enough image not to require a Miltonic precedent.

Another possible connection with Eve may be found in one of Issy's footnotes to the school text of the lessons chapter: "I was so snug off in my apholster's creedle but at long leash I'll stretch more capritious in his dapplepied bed" (276.36–37). If nothing else, this again shows the connection between sexuality and the Fall—his apple pie bed. It also illustrates once more the thematic concern of human generation and development, for here Eden is implicitly identified with childhood and the Fall with sexual maturity. This theme is also indicated in Issy's request to the "master of snakes" made at the mime, during a talk touching on themes of female sexual emancipation. "[P]lease kindly communicake with the original sinse we are only yearning as yet how to burgeon," she asks. That this burgeoning of original sin is actually sexual maturation is perhaps further indicated when she adds, "we can sloughchange in the nip of a napple" (239.4): we can change by sloughing off the old in a moment, in the bite of an apple, in the bite on a nipple (both infantile and sexual), perhaps also in the applelike growth of breasts ("begin to like them at that age. Green apples," as Poldy has it [13.1086]).

A further Eve/Issy connection—and a specifically Miltonic one—may be found in Issy's narcissism, her rapture with herself while looking in the mirror or in the water (see, for example, 486.23–25). In *Paradise Lost*, when Eve is first created, she is captivated by her image in a lake. Indeed, Eve saw her image in the lake and "pined with vain desire" (4.466), much as Issy does before the mirror (see Issy's response to riddle 10, 143ff.).

A reference that seems to link Issy with both Lilith and Eve may be found in the tour of the Earwicker house. Upstairs, we are told, there is "A pussy" (561.9) and "twobirds" (562.17)—Issy and the two boys reduced to their generative organs. When asked, "Has your pussy a pessname?" (561.10; a pet name and, possibly, a "piss-name"), Issy replies, "Yes, indeed . . . she is named Buttercup" (561.10–12). The four evangelists find this charming and connect the butter of her buttercup with the Fall when they say, "now that I come to drink of it filtered, a gracecup fulled of bitterness" (561.14–15). Most often, references to urine are linked with the temptresses, and this transubstantiation of Issy's water into the bitter fruit of the Fall primarily associates her again with this doubled figure of Lilith. However, the name "Buttercup" may also connect her with Eve by way of an opaque comment that appears in the middle of the story about the tailor and the Norwegian captain: "Let be buttercup eve lit by night in the Phoenix" (321.16). If this sentence links Eve with Buttercup and the buttercup or female genitalia with phoenixlike rebirth (and who knows if it does), it makes sense. Once again, the Fall in *Finnegans Wake* is an inevitable part of the "Grand Natural," the course of physical life, death, and birth. Indeed, this is why Issy has some qualities of Eve, and why these are not arrogated wholly to ALP. If the good fortune of the Fall is the cycle of generations, then Issy *must* carry some of her mother's traits—and most particularly her trait as Eve, as generatrix—for she will replace her mother, and be replaced by her own daughter ("Molly. Milly. Same thing watered down" [*U* 6.87]), that daughter ultimately replaced as well, and so on to no last term.

This generational repetition unsurprisingly includes the demonic interloper, the lost lover who stands between husband and wife, the Satanic seducer who effects—or reveals—their lapsarian alienation. In the Senecan soap opera of book 3, chapter 4 (see 573) and in her sexual history (203), ALP is said to have been intimate with Father Michael. Their relationship intertextually recapitulates the relationships between Gretta and Michael Furey, Emma Clery and the priest of *Stephen Hero*, Molly and Lieutenant Gardner. But, more important, it is recapitulated intratextually as well, in the relations between Issy and Father Michael (see, for example, 458, 461, and the response to riddle 10).

Thus Issy, while primarily a Lilith figure, has elements of Eve, some specifically Miltonic. ALP too has both elements, though certainly Eve predominates. The clearest connections of both sorts relate to ALP's sexuality (both libidinous and generative); there is, however, some relevant reference to death as well. Specifically, Kabbalistic writings connect both Lilith and Eve with waters. As already mentioned, there are two Liliths or conceptions of Lilith in Kabbalistic tradition—one erotic, one thanatic. The second Lilith is the demon of certain fishes and of "the waters below" (Waite *Secret Doctrine* 104 n. 1). Joyce has fused these different conceptions, drawing out the connection with fishes, and comically refiguring "the waters below" as urine. The connections between the river and Eve are still more illuminating. As Waite puts it, "Prior to the trespass this river [which passed through Eden] penetrated into the woman and irrigated her waters" (*Secret Doctrine* 98). Thus prelapsarian Eve's bodily water was intimately connected, even identified, with the River of Eden.

At several points Joyce directly connects ALP with this River of Eden, often by way of Christian traditions and at times involving specifically Miltonic elements. Thus in the sexual history of ALP, given by the washerwomen, the Fall—"O happy fault" (202.34)—occurred when "a heavy trudging lurching lieabed of a curraghman . . . gave her the tigris eye!" (202.28–29, 33–34), which is to say, gave her a precious gem (the tiger's eye), looked at her passionately, and looked at her as the Tigris, one of the four rivers that has its source in the river of Eden. This is further, and more strikingly, connected with the Fall by way of Milton. In *Paradise Lost*, Satan, on his way to seduce Eve, reenters Paradise by way of the Tigris where it "[r]ose up a fountain by the Tree of Life" (9.69–76). In this way, the curraghman is akin to Satan; a seducer giving the Tigris eye is linked with a seducer approaching his seduction through the Tigris.

As it turns out, the women find it hard to agree on a first sexual experience/Fall for ALP—predictably, because in *Finnegans Wake* the Fall is recurrent, generational, "always already" (in the popular phrase) or "always again." The second washerwoman thus posits an earlier Fall, something before the curraghman, this one in the "garden of Erin" (203.1)—which links ALP with both the Liffey (the river of Erin) and the river of Eden.

In these two cases, ALP is clearly Eve, specifically the Kabbalistic, rivery Eve. In a still earlier story of the Fall, ALP becomes associated with the Lilith figures as well, and the Miltonic context shifts from *Paradise Lost* to the watery "Lycidas." Here, Anna is penetrated by Michael Arklow—another of the recurrent early Michaels with whom Joyce's Eve-figure is carnally linked. In this case, she is given two names—"Nance the Nixie" and "Nanon L'Escaut"—and thus identified with the temptresses. The second of the two names seems to pun on both *Manon Lescaut* and Ninon l'Enclos, a seventeenth-century prostitute (see McHugh), thus emphasizing their illicit sexuality. Moreover, the act occurs amidst "sycomores"—the trees, but also "more sykos" or "more figs." She is very flirtatious in this instance and her flirtation, as it turns out, draws its vocabulary from "Lycidas":

> By that Vale Vowclose's lucydlac, the reignbeau's heavenarches arronged orranged her. Afrothdizzying galbs, her enamelled eyes indergoading him on to the vierge violetian. Wish a wish! Why a why? Mavro! Letty Lerck's lafing light throw those laurals now on her daphdaph teasesong petrock. Maass! But the majik wavus has elfun anon meshes. And Simba the Slayer of his Oga is slewd. He cuddle not help himself, thurso that hot on him, he had to forget the monk in the man so, rubbing her up and smoothing her down, he baised his lippes in smiling mood, kiss akiss after kisokushk (as he warned her niver to, niver to, nevar) on Anna-na-Poghue's of the freckled forehead. (*FW* 203.26–204.1)

Without examining the entire passage, we should note a few things. Father Michael commits the act of love/thirst-quenching (in some ways recalling the connection between lust and eating in Milton—see 9.740–44, 9.1004–46) after ALP has lured him with her "enamelled eyes" to approach her bank of violets/to violate her virginity. This has occurred by a clear lake ("lucydlac") and Lady Luck has awarded her the laurels in writing teasing petrarchan love poetry or in setting a petrarchan love scene by letting light through the shadowing laurels ("Letty Lerck's lafing light throw [letting light through] those laurals now on her daphdaph teasesong petrock [Petrarch/bedrock]"). Father Michael cannot help himself, and he enters. After the digression in the middle of "Lycidas," Milton calls on the surrounding nature to cast flowers—including "enamelled eyes" (line 139) and "violets" (145)—on "the laureate lease where Lycid lies" (151), hence the water. Joyce almost certainly took "enamelled eyes," "laurel" and the violets of "violetian," and the location, "lucydlac" (lucid lake and Lycid lake), from this poem.

Much as in *Ulysses,* Milton's poem functions here to stress the theme of death—a necessary part of the Fall as part of human generation. Lycidas, Edward King, died in the water. As is clear in *Ulysses,* Milton's monody brings to the fore the destructive aspect of water—also stressed in such rewritings of the poem as "Alastor." It thus serves as an apt marker of the thanatic character of the Fall, and of the river's link with death as well as generation. This theme is developed by the reference to Śiva ("Simba") the Slayer—the destructive aspect of God in the Hindu trinity of Creator (Brahma), Preserver (Viṣṇu), Destroyer. The Fall necessarily involves death, best exemplified, perhaps, in the two Liliths—one who prevents human generation (through seducing to masturbation or nocturnal emission), the other who kills infants, both here linked with destructive waters.

However, human sexuality not only presupposes death, it also ends death. Śiva is "slewd"—both slain and lewd; he is not only the god of destruction, but also an erotic deity whose erect phallus is worshipped by devotees. Śiva the slayer is slain by what is lewd, or sexual, which he too represents. This reproductive aspect of the Grand Natural is associated with Eve, as well as ALP, and both are linked with regenerative waters. In this passage, ALP simultaneously takes on characteristics of the Liliths insofar as her waters have been invaded by Miltonic death.

The washerwomen do appear to come to eventual agreement on an initial Fall, however—a very physical one, but one still associated with Eve: "she sideslipped out by a gap in the Devil's glen" and "fell over a spillway" (205.14–16). This fall, of course, is almost at the very source of the river. According to Catholic doctrine, the fallen condition affects us, determines us in certain ways, from the very beginning of life, due to the weakening or darkening of our souls by original sin. According to Joyce, this fallen condition determines us because of the very nature of our biological condition, not as souls, but as bodies. The slip from a gap here is a birth: ALP's birth, parallel to that of ALP's daughter (as another ALP) at the end of the book. It too is the Fall that brings death but that, at once, slays death through birth.

Before going on to Adam, it is worth looking at one further connection between ALP and Eve, a connection that develops the same ambivalent theme of the Fall. It occurs at the very beginning of the book, when ALP is bringing presents to her children—which is to say, in this context, everyone. "How bootifull and how truetowife of her," Joyce writes, "when strengly forbidden, to steal our historic presents from the past postpropheticals so as to will make us all lordy heirs and lady maidesses of a pretty nice kettle of fruit" (11.29–32). ALP has given to all her children the gift of the forebidden fruit, the Fall; we are all heirs to her historic present, which—as our biological nature, passed from mother to child, from before the time of the prophets—is both true to wife and true to life.

To clarify this further, Joyce goes on: "She is livving in our midst of debt" (11.32)—she, ALP/Eve ("livving" = the Liffey), lives in death in our debt to her. Subsequently, he continues, "Gricks may rise and Troysirs fall . . . for in the byways of high improvidence that's what make lifework leaving" (11.35–12.2). Civilization may pass (Greek and Trojan), but because of carnal relations (rising pricks and falling trousers), we may leave behind new life (our work of life) after we have died; this is what makes life worth living and is, in effect, what replaces divine providence in our improvident lives.

In the years after writing *Ulysses,* Joyce's view of this Eve figure clearly changed. ALP is not Molly, a soiled earth goddess engaging in adulterous sex with a slick charmer. She is sexual, certainly, but her sexuality is affirmative—a gift rather than a failing. Perhaps this is only because she conceives and gives birth; perhaps this is only a sort of Catholic view, relegating sexual activity to propagation. But then it is not clear that the degraded view of sexuality has been transferred to the temptresses. They are referred to as "sluts" and are denounced for their provocative behavior. However, it is clearly HCE and his supporters who have turned their act into the act of Liliths. And Joyce tells us that their lives were ruined by the events. Although the novel is certainly not a feminist critique of sexist attitudes toward female sexuality, it does arguably criticize a number of these attitudes. Joyce connected the temptresses with Lilith. But he probably intended to do so by way of a series of social views that allow them to be seen as Liliths, despite the fact that they are merely ordinary people, much like anyone else. (Of course, it is important to keep in mind that this is a dream and thus has further layers of complication as well, and that Joyce, much like everyone else, shifted in his views, fantasies, and so on, concerning female—and male—sexuality.)

HCE, our Adam, presents fewer complications, if only because his case is ideologically simpler. From his very introduction, HCE is connected with Adam: "Of the first was he to bare arms and a name" (5.5). This echoes a line from *Hamlet* stating that Adam "was the first that ever bore arms" (see McHugh). And certainly Adam was the first human to have a name. Of course, HCE did not exactly bear arms; rather he *bares* arms. In other words, he rolls up his sleeves, due to the lapsarian need to work—in his case, as a publican. Later, at the theater, watching *The Bo' Girl* and *The Lily*, HCE is named "folksforefather": forefather of everyone (as well as "popular author" in Danish). Indeed, the episode in the park is repeatedly referred to as "the case of Mr Adams" (39.24), "Der Fall Adams" (70.5; the Fall or, in German, case of Adam), and so on. At one point he is lionized as "the heroest champion of Eren" (398.5; Erin/Eden)—presumably, therefore, Adam. In the second chapter, "genesis" (30.2), HCE is living "in prefall paradise peace" and is visited by royalty in what is evidently in part a parody of God's visit to Adam (see, for example, *PL* 8.311–459). Even his pole may link him with Adam, for according to the late seventeenth-century *Sepher Rasiel*, one of the few items that Adam took with him from Paradise was a "rod" awarded him by the Almighty (see Rappoport 171).

HCE functions as Adam primarily through his role in the Fall—as "the cause of all our grievances" (220.28)—a role that, once again, combines biblical, Miltonic, and Kabbalistic elements. We have already discussed the Kabbalistic sources and implications of HCE's masturbation. There is, however, one further passage that is important in this context. An HCE figure has appeared on television and "confesses to all his tellavicious nieces." Specifically: (1) "He wollops his mouther with a sword of tusk in as because that he confesses how opten he used be obening her howonton he used be undering her"—he was wanton in speech (that is, with his mouth)/ he committed incest with his mother. (2) "He boundles alltogotter his manucupes with his pedarrests in asmuch as because that he confesses before all his handcomplishies and behind all his comfoderacies" (349.31–35)—he speaks of his manuscripts/manual desires (presumably including masturbation), as well as his pederasty and foot fetishes, and confesses his accomplishments by hand (done before) and his comforting confederacies (done from behind). (3) And "he touched upon this tree of livings in the middenst of the garerden" (350.1–2)—he touched the tree of life/masturbated in the middle of the garden of Eden/Earth (German *Erde*).

Clearly this last is directly connected with the Fall and the expulsion from Eden, for it was due to the Fall that the Tree of Life was forbidden to Adam and Eve and they were condemned to die—living on only through regeneration, hence the penis as the "new" tree of life. By thus connecting the Tree of Life with the male organ, Joyce in part follows a Kabbalistic lead, extending and revising the Judeo-Christian myth in keeping with his thematic concerns. In *Finnegans Wake*, the male organ is indeed the tree of life in that it is, once more, through sexual generation that we gain life. Indeed, this tree is not only in the midst, but in the midden, thus amidst decay and death. And it is firmly rooted in the earth, not associated with a rarified, ethereal Paradise.

HCE later picks up this theme in a Miltonic way when he claims that all men are sinners or lechers, even those who seem pure—"whole men is lepers" (355.33)—that we are nothing but wanderers in the cold wilderness who want children (Hiberno-English *childer*) to carry on our name, which is our true destiny after the Fall of our ancestors: "nobbut wonterers in that chill childerness which is our true name after the allfaulters" (355.33–35). That, he tells us, has been true "from the faust to the lost" (356.1), from first to last, from *Doctor Faustus* to *Paradise Lost*, from the seduction of humankind by Satan until today.

From the Miltonic perspective, perhaps the most interesting reference to HCE as Adam is equally a reference to him as Cain, as his own son—a reference that thus links the male generations in much the way ALP and Issy are linked by the occasional overlap between their characterizations as Eve and Lilith. HCE is being eulogized and comes to be identified momentarily both with Daniel O'Connell, who killed d'Esterre in a duel, and with Cain. The speaker, following the title "Television kills telephony in brothers' broil" (52.18), refers to HCE's gauntlet, with which "in an hour not for him solely evil," he "struck down the might he mighthavebeen d'Esterre" (52.28–30). The "brothers' broil" clearly alludes to the killing of Abel by Cain. But the line in which the act is described alludes to Milton's famous description of Eve's Fall "in evil hour" (*PL* 9.780). The two are not unrelated, however. The Fall "brought Death into the World" (*PL* 1.3), and the death of Abel is the first fulfillment of that aspect of the Fall: "Death . . . In his first shape on man," Michael calls it in *Paradise Lost* (11.466–67).

This leads us to our final character, the son of Adam: Shem, who combines the characteristics of Satan and Cain. This synthesis is in part derived from Byron. However, it is drawn primarily from the Kabbalistic tradition, for in this view Cain was the child of either Samael and Eve or Adam and Lilith. Either way, he was Satanic (see Waite *Secret Doctrine* 101–2). This is indicated, with a slight change, in the dialogue between Shemian Mercy and Shaunian Justice (see 187.24, 193.31)—where the brothers take up the two aspects of divine judgment, according to a number of writers, including Milton (see, for example, 3.132, 10.59, and 10.78). As Mercius, speaking "of hisself" (193.31), "cannibal Cain" (193.32), Shem refers to himself as "firstborn and firstfruit of woe" (194.12; perhaps alluding to Milton's "fruit" that brought "all our woe") and "tree of the knowledge of beautiful andevil" (194.15), "the child of Nilfit's father, blzb . . . woewoewoe! bab's baby" (194.17, 24). Shem is then the fruit of the tree of the knowledge of good and evil insofar as he is the first lapsarian child and the one who "brought death into the world" in killing Abel. But he is equally the fruit of the tree of beautiful Eve and the devil—Beelzebub (blzb), who, as we have already seen, was connected with Samael (and Asmodeus) as the demon of death. He is, then, woefully, Bab's/Beelzebub's baby.

Indeed, in keeping with this, HCE is later referred to as Beelzebub, precisely when he is going upstairs with ALP (herself assimilated to Lilith) in order to see the children. They are "bullseaboob and rivishy divil" (580.14)—the dull-witted, sexually bullish, seafaring Beelzebub, and the ravishing rivery devil (that is, Lilith). Thus they combine both possibilities for Cain's demonic parentage—Adam/Lilith and Eve/Samael (or Beelzebub)—and thereby explain Issy's Lilith character also.

For the most part, however, Shem develops as a more heavily ironized version of Stephen, another romantic Satan in part modeling (and ironizing) Joyce himself. Joyce had of course already connected himself with Satan through Stephen Dedalus, and one reason for his choice of "Shem" as the Satanic name is that it is the Irish version of "James." However, there are other reasons also. Most important, Joyce was probably aware that "Samael" was thought to derive from "Shemal" (as noted in the *Jewish Encyclopedia* entry for "Samael"); in this way, the name "Shem" contains just what is common to "Seamus" or "Shemus" (James) and "Shemal." Moreover, there is a further Satanic link by way of the fallen Seraphim lured by the temptresses of Earth—Seraphim with whom Stephen identified himself in the villanelle of *A Portrait*. In the pseudepigraphic Book of Enoch, the leader of this salacious angelic band is named Shemhaza (see Rappoport 62–63).

Of course, Shem's demonic characteristics go well beyond his name. He is the Miltonic "manroot of all evil" (*FW* 169.18–19), no doubt in part because Milton's Satan sought "to confound the race / Of mankind in one root" (*PL* 2.382–83) as the means whereby "out of good still to find means of evil" (1.165). He travels in "the shipsteam *Pridewin*" (*FW* 171.35) and took a fall "off Eden Quay" (172.15). We discover that, as Glugg, "the duveln sulpp"—the devil himself—was in him (222.25). As Dave the Dancekerl, he's "lost" and seems to have fallen "out of space" (462.17, 31), like the rebellious angels. He has other Satanic characteristics as well (see 464.11–12).

More suggestively, Shaun asks Shem if he, Satan-like, thinks he is the son of God and thus will not serve: "Do you hold yourself then for some god in the manger, Shehohem, that you will neither serve nor let serve, pray nor let pray?" (188.18–19). Likewise, Milton's Satan refuses to serve God or let other angels serve God and he begins this rebellion precisely when the son (who will become "god in the manger") is declared by the Father equal to Himself and above all others (*PL* 5.603–6), a superiority Satan rejects (5.772–802). In the same passage, Shaun also calls Shem an "anarch," thereby connecting him not only with anarchism (and thus political revolution, both Irish and Satanic) but with Satan's ally in his battle against God, the ruler of Chaos, the "Anarch" of book 2 (*PL* 2.988).

Elsewhere, Shem is uncertain, tempted by demons. For example, in the Mime, a good angel and a bad angel sit, cartoonlike, on his shoulders, advising: "he was ambothed upon . . . first on the cheekside by Michelangelo and, besouns thats, over on the owld jowly side by Bill C. Babby [Beelzebub]" (230.2–4). This is not inconsistent with his being Satan, for in *Paradise Lost*, Satan repeatedly suffers from self-doubt in the course of his mission. Indeed, he took up this mission during the pandemonic "demoncracy" (*FW* 167.25) at the suggestion of, precisely, Bill C. Babby, as a sort of revenge against God and his army, led by Angel Michael/Michelangelo. Moreover, when, on the same page, Shem thinks of his loss to angelic Shaun (a Michael figure), he behaves in the most Satan-like fashion: "With tears for his coronaichon, such as engines weep" (230.24–25). Clearly this echoes and parodies Milton's famous description of Satan's efforts to speak to the assembled demons after their defeat in Heaven: "Thrice he assay'd, and thrice in spite of scorn, / Tears such as Angels weep, burst forth" (1.619–20). "Coronaichon" is a suggestive addition. It is Shaun's coronation, just as it was the triumph of both the Son and, at least to some degree, of Michael. Correlatively, it is Shem's/Satan's complete destruction, his *coronach*, Irish for funeral dirge. Thus he weeps for Shaun's/Michael's/the Son's coronation, and for his own funeral.

But why does he weep as *engines* weep rather than as *angels* weep? No doubt "engine" here derives from Milton's use of the term to signify a machine of war (see, for example, 2.65 and 4.17). In general terms, the angelic Fall—which Shem's loss repeats—entailed for humankind a continual state of war, of massive destruction wreaked all around by Hellish engines. Moreover, in this particular case, Shem, like Satan, will continue to engage in battle, if indirectly. Specifically, Shem's war, like that of his creator, is a war in writing, his only engine of war, the inkpen. Indeed, Shem has at this point just gone through some of the ways in which he will flay his enemies in print. He, like Stephen, plans to follow Marie Corelli in skewering his antagonists on a quill; he will catalogue "all the sorrors of Sexton" (230.10–11). For this task, Shem earlier took up Satanic residence at "the Haunted Inkbottle, no number Brimstone Walk" (182; compare the "firm brimstone" [1.350] that surrounds the lake of fire and allows the demons of *Paradise Lost* to establish their dwelling in Hell). Finally, "engines" here puns on the Irish *Ingean*, daughter, making these into tears such as daughters weep: Issy weeping for Shem's defeat or, more generally, the keening of daughters (sisters, mothers, wives) for the men dead in battle— or for themselves, fated like their mothers before them, to perpetuate death through birth.

As one might expect, Shem/Satan and his father Bab are not the only Miltonic demons to put in an appearance in *Finnegans Wake*. The demonic is, in fact, widespread. Dublin appears as "diablen" (72.34; French *diable* = devil), when one of HCE's attackers is pacing outside his gates (guarded like the gates of Paradise or Hell). In a related event, another of HCE's demonic attackers makes a "belzey babble," a Beelzebubian rattle, at his gates. Even the boozy evangelists—usually referred to as Mamalujo (*Mat*thew, *Ma*rk, *Lu*ke, and *Jo*hn)—are at once associated with Joyce and transformed into Mammon, the angel of greed and third speaker in Milton's demonic congress. Specifically, they become the Irish Herodotos: "our herodotary Mammon Lujius" (13.20), who has written the "bluest book in baile's annals" (13.21–22)—presumably the "usylessly unreadable blue book" (179.26–27), useless *Ulysses*.

Shem himself is at times connected with other demons also. For example, as Dave the Dancekerl, he and Shaun are "the closest of chems" (464.3), perhaps indicating a relation with Chemos (see *PL* 1.406–17), an orgiastic sex god. (Elsewhere, we read that the houris in hell appropriately wear "chems" [177.10], Chemotic versions of gems). He may also be linked with the Middle Eastern monarch Ahaz, a worshipper of Rimmon (*PL* 1.467–72), when—in a partially orientalized parody of Synge's *Playboy of the Western World*—he flees the Irish civil war "in a bad fit of pyjamas [in the sense of loose pants worn in Persia, India, and elsewhere] . . . like a leveret [hare, with a possible pun on *levirate*, a Jewish marriage custom] for his bare lives, to Talviland, ahone [Irish *ochon* = alas] *ahaza*, pursued by the scented curses of all the village belles and, without having struck one blow" (176.26–29; emphasis added).

Of the remaining references to demons, the most interesting for our purposes are probably those surrounding Baalim and Astaroth (singular, Astarte). These male and female fertility deities are introduced conjunctively and collectively in *Paradise Lost* (1.422, see also Blake's *Milton* 1.337). In *Finnegans Wake*, they are similarly conjoined—though in their singular forms—by a Shem figure, Pegger Festy. Defending himself against accusations of cadlike behavior, Pegger says that his accusers "might walk to Baalastartey" (91.14), which is to say, go to Hell, the dwelling of Baal and Astarte. More significantly, Issy and the rainbow girls are linked with Astaroth in the phrase, "Hwy, dairmaidens? Astoreths, assay!" (601.8)—an appropriate link, for insofar as Issy is identified with Lilith, her troupe should be both sexual and demonic as well. (Elsewhere, the mime in which they are involved is twice referred to as a sort of Pandemonium [see 285 and 455].) In a similar vein, Issy is connected with a wounded dove that "astarted" toward Satanic Shem, thus linking her more narrowly with Astarte (232.12). The sexual implication here is important, for, as Rappoport points out, the earthly consort of fallen Shemhazai was Istahar, a version of Astarte (61). Moreover, Manfred's sister, ruined by incestuous love, was named Astarte.

All Tombed to the Mound: Death and War after the Fall

One prime result of the Fall is hateful conflict. The crucial prototypes for this are Satan vs. Michael and Cain vs. Abel. The conflict between Shem and Shaun reconfigures both. At times, the Michael/Satan or Mick/Nick opposition shifts to an opposition between the representatives of God (the church or saints) and the demon Belial, last of the demonic processants in *Paradise Lost* (1.490). (Scholem notes that Belial, Samael, and Satan are identified in some Kabbalistic works [385].) In both cases, the opposition is further assimilated to a sporting conflict between two Oxford colleges: "All Saints beat Belial [= Balliol]! Mickil Goals to Nichil!" (175.5). And "Christ's

Church varses Bellial" (301.9–10). The first of these phrases occurs as Shaun gloats over a beating received by Shem. The second appears in the context of a more sublimated Shaun/Shem conflict, partially assimilated to a conflict between Shaun and HCE: "Sure you could wright anny pippap passage, Eye bet, as foyne as that moultylousy Erewhig, yerself, mick! Nock the muddy nickers! Christ's Church varses Bellial!" (301.6–10). The speaker says that Shaun could easily write as well as Shem (or his father HCE) and urges Shaun/Mick/All Saints/Christ's Church to defeat Shem/Satan/Nick/Belial in this scriptorial war, now transformed into a sports contest.

Unfortunately, the battling of Mick, Nick, and others is not confined to sports and poetry. It is, most often, far more consequential. For Joyce as for Milton, death, even more than perverse sexuality, defines our lapsarian condition. Moreover, just as sex is not always regenerative, death is not always natural. And neither murder nor war is absent from the fallen world of *Finnegans Wake*.

A good example of lapsarian, mortal conflict—indeed, a good Miltonic example—may be found in the scene where Butt/Buckley shoots the Russian general. Butt/Buckley is a soldier fighting on the side of Britain against Russia in the Crimean War. He locates a Russian general, but has qualms about killing him as he defecates. Finally, he does shoot when the general wipes his arse on a sod of turf—an "insult to Ireland," for obscure reasons (the battle could hardly have taken place there; evidently it is simply a matter of the words "sod" and "turf"). In any event, Butt gets the general in his sights. At first he is frightened, but then he thinks "Of manifest 'tis obedience and the. Flute!" (343.36). In other words, he tells himself ("the"/thee) that this is manifestly a matter of obedience and orders himself to shoot ("Flute!"). In response to this, Taff shouts out "Your partridge's last!" (344.7). Both utterances refer to Milton and to the Fall. Butt, in ordering himself to shoot, recalls the theme of *Paradise Lost*, "Of man's first disobedience and the fruit ["Of manifest 'tis obedience and the. Flute!"] / Of that forbidden tree whose mortal taste / Brought death into the world, and all our woe" (1.1–3). Thus Butt implicitly connects the obedient soldier's killing in a war with humankind's (disobedient) Fall. Taff does likewise in shouting at the general that his paradise is lost through the last shot from a cartridge.

This is a recurrent theme in *Finnegans Wake*. However, before going on to other examples, it is worth lingering for a moment over one unexplained item in the previous assassination—the flute. In part it combines "flew" with "fruit," linking the general to flight and the partridge, as well as the forbidden act that caused our Fall (that is, eating of the fruit). It also alludes to a peculiarly Miltonic belief that flute music is played in Hell (see 1.551; the harp, the dulcimer, and "the solemn Pipe" are, in contrast, the instruments of celestial melody [7.594–96]). Elsewhere, Joyce alludes to this. Thus he alters the common ejaculation, "Hell's bells!" making it into the more Miltonic "hell's flutes" (520.20; the context is yet another retelling of the Fall in the park). Flutes turn up in other, related contexts as well. Thus HCE's business losses (usually fortunate Falls, due to good insurance coverage—see 589–90) include, not surprisingly, a postlapsarian flood (the major biblical account of death), a "sinflute" (590.1; German = flood)—not only a flood, but a flute, both connected with sin. At other points the flute is linked with the sexual Fall. Oscar Wilde is recalled as "Poor Felix Culapert"—both the fortunate fault and the happy, bold spread-butt (French *cul* = buttocks, apert = a pert and apart), an obvious reference to sodomy. He, we are told, still has a "flautish," or flutelike, voice (536), even in the other world. At the singing of the ballad recounting the Fall, flute music is played and the flute itself is implicitly sexualized as the "onecrooned king of inscrewments" (43.32), the king of instruments that one screws together, but also the crown-bearing male instrument that one screws in. Moreover, by association with the phrase, "the uncrowned King of Ireland," a common epithet for Parnell, Joyce implicitly associates adultery with the flute as well. The "fluteous" (297.23) is subsequently connected with the "midden wedge" (297.23), the "triagonal delta" (297.24), and the "vulve" of ALP (297.27), again lending the instrument a coital aspect. Finally, there may be an implicit connection with the sexualized, demonic Pan, who is frequently represented as playing a flute (see, for example, Stephens 50, where flute-playing Pan is clearly a sexualized Miltonic/romantic Satan).

Other developments of the thanatic aspect of the Fall may be found from the very beginning of the book. Finnegan's mortal fall/Fall is the most obvious instance: "The great fall of the offwall entailed at such short notice the pftjschute of Finnegan" (3.18–19). A more specifically Miltonic connection may be found later in the first chapter. Speaking, it seems, of HCE and ALP, the narrator tells us that we will hear "of a pomme [French, apple] full grave" and clearly connects ALP with Eve (and Lilith), referring to her as "this snaky woman" (20.33). Just after this reference, we are told that she has a "trippiery toe," a toe to dance a trippiere, no doubt, but also the toe of Mirth in "L'Allegro," who is adjured: "Come, and trip it as ye go / On the light, fantastic toe" (11.33–34; we have already seen that Joyce alludes to this line elsewhere in *Finnegans Wake*). Why Joyce might refer to this line in the context of a "pomme full grave" is not entirely clear, but may involve a pun on "trip." Thus, unlike Mirth, the "snaky woman"—a "Hohore" with "volantine valentine eyes" (20.36, 34)—will not dance, but (like Finnegan) fall. Shortly after this, the judgment of God upon Eve and Adam, that they shall earn their bread by the sweat of their face, is reworked to emphasize the inevitability of lapsarian death. In what is perhaps his earliest incarnation, HCE as Adam "urned his dread" (24.5). Thus he earned his bread, but he also placed in funerary urns the remains of his dead, those who have met their dreaded end. (Recall the similar judgment on Issy, that she must "eurn bitter bed by the sweet of her face" [291.6].)

Significant references to lapsarian mortality are scattered throughout the book. Another Miltonic example may be found in Joyce's retelling of the story of Tristan and Isolde—a story of both love and death. Here Joyce refashions a line from Thomas Moore, "O Weep for the Hour When to Eveleen's bower," in order to make it refer to the sorrows of the Fall: "O weep for the hower when eve aleaves bower!" (389.20). According to Milton, the Fall—with all its consequences, including sexual shame and the consequent wearing of leaves—was made possible by the fact that Eve left her bower without Adam (see 9.204–410).

But, once again, the worst result of the Fall is not death per se, natural death, but war. It was only in "prefall paradise" that we might find "peace" (30.15). Now, "the world, mind, is, was and will be writing its own wrunes for ever" (19.35–36)—the postfall world will always be writing the runes of its history, and seeking to set right the wrongs that have led to the ruins. After the Fall, war is unending. It is also pointless. In an obscure passage where they are denouncing HCE, the evangelists state this theme, shouting "Woes to the wormquashed, aye and wor to the winner!" (379.10–11). This line neatly combines the themes of the Fall, death, and war. The vanquished have woe, but the winners really have only *more woeful war*—even victory being only a mixed blessing. Furthermore, the vanquished are *wormquashed*. Thus they are "food for worms," (compare Hamlet's dialogue with the king 4.3.19–38, alluded to a few lines earlier at 379.1–2). Or they are merely mortal, having been defeated by the serpent, Satan, "that false Worm," in Milton's phrase (9.1068), "snake wurrums" in Joyce's (19.12; note that these "snake wurrums" are found in "the midst of the cargon of prohibitive pomefructs," thus the Garden of Eden [French *pomme* = apple]—the "prohibitive" perhaps echoing Milton's "tree / Of prohibition" [9.645]).

This endless, devastating warfare is often justified by reference to religion—each side "of course, on the purely doffensive [that is, each side pretending to be on the defensive when in fact on the offensive] since the eternals were owlwise [always wisely] on their side everytime," since— each side insisted—God is on our side (78.29–31; one recalls Milton's use of this tactic in celebrating Cromwell, as well as its importance to the angelic combat of *Paradise Lost*). This too is exemplified in the case of Buckley/Butt and the Russian general. Amidst a medley of Irish rebel songs, we find that Butt and Taff's "fight" has been "upheld to right" (354.8) and that "Old Erssia's magisquammythical mulattomilitiaman . . . too foul for hell, under boiling Mauses' burning brand . . . falls by Goll's gillie" (354.10, 12–13). The passage is complex, and obscure in spots, but at one level refers to Old Russia's great military man, the general, killed by God, through the Gaul Buckley, God's aid or gillie. Moreover, Butt/Buckley is a mauser rifle-carrying Moses and an Archangel carrying a burning brand like the "flaming Brand" wielded by Michael in *Paradise Lost* (12.643).

The following speech of Butt and Taff continues to develop the link between war and the Fall. "When old the wormd was a gadden," they begin—when of old the world was a worm-quashed, snake fallen (Pan-slavonic *gad* = snake) garden—"wanderloot was the way," wandering and looting, or natural lawlessness, ruled. "[O]pter and apter were samuraised twimbs," after and aptly warriors (samurai), paired like Siamese twins, raised their limbs (presumably in battle). "[T]hey had their . . . murdhering idies"—their Ides of March (day of Julius Caesar's murder), their murderous ideas (354.22–25). Evidently returning to the Russian General/HCE, they further elaborate this theme, saying, "he's dancing figgies to the spittle side and shoving outs the soord . . . while myanthys playing lancifer lucifug . . . till butagain budly shoots thon rising germinal" (354.29–35). Until, with lapsus-marking thunder ("thon"), Butt/Buckley shoots the Russian general again (in the cycle of recurrent violence and death that is as much a part of our fallen condition as the cycle of birth and life), we *all* ("myanthys") will be like Satanic rebels fighting with the lance ("lancifer") and eating the sexual fruit of the Fall ("lucifug" = lucifer + fig + fuck). Correspondingly, he'll be fighting with his sword (and having sexual relations) and dancing lapsarian jigs ("figgies"). (There are also hints of rebirth here in "rising" and in "germinal," the first month.)

As this last passage hints, Satan's rebellion is closely related to lapsarian wars. Early and late in the book, Joyce explicitly connects the fallen angels with the beginning of warfare—often in a comic way. We find this, for example, during the story of the prankquean, which explains how "skirtmisshes [or skirmishes] began" (21.19). After she steals the first child, "there was a brannewail that same sabboath night of falling angles" (21.25)—a fire cry that sabbath night/an army (Hebrew *sabboath*) of falling angels. (These are also falling Angles, or English, due to the nature of the enemy in Irish history.) Similarly, the evangelists ask Shem how a fight broke out at a wedding: "was that how in the annusual curse of things . . . their celicolar subtler angelic warfare . . . started?" (516.32–33, 35–36)—was that how, in the usual, annual course of cursed (fallen) things their battle, like the battle of the angels, started? Subsequently, they explain that the parties were "struggling diabolically . . . their virtues *pro* and his principality *con* [virtues and principalities being sorts of angels—also, both sides are claiming that they alone are virtuous and principled] . . . kicking up the devil's own dust" (518.4–6).

Perhaps the most significant and poetically powerful reference to war takes place early in the book, beginning with Mutt's introduction to "ye plaine of my Elters, hunfree and ours" (17), the plain of his ancestors, and the lament (French *plaindre*) of these ancestors. "Countlessness of livestories," he tells us, "have netherfallen by this plage, flick as flowflakes, litters from aloft, like a waast wizzard all of whirlworlds. Now are all tombed to the mound, isges to isges, erde from erde. Pride, O pride, thy prize!" (17.26–30). Countless lives with all their stories have fallen down by this beach, have been felled by this plague (of death), thick as snowflakes, flowing, whole families falling, the remains of their lives like letters from the past, all whirling, a vast blizzard, a waste of what was magic, whole worlds of the dead. Now all are fallen (French *tomber* = fall) and entombed in the mound, ashes to ashes, earth to earth. This, O pride, is thy prize! Pride, the sin of Satan, the cause of war—angelic, and human. He continues: "Hereinunder lyethey. . . . And thanacestross mound have swollup them all. This ourth of years is not save brickdust and being humus the same roturns. He who runes may rede it on all fours" (17.32, 18.3–6). Here, underneath, they are buried in lye. And the ancestral mound, the mound of death (Greek *thanatos*) has swallowed them all and become swollen with them. This earth, which is us, is only dust and being human/fertile it returns always and the same happens again and again. He who can interpret runes and ruins can read it—this human fate—even in the crawling child.

Much of this passage, and many of the broader thematic concerns it expresses, are drawn in part from Byron's (highly Miltonic) *Cain*. Byron's Lucifer places particular stress on war as an outcome of the Fall: "Cain. But why *war*? / Lucifer. You have forgotten the denunciation / Which drove your race from Eden: war with all things" (2.2.147–49). Moreover, Byron in this play seeks, like Joyce, to imagine and articulate the inexorable accumulation of death and suffering, generation after generation. Specifically, Lucifer speaks of the "oceans" filled with tears from "[t]he million millions, / The myriad myriads, the all-peopled earth, / The unpeopled earth" (1.1.520–23). And Cain mourns that bearing children "is merely propagating death / And multiplying murder" (2.1.70–71).

There are more direct Miltonic connections as well. At the end of the dialogue of Mutt and Jute, Joyce explicitly links death and war with Milton's vanquished archangels. Almost immediately after the litany of death, Mutt asks: "Ore you astoneaged, jute you?" and Jute answers, "Oye am thonthorstrock, thing mud" (18.15–16). They are thunderstruck and astonished like Satan and Beelzebub waking from their defeat in heaven: "Here Satan with his angels lying on the burning Lake, thunder-struck and astonisht" (the argument to *PL* book 1). From here, we enter the museum and we read, "the same told of all. Many. Miscegenations and miscegenations. . . . They lived und laughed ant loved end left. Forsin" (*FW* 18.18–20). The same returns, the story repeats. Many people. Generations and generations. They lived and laughed and loved, and, in the end left. Because of sin. Because of the Fall.

The Fortunate Fall and the Design of Nature: O Ferax Cupla!

For Milton and for Joyce, the Fall had many woeful consequences. It brought death into the world and subjected us to war, made us earn our bread in the sweat of our face and bring forth in pain, deprived us of sexual purity, and inflicted us instead with shame and perversion. But again, despite suffering, death, the distortions of lust, the tortures of childbirth, the ravages of war, the Fall for Joyce, as for Milton, was fortunate. To a great extent, both Milton and Joyce sought in their major works to answer the question asked by a lisping voice through the medium of Shaun: "Have you ever weflected . . . that the evil what though it was willed might nevewtheless lead somehow on to good towawd the genewality?" (523.2–4; see also 23.16–17). Both answer Yes, though Joyce does so more hesitantly, more ambiguously. The purpose of Milton's epic was in part to support this answer by "assert[ing] Eternal Providence" (1.25). In Joyce's view, in contrast, it is the structure of natural life—generation, love, birth—which, perhaps, makes the Fall happy. It is not providence, but something more like design without a designer, the design of nature.

The most obvious sign that this is Joyce's view may be found in the repeated transformations of St. Augustine's exclamation "O felix culpa!" Some make humorous reference to the Fall in its wakean form. For example, "O ferax cupla!" (606.23), "O Fruitful pair," clearly refers to the fig- and apple-related temptresses and implies regenerative human fertility, linking that fertility with the fruit of the Fall. Similarly, "O foenix culprit" refers to the rising phoenix and thus to rebirth, specifically the rebirth of humankind, as the rebirth of Adam/HCE ("Here comes everybody" [32.18–19]), the culprit from the Phoenix Park. As the following sentence comments "Ex nickylow malo comes mickelmassed bonum" (23.16–17; out of low Satan's evil/apple comes the Michaelmade good).

On the other hand, sometimes the echoes of Augustine's phrase are less clearly comic, more haunted by Joycean and un-Miltonic doubt. One particularly interesting example of this sort is "happy finish," the end of a play that has been "running strong since creation" (32.32–33). The play is a version of the ever-recurring Fall and it is a typically Joycean version of the Fall as a natural condition—for it has been running strong since creation itself, not since the primal disobedience. But this play has the infelicitous-sounding title *A Royal Divorce*, a title that at least raises a doubt as to whether the finish is genuinely happy. The phrase itself calls to mind the mutual alienation of Adam and Eve following the Fall, a motif we have seen in "The Dead," *Exiles*, and, especially, *Ulysses*—though this does not seem to fit the thematics of *Finnegans Wake* itself. In any case, whatever its specific reference, it clearly implies a lapsarian disunion—a division between spouses, first of all, but also, by extension, between siblings, nations, and so on—a lapsarian rift to which one could, at best, apply Stephen's dictum: "There can be no reconciliation . . . if there has not been a sundering" (9.397–98).

This passage might also contain a Miltonic reference—although one that does not resolve but repeats the ambiguity we have been considering. Specifically, late in *Paradise Lost*, Satan returns to Hell triumphant after his seduction of Eve. He is "plac't in *regal lustre*" in Pandemonium and awaits "*universal* shout and high *applause*" (10.447, 10.505; emphasis added). In *Finnegans Wake*, the audience, watching "from good start to happy finish" has "gathered together in that *king*'s treat house of *satin* [Satan enthroned] a*lustre*like [in regal lustre] . . . *unanimously* to cl*applaud* [universal shout and high applause]" (32.24–28; emphasis added). This may seem indeed a happy finish. But it is important to recall that Satan never hears the intended and expected applause. Instead, he hears the hiss of many snakes and tastes in his mouth the ashes of the mortal fruit. It is difficult to say whether Joyce intends to contrast this scene with his own happy finish or to show that there is not a happy finish after all. Again, the entire passage is ambiguous. Indeed, the ambiguity might itself be the main point. As we saw in *Exiles*, uncertainty is part of our natural, lapsarian condition. It is, it seems, one necessary result of trading providence for natural design.

Indeed, this exchange, this materialist revision of providence, is itself thematically important in *Finnegans Wake*. Joyce refers frequently to providence and even connects it Miltonically with foreknowledge and determinism. However, he repeatedly addresses or alludes to providence in contexts that render it secular—or Satanic—rather than divine. Often these references concern the protection of HCE/Adam. Thus when HCE flees the threat of "diversified outrages" (61.31) after his fall, it is due to "devine previdence" (62.7–8)—not so much providence as foresight (pre-vidence), a devious divination, no more divine than demonic ("devine"). We come upon the same, secular "Devine's Previdence" (325.1–2) after a "[g]iant crash in Aden" (324.36) when Kersse the Tailor and the Norwegian captain bury the hatchet and the nuptials of the captain and the tailor's daughter (or HCE and ALP—see Rose and O'Hanlon 196 n. 5) are announced.

At least two references to providence allude directly to *Paradise Lost*. One concerns the protection of HCE by the "gracious providence" (69.28) of several citizens who locked him in his own home. The gate, we are told, was ancient, from the time of the "garthen of Odin" and the "lost paladays" (69.10)—Garden of Eden and Paradise Lost + paladays or days long ago (Greek *palai* = long ago). Despite the Miltonic connection, however, the providence is strictly human—and not unambiguous. (Note also how this passage repeats the Joycean/Kabbalistic theme of the Fall leading to enclosure rather than to expulsion from Eden.)

A more complex case is to be found in the lessons chapter. Beside the text where the Earwicker family arrives at the bar, we find a Shaunian marginal note: "GNOSIS OF PRECREATE DETERMINATION. AGNOSIS OF POST-CREATE DETERMINISM" (262.20–27). The point is somewhat unclear, but at the very least, Joyce is touching on the problem of predestination. Most literally it seems to refer to a normal process by which a creator sets out with knowledge (gnosis) and action-guiding (free?) determination to create an object. But this object, once created, it has a sort of deterministic autonomy, separate from the knowledge of the creator. In the case of Adam and Eve, this would accord with Milton's view insofar as it means that Adam and Eve were autonomous when they fell, but it is incoherent with Milton's view insofar as it indicates that their autonomy was not free, but determined. Another reading is also possible, according to which it is only believers who see divine determination (and thus providence and free will?) while unbelievers (agnostics) see mere determinism.

The passage continues with a discussion of how HCE has appeared in many guises in many countries. Things continually recur "since primal made alter in the garden of Idem" (263.20–21)—since our earliest (primal) ancestors were altered in the Garden of Eden, and since that first sexual act produced a second or different generation in the garden of Same, which is to say, the garden where all were/are condemned continually to repeat that first generational act (the Fall) in reproducing themselves. To clarify, Joyce then points out that this repetition has occurred "under one . . . original sun" (263.27)—the original sin, which we continually repeat, represented as a sun around which we continually orbit.

Here the text includes a further felix culpa: "O felicitous culpability," with two comments. The Shemian marginal comment, beside "O felicitous culpability" is "Hearasay in paradox lust." The textual comment is "sweet bad cess to you for an archetypt" (263.29–30). The textual comment clearly shows more than skepticism about the providential doctrine; it shows contempt. The marginal note is kinder, finding Milton's optimism a matter of hearsay combined with heresy. The title Shem gives to *Paradise Lost* is particularly revealing, both in general and in this particular context. *Paradise Lost* is a poem about a paradox, the paradox of divine foreknowledge and human will, a paradox supposedly resolved in providence. It is also a poem about lust—the sexual lust caused by the Fall, but also the lust for godlike attributes that leads to Eve's downfall, and the prelapsarian desire of Adam that led to his Fall as well.

Furthermore, read in conjunction with the preceding marginal comment of Shaun, we could see this title as proposing yet a further paradox, one that strikes at the heart of Milton's justification of God's ways, and thus at his notion of providence. The problem is something like this: If Eve and Adam fell, they fell because—in terms of Renaissance and classical moral psychology—their lust was stronger than their reason. Clearly God created them to have a particular strength of reason and a particular strength of desire ("precreate determination," in Shaun's terms). Thus He must have designed them in such a way that, faced with Satanic temptation, their desire would necessarily overwhelm their reason and they would fall. Little wonder the narrator's response to the notion of divine providence is "sweet bad cess to you"—bad luck, a secular opposite of providence.

But again, Joyce has an alternative to the heretical hearsay and "bad cess" of Miltonic providence—natural design, a notion articulated later in the same chapter. The children are in their home, which is attached to their parents' pub, "The Goat and Compasses" (275.16). They begin to work on mathematics, but there are difficulties; everything is "Equal to aosch" or a chaotic version of *chaos*. They set out to restore some order: "Problem ye ferst, construct ann aquilittoral dryankle" (286.19–20). Their first problem is to construct an equilateral triangle (or to keep a dry ankle on Ann's watery shore). The textbook instructs Shem and Shaun to "unbox [their] compasses" (287.11). They construct two intersecting circles and, in the overlapping space, an equilateral triangle. These, Shem explains, are the buttocks and genitalia of their mother ALP (297–98).

Before going on to discuss how this contributes to the notion of design, it is important to point out that this entire exercise is a parody of Milton's account of God's creation of the universe. According to Milton, God went into Chaos (recall "Equal to aosch") and took "the golden compasses" (7.225; compare not only the compasses, but the pub name, "The Goat and Compasses" [275.16], a connection pointed out by Schork) "to circumscribe this universe, and all created things" (*PL* 7.226–27). God uses Golden Compasses to make the world out of Chaos—or "the womb / Of . . . Chaos" as it is called elsewhere (10.476–77)—to allow for his providence. Blake revised Milton's creation, rendering it sinister and unprovidential, when in "The Book of Urizen," he had his version of Milton's deity mark out "a garden of fruits" with "golden compasses" on "the Abyss" (lines 409–10), shortly before he spins from his sorrow "[t]he Net of Religion" (line 469). Joyce revises both; however, his focus is more on Milton than on Blake, for Satanic (and thus goat-footed?) Shem, in the Goat and Compasses, uses compasses to transform the womb of chaos into the maternal womb.

This maternal womb is, again, the true design of nature—of all that is born, *natus*—and thus it is true human providence. More exactly, Shem describes looking at the geometric construction as a peek under his mother's skirts. "Hissss!" he wheezes, aptly snakelike. "Outer serpumstances beiug ekewilled, we carefully, if she pleats, lift by her seam hem and jabote at the spidsiest of her trickkikant (like thousands done before since fillies calpered. Ocone! Ocone!)" (297.4, 7–11). Other circumstances being equal—which is to say the relation to the serpent ("serpumstances") being willed—we carefully, if it pleases her, with her pleats, lift her seam, hem, and frills at the side or point where we can best spy her tricky triangular (Danish *trekant* = triangular) cunt (kant). Thousands have done this before, ever since the happy Fall when fillies or young girls capered about—Alas! Alas!

An ocean of them. In other words, just as so many died on the plain discussed by Mutt and Jute, so too so many have been born from the womb of nature since the Fall. (Shem continues, making the obvious connection between the river's delta and the vulva.)

This is a fairly clear statement about the natural succession of generations, and the relation between the Fall and birth. Shaun, to clarify, comments in the margins: "Destiny, Influence of Design upon" and, alluding to Shelley, "Prometheus or the Promise of Provision" (297.4–6, 14–16). The design of nature—the simple pattern of generation succeeding generation—endlessly flows in (in-fluence), like a river (like Eve, like ALP), upon our destiny. Provision/providence, however, is only promised; like the freeing of Shelley's Prometheus, it defines the telos or culmination of time, the beginning of a utopian age, a new Paradise where all is love. In contrast with Shelley's drama, Joyce's novel includes no such great culminating event. It is rather a series of cycles, written in the circular form of a cycle—a design of destiny rather than a promise of provision.

This reference to design emphasizes its regenerative aspect. Unsurprisingly, Joyce also uses the term in connection with mortality. A good example of this sort may be found at the very end of the book. When speaking to Finnegan in the course of her final monologue, Anna says "And people thinks you missed the scaffold. Of fell design" (621.29). Finnegan did not die precisely by accident. His death was, rather, part of the design of fallen nature, the *Apfel* (German, apple) design of death and birth.

These themes of lapsarian design are brought together nicely in the discussion of the great tree in the park, a tree with "Orania epples"—among other things, apples of Urania, the muse of *Paradise Lost* (see 7.1, 7.31). This is the tree of generation: "all over again in their new world through the germination of its gemination from Ond's outset till Odd's end. And encircle him circuly" (505.11–13). From seed to twinning (gemini/gemination) or repetition, all over again, each new world from the beginning of evil (Danish *onde*) to the odd end of death (perhaps God's end also), is a circle forever (Latin *in saeculum saeculi* = forever). Moreover, this generative tree is Eve all-mother herself, "after . . . her downslyder in that snakedst-tu-naughsy whimmering woman't seeleib such a fashionaping sathinous dress out of that exquisitive creation and her leaves . . . sin-sinsinning since the night of time" (505.6–10). The "downslyder" serpent coiled about her and tempted her woman's soul and body and womb ("woman't seeleib," German *Seele* = soul, and *Leib* = body, womb). As a result, she now wears a fascinating, fashionable dress that is satin/Sathanic ("sathinous"—in a number of writers, including Dryden, our Adversary is named Sathan, not Satan), but that is also made of leaves (connected both with the fig leaves of sexual shame and with the greenery of regenerative springtime). The leaves whisper in the wind: "sinsinsinning," as they have done since time began in the darkness of the Fall ("since the night of time").

As this passage indicates, the tree of generation and life is also the tree of sexual Fall. It is, in fact, a "shrub of libertine" (505.21)—both liberty and free sexuality. And it is an "Upfellbowm"—an apple tree (German *Apfelbaum*), but also a tree that helps us up, only to let us fall down (with a thunderlike boom). Thus "[i]t reminds of the weeping of daughters" (505.29–30)—whose curse it is to bring forth in agony and, as stressed by Byron's Cain, to perpetuate not only the cycle of life but that of death. "[W]hat stiles its neming?" what is it called, the four inquire: "Tod, tod, too hard parted!" (505.22–23)—it is death (German *Tod*). In nature, unlike in Paradise, the Tree of Life is also the Tree of Death. "Oh Finlay's coldpalled!" (506.9). Felix culpa: Finn lay cold in the pall. "Is it so exalted?" they ask. And Shaun replies that he has never seen its equal amongst "trees like angels weeping" (505). Here Joyce combines a reference to the fallen Satan, struggling to speak to the gathered demons after their defeat, with another Miltonic reference. In Paradise, the river watered "rich trees," which "wept odorous gums and balm" (4.248). On the one hand, this tree is compared with the rebel angels, wracked by the physical torments of Hell and by the inner torment of shame and remorse. On the other hand, it is compared with the Edenic medicinal trees that soothe and heal. Again, of both Death and Life, both degraded lust and regenerative love, in short the Fall—the partially destructive, partially redemptive design of nature.

Though the tone of the passage is comic, it does not represent the optimism of, for example, serious-toned Milton. Indeed it is a passage in which, as in much of the book, the writer seems to be laughing through his tears. In *Finnegans Wake,* Joyce gives us some idea of his views on life and art. At the end of the chapter at the "Feenichts Playhouse"—the no fee, phoenix theater—we find that we are "the unhappitents of the earth" (258.22): unhappy, hapless, inhabitants of the earth. Joyce ends the chapter with a sort of prayer related to our condition and to his aims in writing: "Loud, heap miseries upon us yet entwine our arts with laughters low! Ha he hi ho hu. Mummum." Loud lord have mercy, even if you heap miseries upon us, allow us art to keep laughing, not so loudly, but in our hearts. Ha ha! Ho ho! Then, Joyce turns: Mummum. Quiet! but also Courage! (German *Mumm*), but also—Mother.

Mother and Child

If the maternal womb is the source of joyful regeneration for Joyce, it is only apt that he should end his work with the mother, the mother who perhaps has dreamed the dream of *Finnegans Wake*. As in *Ulysses*, Joyce follows the "Life of Adam and Eve" in ending with Eve's monologue on the Fall and its consequences—though here the parallel is closer, for in the pseudepigraphic work Eve is on her deathbed, and the speech concludes with her demise (Charles 152–53). Here Anna (or Eve or May Murray Joyce) is dying. She recalls in the final moments the "paladays last," the lost paradise of days long gone (Greek *palai* = long ago), the last, lost days mentioned in her letter (615.25). She speaks in a dream to her husband. It is morning. There is a soft mist. As in the cliché, her life flashes before her eyes. It is "the day one, come back" (619.34–35), the first day—her birth, her marriage, also the first day of the world. She calls to her husband to "rise up . . . you have slept so long." One imagines her husband long dead, his death half-forgotten in sleep, as at the beginning of *Nectar in a Sieve*, Kamala Markandaya writes: "Sometimes at night I think that my husband is with me again, coming gently through the mists, and we are tranquil together. Then morning comes, the wavering grey turns to gold, there is a stirring within as the sleepers awake, and he softly departs" (9). "I am leafy speafing"—Liffy, Livia, Eve, fallen Eve with her fig leaf—for even at the end, her "leaves have all drifted from [her]. But one clings still" (628.6–7). A final dream of Eve, perhaps parallel to the dream of Eve in book 12 of *Paradise Lost*, the dream in which divine providence is revealed.

But in Anna's dream, there is, again, no providence. She does suggest, "Let's our joornee saintomichael make it. Since the lausafire has lost and the book of the depth is. Closed" (621.2–3). But the book of life and death—the prophetic book carried by Adam out of the Garden (see Rappoport 148, 171)—is not closed. And this hope of providence is unstable. Later she suggests, "We might call on the Old Lord"—he'll take us in, since you invited him last Easter (623.4). But in each case, the optimism barely conceals despair. There is no providence, only death "Of fell design." At the thought of her husband's death, she closes her eyes "So not to see. Or see only a youth in his florizel, a boy in innocence, peeling a twig, a child beside a weenywhite steed. The child we all love to place our hope in for ever" (621.29–32). Our hope, if there is any, is in generation, in childhood. But childhood too is always already lost—what could be clearer from *Dubliners* to *Ulysses*? Recall Dilly Dedalus drowning in poverty and hopelessness, her brother paralyzed by fear of being dragged to a watery grave himself.

If there is any compensation in life, then it is the beauty and strength of ordinary people, fallible humanity. "All men has done something," Anna laments, lovingly, forgivingly to her dead husband, to the husband whose death she is trying to deny in a dream leading to her own death, "Be the time they've come to the weight of old fletch." But, not wishing to hurt, she stops, "We'll lave it [leave it/wash it clean]. So" (621.29–33). She recalls walks and love and trips planned but never taken. She talks of the boys, how much they are like their father. How they fight! Their happy young girl—"'Twould be sore should ledden sorrow. I'll wait. And I'll wait" (620.30–31). Was she later to become one of the two girls whose life was ruined, or Joyce's own daughter, racked by mental illness—a new life for which he could hardly think life meaningful? She talks of the playful, silly trivialities that mark intimacy, ease, affection. Then, "It seems so long since, ages since. As if you had been long far away" (622.13–14). She dreams and remembers. Why is it so distant? How did everything change? Ordinary feelings. But tragic precisely because they are ordinary. In her dream, she takes him—"You know where I am bringing you? You remember?" (622.16–17). A picnic. They are very young. She picks berries. He bombards her with hazelnuts from his hammock. "I could lead you there and I still by you in bed" (622.19–20).

But the ordinary sufferings of ordinary life are never far from her mind. "Beauties don't answer and the rich never pays" (622.32–33). And yet, like Joyce, she doesn't care about them, but about the people who do answer and who do pay. Was he brought up in an orphanage? because his parents were drunkards (624.31–35)? She looks about at the little lentil peas and the dear small seeds: "Pretty mites, my sweetthings, was they poorloves abandoned by wholeawidey world?" she asks motherlike. But then she remembers again death and loss and time. "Why I'm all these years within years in soffran, allbeleaved" (625.24–30)—Beloved, leaf-clothed Adam, for years, for days and weeks that feel like years, I have suffered. "To hide away the tear, the parted"—only trying to hide it, to forget the dear ones for whom I should have wept or might have wept, those who have departed. "It's thinking of all"—her voice falters. "The brave that gave their. The fair that wore. All them that's gunne" (625.30–32)—all who have died in war after war after war. Fears overcome her, both for all the ordinary people who have died and for her husband, whose death she is suppressing, and for her own death. "I'll begin again in a jiffey"—begin to speak, begin to live in the cycle of regeneration. "How glad you'll be I waked you!" she says, unaware of what she means. But not entirely unaware.

She remembers providence. "I only hope whole the heavens sees us. For I feel I could near to faint away. Into the deeps" (625.36–626.1)—here we begin to sense Anna's impending death, and her fear. Dying, she hopes for heaven. She calls on her husband to support her because he's "adamant ever" (626.3)—his identity as Adam entering with the hint of her death. And now her husband becomes her father. She remembers confusedly childhood scenes, her father a big man, admired by everyone. She worries, like a child, pathetically, at her father's premature death—who'll find her coloring book? And what about the "sealskers" in "Tobecontinued's" bedtime story? "There'll be others but non so for me" (626.18–20). She recalls games when "[m]y lips went livid for from the joy of fear," then adds, [l]ike almost now" (626.29–30)—almost now, perhaps because now there is fear only, and no joy?

Her thoughts switch to courting and her husband. "How you said how you'd give me the keys of me heart. And we'd be married till delth to uspart. And though dev do espart" (626.30–31). Like the word "uspart," they were joined until death tore them apart—"the tear [now as in "a tear in the fabric"], the parted." And even then, though death parts them, tears them apart, they have hope (French *espoir*) in God (Sanskrit *dev*), that they will be joined again. But now it is in death: "O mine! Only, no, now it's me who's got to give. . . . And can it be it's nnow fforvell?" (626.32–33)—and can it be it's now farewell (Danish *farvel* = goodbye) forever? Here, generation. She dies. Her husband dies. Her daughter and son take their places. "Yes, you're changing, sonhusband, and your turning, I can feel you, for a daughterwife. . . . Now a younger's there. . . . For she'll be sweet for you as I was sweet when I came down out of me mother" (627.1–2, 6–9). Birth, the start of a new cycle. "First we feel. Then we fall. . . . Anyway, let her rain [reign/fall like rain] for my time is come" (627.12–13).

Thousands and thousands, flick as flowflakes. Death thickens about her; she recalls a "hundred cares, a tithe of troubles" as she rushes to the sea of souls. She blames those about her for her absolute aloneness, her impenetrable isolation in death: "is there one who understands me?" (627.14–15). She hates even her husband now, even her father—for having died, for letting her die: "I thought you the great in all things, in guilt and in glory. You're but a puny" (627.23–24). "I am passing out. O bitter ending!"—bitter like the fruit of the Fall, like "the frucht of this hour" (148.29), like the "knowledge's fructos" (155.21–22).

But here her thoughts return to her children. As if she were going on a journey, just leaving, hoping not to disturb them, like a walk with their father: "I'll slip away before they're up. They'll never see. Nor know. Nor miss me" (627.35–36). Now she is old, old and sad and weary. She sees death, the ocean of death, of new life perhaps, the endlessness of death—all the miles and miles of the moaning dead. She begs for more time, "Two more. Onetwo moremens more" (628.5–6). Hail and farewell! "My leaves have drifted from me. All. But one clings still. I'll bear it on me. To remind me of" (628.6–7)—of the Fall, and all that follows. A child in death she calls out, "Carry me along, taddy, like you done through the toy fair!" then thinks, "If I seen him bearing down on me now under whitespread wings like he'd come from Arkangels, I sink I'd die down over his feet, humbly dumbly, only to washup" (628.8–11). If I see my father, God, Michael the Archangel, Death bearing down on me under white, widespread wings, flying from heaven, I think I would sink to his feet, die at his feet, humbly, silently (but also like Humpty Dumpty, fallenly—entwine our arts with laughters low) only to worship. Now she sees . . . Eden: "There's where. First" (628.12). A long way since. "Coming, far! End here. Us then" (628.13–14). To those around her deathbed—one kisses her softly, perhaps—perhaps a child, fruit of generation, happiness of the Fall: "Bussoftlhee, mememormee. Till thousendsthee" (628.14–15)—kiss (slang, buss) me softly, remember me. Till you too, like thousands before, send yourself. "Lps"—lips touch her face. Now "the keys to. Given!" (628.15). For a moment the presence of children, their love—a kiss as she is dying, give her the keys to her heart, promised so many years earlier, make the Fall almost fortunate. But, however irrelevant to the book, we cannot help think that this kiss is related to a kiss Joyce could not give his mother as she lay in a coma dying, and we cannot forget that, later, when Joyce himself awoke on his deathbed, only briefly, and called out for his wife and son, whom he had begged to wait at his bedside—no one was there; he drifted back into a coma and died.

The book ends as Anna/May/any of us fades into death—"A way a lone a last a loved a long the" (628.15–16). Joyce insisted that *the* is almost "not even a word . . . a breath, a nothing" (quoted in Rose and O'Hanlon 320). But he did not mean it. *A* is almost not a word—and in many languages there is no indefinite article. *The* is perfectly suited to Joyce's purposes because it is in fact a very strong word. As a definite article, it is closely linked with a noun. Ending with "the" gives a strong sense of the irresolution of the book, forcefully leading us back to the beginning. At the same time it is ambiguous, meaning *thee* as well—the child at the bedside kissing her softly, remembering her, or—on the other side of death, a spirit folded in the memory of nature—her husband, her father.

But what does this ending mean? Is Anna "alone" or "along thee"?—is she a loved (one) or unloved? The sentence in some ways echoes the end of *Paradise Lost*, lines to which Joyce referred more directly in *Ulysses* and elsewhere. The keys to Paradise not given, but withheld, Adam and Eve stand outside the gate, now to begin their fallen life:

Some natural tears they dropp'd, but wip'd them soon;
The World was all before them, where to choose
Thir place of rest, and Providence thir guide:
They hand in hand with wand'ring steps and slow,
Through *Eden* took thir solitary way. (12.645–49)

Away alone/through Eden took their solitary way. A last/alas/Some natural tears they dropped. A loved along the/Hand in hand. The phrase is positive. Anna, it seems, finds peace in death. Or, rather, in a final thought of death, a final expectation, unconfirmed if also undenied. Joyce's lines again contain no providence. At least for a reader who does not believe, this happy finish belies a wrenching sadness, a deep unhealable sense of mourning.

And what did Joyce himself feel in writing these lines? It is unclear. It seems he has not taken a stand. He has not told us. Perhaps this was the only honest way for him to write—for he had not died. But he had seen others die. And he had little reason to believe that his children's lives, especially the life of his daughter, would in any way compensate for the suffering in his own life, or in the lives of his parents, or his sisters, or the thousands and thousands of others, swirling worlds of the dead, thick as snowflakes, fields and fields of them. And yet, at the end of the book, he seems to have had the Miltonic hope that allowed Adam and Eve to wander through Eden on their solitary way—however unjustified, however absurd this hope may have been.

Appendix

Joyce's Milton: The Contents and Annotations of Volumes from Joyce's Trieste Library Now Contained in the Harry Ransom Humanities Research Center of the University of Texas at Austin

There are at least six volumes in this collection that contain works or parts of works by John Milton. The fullest volume is *The Poetical Works* of John Milton, which includes a life of the poet. It was published by Gall and Inglis of Edinburgh and is undated, but Gillespie conjectures a printing date between 1875 and 1880 for an edition first published between 1872 and 1874 (see Gillespie 166–67). Second to this is the A. W. Verity edition of *Ode on the Morning of Christ's Nativity, L'Allegro, Il Penseroso, and Lycidas,* published by the Cambridge University Press in 1911. In addition, there are four collections that contain work of Milton: (1) *An Anthology of English Prose (1332 to 1740),* edited by Annie Barnett and Lucy Dale, with a preface by Andrew Lang (London: Longmans, Green, 1912); (2) *Selections from the Best English Authors (Beowulf to the Present Time),* ed. A. F. Murison (London: W. and R. Chambers, 1907); (3) *English Prose from Mandeville to Ruskin (The World's Classics, 45),* chosen and arranged by W. Peacock (London: Henry Frowde, Oxford University Press, 1912); (4) *English Prose: Narrative, Descriptive, and Dramatic (The World's Classics, 204),* compiled by H. A. Treble (London: Humphrey Milford, Oxford University Press, 1917).

The Barnett and Dale anthology runs from Maundeville to Pope and is virtually lacking in annotation—except for an obscure inscription at the outset of the volume. From Milton, the editors include four selections. The first, from the letter on education, is an invigorating disquision on the benefits of sport. The selection begins: "This institution of breeding which I here delineate shall be equally good both for peace and war." (Unless otherwise noted, quotations from Milton are taken from Merritt Hughes's edition. Joyce's editions may differ in matters of spelling, punctuation, or other incidentals.) The passage urges practical study for young boys in "the exact use of their weapon," most particularly when they are engaged in "their military motions." Milton also covers the important topic of "the interim of unsweating." The selection ends with a complaint about the "slight and prodigal" Parisians who transform our youth "into mimics, apes, and kickshaws"—one recalls Buck's attitude toward Stephen with his damn Paris fads (*U* 1.343)—and an expression of fervent hope that "other nations will be glad to visit us for their breeding, or else to imitate us in their own country."

The other selections included by the editors are all drawn from *Areopagitica*. The first is given the title "Of Temperance" and was no doubt for that reason dearer to Stanislaus than to James. It begins, "How great a virtue is temperance, how much of movement through the whole life of man!" An inauspicious opening, no doubt, but the essay covers such important concerns as how God overfed the Hebrews, giving them "more than might have well sufficed the heartiest feeder thrice as many meals" and relates this to the disquieting fact that "much reading is a weariness to the flesh"—whether one's flesh is or is not the result of excessive divine nurturance. More seriously, Milton concludes with a fine argument against religious justifications for book burning, and the passage ends with an edifying reference to Spenser "describing true temperance under the person of Guyon, bring[ing] him in with his palmer through the cave of Mammon and the bower of earthly bliss, that he might see and know, and yet abstain."

The second selection from *Areopagitica* included in Barnett and Dale is entitled "Of Truth." It begins, "And though all the winds of doctrine were let loose to play upon the earth, so Truth be in the field, we do injuriously by licensing and prohibiting to misdoubt her strength." It continues through a remarkably optimistic discussion of the inevitable victory of truth over falsity. In conclusion, Milton concedes, reasonably, that "all cannot be of one mind," but he admirably maintains, nonetheless, that it is "doubtless . . . more wholesome, more prudent, and more Christian, that many be tolerated, rather than all compelled."

The final selection is entitled "Occasional Religion." This is a condemnation of those who seek to fulfill their religious obligations by merely external means, never cultivating a true, inner spirituality. It begins, "Truth is compared in scripture to a streaming fountain" and ends with "his religion walks abroad at eight, and leaves his kind entertainer in the shop trading all day without his religion."

Turning to Treble, this too is virtually unmarked by Joyce. It contains one selection of Milton, from "The Reason of Church Government Urged against Prelaty." Now entitled "He Announces His Intention of Writing an Epic," this selection begins, "For although a poet, soaring in the high region of his fancies," ends, "with the taste of virtuous documents harsh and sour," and includes the phrase to which Gabriel Conroy alludes in "The Dead": "I might perhaps leave something so written to aftertimes, as they should not willingly let it die." The selection treats Milton's early realization that he was a talented poet. Milton discusses the aid lent him by his father and his successes in Italy—neither of which was the good fortune of Joyce. He goes on to explain his decision to write in English, and concludes with a discussion of the nationalist and moral purposes of his work, criticizing those "libidinous" writers who (perhaps like Joyce) fail to realize the importance of the latter.

Murison also has no relevant markings. It contains selections of both prose and poetry, extensive annotations, a biographical notice, and a reproduction of Pieter Van der Plaas's rather proboscidian portrait of England's national epicist. The biographical note emphasizes Milton's libertarianism and ends by quoting Landor on Milton's superiority to all men at all times in all ways. The poems included are: "An Epitaph on the Admirable Dramatic Poet, W. Shakespeare"; "Sonnet to the Lord General Cromwell, May 1652," no doubt one of Joyce's personal favorites; lines 192–238, 283–315, and 670–730 of *Paradise Lost* 1; lines 634–78 of *Paradise Lost* 6; lines 409–38 of *Paradise Regained* 4. There is little to remark upon in any of this. Ironically, the notes on Milton's Cromwell poem state, unselfconsciously, that "[f]reedom in every form, domestic and civil as well as religious, was what Milton ever struggled most earnestly for" (183 n. 13). Several lines alluded to by Joyce in *A Portrait*, *Ulysses*, and *Finnegans Wake* ("hurled headlong," "ocean stream," and so on) are highlighted in the headnote and endnotes to the *Paradise Lost* sections, but this is probably not significant, for the notes also stress lines unimportant to Joyce. It is interesting, however, that in a note to line 434 of *Paradise Regained* 4, Murison discusses, disapprovingly, Milton's penchant for wordplay.

From Milton's prose, Murison includes the section of *Areopagitica* from "I proceed from the no good it can do" to "without the castle of St. Angelo of an imprimatur." The passage concerns the licensing of books. Milton argues that the practice is demeaning to the public as well as the author and, for quite practical reasons, damaging to the text.

The Peacock volume is significantly annotated, but the brief selection from Milton is unmarked. Entitled "On the Licensing of Books," it is drawn from *Areopagitica* and begins "Good and evil we know in the field of this world grow up together." The first section ends with "And this is the benefit which may be had of books promiscuously read." There is a lengthy ellipsis here and the second section begins, "To sequester out of the world" and ends with "what gramercy to be sober, just, or continent?" In this selection, Milton argues that it is only by being acquainted with evil—as for example in books—that one's goodness may be tested, and that goodness untested does not deserve the name of goodness.

The most obvious relevance of these collections is to the parodies of "Oxen of the Sun." However, they are of only minimal value in this regard.

Turning to the A. W. Verity edition of the Nativity ode, "L'Allegro," "Il Penseroso," and "Lycidas," we find several scratchings, primarily in "L'Allegro." Ignoring what appear to be accidental marks, and a peculiar "47" in one margin, we find the following lines of "L'Allegro" marked by horizontal dashes in the left margin: "To Ivy-crowned *Bacchus* bore" (line 16); "And Laughter holding both his sides. / Come, and trip it as ye go / On the light fantastic toe" (32–34); "And if I give thee honor due" (37); "To live with her, and live with thee, / In unreproved pleasures free" (39–40); "Stoutly struts his Dames before" (52); "While the Plowman near at hand, / Whistles o'er the Furrow'd Land" (63–64); "And every Shepherd tells his tale / Under the Hawthorn in the dale" (67–68); "Where perhaps some beauty lies, the Cynosure of neighboring eyes" (79–80); "To many a youth, and many a maid, / Dancing in the Checker'd shade" (95–96); "Thus done the Tales, to bed they creep, / By whispering Winds soon lull'd asleep" (115–16); "Or sweetest *Shakespeare*, fancy's child, / Warble his native Wood-notes wild" (133–34). In addition, there are two diagonal slashes, one at the end of line 68 ("Under the Hawthorn in the dale"), the other at the end of line 90 ("To the tann'd Haycock in the Mead").

There are references to some of these lines in Joyce's works. For example, lines 33–34, "Come, and trip it as ye go / On the light fantastic toe," are alluded to in *Finnegans Wake* by way of a "trippiery toe" (20) and a "light phantastic of his gnose's glow" (182). However, not only are these some of the more widely quoted lines from the poem, we know that Joyce had the whole of "L'Allegro" by heart (see Gillespie 166). Moreover, at least one allusion to the poem, in *Ulysses*—"Through the twisted eglantine" (9.873)—refers to two lines (47–48) that are unmarked in this copy. Thus we do not have any very good reason to assume that this particular volume had any special importance for Joyce either personally or compositionally, or that the lines marked are of any particular significance for an understanding of Joyce's relation to Milton.

There is, however, one textual point that might be of interest. Verity isolates lines 165–85 of "Lycidas" as "the concluding passage of the monody," insisting that "the last eight lines are a kind of epilogue" (158). This may add some weight to the conjecture discussed in chapter 4 that lines 165–85 constitute the section memorized, or rather not memorized, by Stephen's students in the "Nestor" episode.

Turning finally to *The Complete Poetical Works of John Milton*, we find the heaviest annotations. Moreover, beyond what remains legible, "there is evidence of extensive glossing in German of words and phrases, subsequently erased" (Gillespie 168). Unfortunately, it is not clear that these heavy annotations, legible or not, are any more useful than the light annotations of the works already discussed. As Gillespie explains, "This text was apparently used in language instruction, possibly by Stanislaus" (168).

There are erasures throughout a number of poems: "Song: On May Morning," sonnet 1 ("O Nightingale"), "The Passion," "On the University Carrier" and "Another on the Same," "An Epitaph on the Marchioness of Winchester," "On Time," and "At a Solemn Music." In "On the Morning of Christ's Nativity," we find "wrapt" underlined in line 30 and "eingewickelt" written in the right margin; "doff't" underlined in line 33, and something written in the right margin (Gillespie conjectures "abgelegt"). Line 142, "Will down return to men," is marked. Lines 143–44 are given in the 1673 version, "Orb'd in a Rainbow; and like glories wearing / Mercy will sit between," and "Heiligenschein" is written above "glories." There are many erased marks in stanzas 22 through 25. And, finally, in line 233—"Troop to th' infernal jail"—"eilen" is written above the word "Troop."

Paradise Lost—certainly the Miltonic work most present in Joyce's writings—has numerous annotations, some erased, some not. After some textual emendations, to which I turn below, the first mark in the text follows line 124, "Sole reigning holds the Tyranny of Heav'n." Following this, we find a quote from Vergil—"Talia voce refert, carisque ingendibus / aeser / Spem vultu simulat, premit altum corde dolorem" (6). Gillespie judges the handwriting to be that of Stanislaus. As he points out, the line is believed to have suggested *Paradise Lost* 1.125–27; he translates, "Such things he said in voice, and sick with great grief, he pretends hope with his face, and represses deep sorrow in his heart." There is a slash at the end of the deservedly famous line 191—"What reinforcement we may gain from Hope, / If not what resolution from despair." A mark follows the somewhat less memorable "*Titanian, or Earth-born*, that warr'd on *Jove*," and another slash follows line 241, "Not by the sufferance of supernal Power." Lines 244–45, "The mind is its own place, and in itself / Can make a Heav'n of Hell, a Hell of Heav'n," are marked on the left, and "To reign is worth ambition though in Hell: / Better to reign in Hell, than serve in Heav'n" are marked both right and left.

An enigmatic *F* graces the right margin of line 270, "Regain'd in Heav'n, or what more lost in Hell?" Lines 291–94 have annotations that have been erased. The first vowel in "scatter'd" is underlined on line 304. There are slashes beside and below lines 313, "Under amazement of thir hideous change" and 330, "Awake, arise, or be for ever fall'n." Another *F* appears beside the word "Innumerable" in line 338. There are a couple of erasures between 370 and 385, and a dot between 396 and 397—"Him the *Ammonite* / Worshipt in *Rabba*." Line 418, "Till good *Josiah* drove them thence to Hell" has been marked, and something in German has been erased. A number of marks have been erased between 445 and 460. Line 466, "And *Accaron* and *Gaza's* [*Gazar's* in Joyce's edition] frontier bounds," is marked by an *x* and an *F*. Line 475, "Whom he vanquisht. After these appear'd" is broken by a slash. Lines 537 and 540, "Shone like a Meteor streaming to the Wind" and "Sonorous metal blowing Martial sounds," are marked to the left. There were many marks between lines 550 and 651 that have been erased.

The final mark in book 1 is a dot to the left of line 740, "Men call'd him *Mulciber*." Book 2 has two marginal *x*'s. The first appears at line 10, "His proud imaginations thus display'd," the second at line 50, "He reck'd not, and these words thereafter spake." There is a concluding slash after "The steadfast Earth" in line 927.

These annotations are not, needless to say, every scholar's dream—though readers no doubt can recognize their somnolent properties. Again, there are some connections with lines present in Joyce's works. The most interesting is perhaps "Shone like a Meteor." James Atherton has maintained that "clothed upon with the metuor and shimmering like the horescens" (*FW* 194.15–16) combines two lines from *Paradise Lost*, one being "shone like a meteor." Perhaps the marking of this line makes Atherton's surmise more plausible.

But it is difficult to tell what evidential value the markings in this text might have—either for past conjecture or future research. As already noted, the volume appears to have been used by Stanislaus, but we have no way of knowing if it was used by James as well. Certainly a number of lines that are marked have no echoes in Joyce's writing—and certainly a number of lines that find echoes in Joyce's writings (for example, 1.619–20) are unmarked. Perhaps most important, there is evidence that this edition of *Paradise Lost* was compared with another and thus that there was at least one further volume of Milton in the house—perhaps the volume used by James. Specifically, there are four textual emendations in this copy. The first, and least interesting, is to be found in 1.58 and is simply an accent on the second syllable of "obdurate." The second involves the substitution of a semicolon for a comma at the end of 1.108 and the third consists in the insertion of a question mark at the end of 1.109. The final emendation alters "Wings" to "Winds" in "Levied to side with warring Wings" (2:905). It is unlikely that these were successful conjectures or emendations from memory; it seems more plausible that there was another edition of *Paradise Lost* upon which they were based.

Unfortunately, none of this leads to terribly interesting conclusions. Beyond a very few points that they might possibly help somewhat to illuminate—for example, the length of the passage from "Lycidas" recited in "Nestor," as mentioned above—the Trieste library copies of Milton seem to have little value for a study of Milton's influence on Joyce. Perhaps they tell us only two things of general importance, and even these are tentative. First, they show us that Stanislaus and, perhaps, James scrutinized Milton's language, in a large number of poems, with the care and detailed attention of language instructors. Second, they present us with some evidence that there was another copy of Milton owned by James, a copy that, if recovered, could perhaps be genuinely useful.

Bibliography

Abhinavagupta. *The Aesthetic Experience According to Abhinavagupta*. Ed. and trans. Raniero Gnoli. 2d ed. Varanasi: Chowkhamba Sanskrit Series, 1968.
———. *The Dhvanyāloka of Ānandavardhana with the Locana of Abhinavagupta*. Ed. Daniel H. H. Ingalls. Trans. Daniel H. H. Ingalls, Jeffrey Moussaieff Masson, and M. V. Patwardhan. Cambridge: Harvard University Press, 1990.
Adams, Robert Martin. *James Joyce: Common Sense and Beyond*. New York: Random House, 1966.
———. *Surface and Symbol: The Consistency of James Joyce's "Ulysses."* New York: Oxford University Press, 1962.
Aitchison, Jean. *Words in the Mind: An Introduction to the Mental Lexicon*. Oxford: Basil Blackwell, 1987.
Amaladass, Anand. *Philosophical Implications of Dhvani: Experience of Symbol Language in Indian Aesthetics*. Vienna: De Nobili Research Library, 1984.
Ānandavardhana. *The Dhvanyāloka of Ānandavardhana with the Locana of Abhinavagupta*. Ed. Daniel H. H. Ingalls. Trans. Daniel H. H. Ingalls, Jeffrey Moussaieff Masson, and M. V. Patwardhan. Cambridge: Harvard University Press, 1990.
Aristotle. *Peri Poietikes*. In Butcher.
Atherton, James. *The Books at the Wake: A Study of Literary Allusions in James Joyce's "Finnegans Wake."* New York: Viking, 1960.
———. "The Oxen of the Sun." In Hart and Hayman, eds.
Barnett, Annie, and Lucy Dale, eds. *An Anthology of English Prose (1332–1740)*. London: Longmans, Green, 1912.

Bate, Walter Jackson. *The Burden of the Past and the English Poet.* Cambridge: Harvard University Press, 1970.

Batho, Edith. *The Later Wordsworth.* New York: Russell and Russell, 1963.

Begnal, Michael H., and Fritz Senn. *A Conceptual Guide to "Finnegans Wake."* University Park: Pennsylvania State University Press, 1974.

Ben-Merre, Diana, and Maureen Murphy, eds. *James Joyce and His Contemporaries.* Westport, Conn.: Greenwood Press, 1989.

Benstock, Bernard. *James Joyce: The Undiscover'd Country.* Dublin: Gill and Macmillan, 1977.

———. *Joyce-Again's Wake: An Analysis of "Finnegans Wake."* Seattle: University of Washington Press, 1965.

Bigland, Eileen. *Marie Corelli: The Woman and the Legend.* London: Jarrolds, 1953.

Black, Martha Fodaski. *Shaw and Joyce: "The Last Word in Stolentelling."* Gainesville: University Press of Florida, 1995.

Blake, William. *The Poems of William Blake.* Ed. W. B. Yeats. London: Routledge, 1905.

Blamires, Harry. *The Bloomsday Book: A Guide through Joyce's "Ulysses."* London: Methuen, 1966.

———. "Influence on Twentieth-Century Literature, Milton's." In *A Milton Encyclopedia,* 4:136–46. Lewisburg, Penn.: Bucknell University Press, 1978.

Blavatsky, H. P. *Theosophical Glossary.* New Delhi: Asian Publications Services, 1986. (Reprint of 1892 edition.)

Bloom, Harold. *The Anxiety of Influence: A Theory of Poetry.* New York: Oxford University Press, 1973.

———. *A Map of Misreading.* New York: Oxford University Press, 1975.

Bordwell, David. *Making Meaning: Inference and Rhetoric in the Interpretation of Cinema.* Cambridge: Harvard University Press, 1989.

Bornstein, George. *Poetic Remaking: The Art of Browning, Yeats, and Pound.* University Park: Pennsylvania State University Press, 1988.

Boss, Valentin. *Milton and the Rise of Russian Satanism.* Toronto: University of Toronto Press, 1991.

Bradley, Bruce. *James Joyce's Schooldays.* New York: St. Martin's Press, 1982.

Brivic, Sheldon. *Joyce the Creator.* Madison: University of Wisconsin Press, 1985.

———. "The Mind Factory." *James Joyce Quarterly* 21, no. 1 (fall 1983).

Budgen, Frank. *James Joyce and the Making of "Ulysses."* New York: Harrison Smith and Robert Haas, 1934.

Bush, Douglas. Introduction to *The Portable Milton.* Ed. Douglas Bush. New York: Viking, 1962.

Butcher, S. H. *Aristotle's Theory of Poetry and Fine Art, with a Critical Text and Translation of the Poetics.* 4th ed. New York: Dover, 1951.

Byron, Lord [George Gordon]. *Cain: A Mystery.* In Steffan.

———. "Parliamentary Speeches." In Stoddard, ed., vol. 16.

Charles, R.H., ed. *The Apocrypha and Pseudepigrapha of the Old Testament in English.* Vol. 2, *Pseudepigrapha.* Oxford: Clarendon Press, 1913.
Chomsky, Noam. *Knowledge of Language: Its Nature, Origin, and Use.* New York: Praeger, 1986.
Clark, David Lee, ed. *Shelley's Prose, or The Trumpet of a Prophecy.* Albuquerque: University of New Mexico Press, 1954.
Clarke, Aidan. "The Colonisation of Ulster and the Rebellion of 1641 (1603–60)." In Moody and Martin, 189–203.
Cope, Jackson I. *Joyce's Cities: Archaeologies of the Soul.* Baltimore: Johns Hopkins University Press, 1981.
Corelli, Marie. *The Sorrows of Satan, or The Strange Experience of One Geoffrey Tempest, Millionaire: A Romance.* New York: Grosset and Dunlap, 1895.
Costello, Peter. *James Joyce: The Years of Growth, 1882–1915.* New York: Pantheon, 1992.
Cross, Richard K. *Flaubert and Joyce: The Rite of Fiction.* Princeton: Princeton University Press, 1971.
Curtis, L. Perry. *Apes and Angels: The Irishman in Victorian Caricature.* Washington, D.C.: Smithsonian Institution Press, 1971.
Damon, S. Foster. "S. Foster Damon on *Ulysses* and Dublin: 1929." In Deming.
Dante Alighieri. "De Monarchia." In Milano, ed.
———. "La Vita Nuova." Trans. D. G. Rossetti. In Milano, ed.
Dasenbrock, Reed Way. *Imitating the Italians: Wiatt, Spenser, Synge, Pound, Joyce.* Baltimore: Johns Hopkins University Press, 1991.
de Almeida, Hermione. *Byron and Joyce through Homer: "Don Juan" and "Ulysses."* New York: Columbia University Press, 1981.
Deming, Robert H. *James Joyce: The Critical Heritage (Volume 2: 1928–1941).* New York: Barnes and Noble, 1970.
Dickens, Charles. *Great Expectations.* New York: Holt, Rinehart, Winston, 1961.
Dimock, Edward. Introduction to *In Praise of Krishna: Songs from the Bengali.* Chicago: University of Chicago Press, 1967.
Dryden, John. *The State of Innocence and Fall of Man: An Opera.* In Montague Summers, ed., *Dryden: The Dramatic Works.* New York: Gordian Press, 1968.
Dufrenne, Mikel. *Main Trends in Aesthetics and the Sciences of Art.* New York: Holmes and Meier, 1979.
Eliot, T. S. *Collected Poems, 1909–1962.* New York: Harcourt, Brace and World, 1963.
———. "Ulysses, Order, and Myth." In Bernard Benstock, ed., *Critical Essays on James Joyce.* Boston: G. K. Hall, 1985.
Ellmann, Richard. *Eminent Domain.* New York: Oxford University Press, 1967.
———. *James Joyce.* 2d ed. New York: Oxford University Press, 1982.
Erlich, Heyward, ed. *Light Rays: James Joyce and Modernism.* New York: New Horizon, 1984.

Fiedler, Leslie. "To Whom Does Joyce Belong? *Ulysses* as Parody, Pop, and Porn." In Erlich, ed., 26–37.

Flaubert, Gustave. *Madame Bovary.* Trans. Francis Steegmuller. New York: Random House, 1957.

Fletcher, Harris Francis. *Milton's Rabbinical Readings.* Urbana: University of Illinois Press, 1930.

Fogel, Daniel Mark. *Covert Relations: James Joyce, Virginia Woolf, and Henry James.* Charlottesville: University of Virginia Press, 1990.

Ford, Jane. "James Joyce and the Conrad Connection: The Anxiety of Influence." *Conradiana* 17, no. 1 (spring 1985): 3–18.

Frye, Northrop. *Fearful Symmetry: A Study of William Blake.* Princeton: Princeton University Press, 1947.

Funk, S. *Die Entstehung des Talmuds.* Leipzig: G. J. Goschen'sche, 1910.

Garman, Michael. *Psycholinguistics.* Cambridge: Cambridge University Press, 1990.

Gifford, Don. *Joyce Annotated: Notes for "Dubliners" and "A Portrait of the Artist as a Young Man."* 2d ed. Berkeley: University of California Press, 1982.

Gifford, Don, with Robert Seidman. *Notes for Joyce.* 2d ed. Berkeley: University of California Press, 1988.

Gilbert, Sandra, and Susan Gubar. *The Madwoman in the Attic: The Woman Writer and the Nineteenth-Century Literary Imagination.* New Haven: Yale University Press, 1979.

Gilbert, Stuart. *James Joyce's "Ulysses."* New York: Vintage Books, 1955.

Gillespie, Michael Patrick. *James Joyce's Trieste Library: A Catalogue of Materials at the Harry Ransom Humanities Research Center the University of Texas at Austin.* Austin: Harry Ransom Humanities Research Center, 1986.

Glasheen, Adaline. *A Second Census of "Finnegans Wake."* Evanston, Ill.: Northwestern University Press, 1963.

Gombrich, E. H. *Art and Illusion: A Study in the Psychology of Pictorial Representation.* New York: Pantheon, 1959.

Good, John Walter. *Studies in the Milton Tradition.* New York: AMS Press, 1971 (1915).

Gordon, John. *"Finnegans Wake": A Plot Summary.* Syracuse: Syracuse University Press, 1986.

Gregory, Lady Augusta. *Cuchulain of Muirthemne.* Gerrards Cross, Buckinghamshire: Colin Smythe, 1973.

Griffin, Dustin. *Regaining Paradise: Milton and the Eighteenth Century.* Cambridge: Cambridge University Press, 1986.

Guillen, Claudio. "The Aesthetics of Literary Influence." In Ronald Primeau, ed., *Influx: Essays on Literary Influence,* 49–73. London: Kennikat, 1977.

Halasz, Laszlo. "Emotional Effect and Reminding in Literary Processing." *Poetics* 20 (1991): 247–72.

Hart, Clive. *Structure and Motif in "Finnegans Wake."* Evanston, Ill.: Northwestern University Press, 1962.
Hart, Clive, and David Hayman, eds. *James Joyce's "Ulysses": Critical Essays.* Berkeley: University of California Press, 1974.
Hauser, Arnold. *The Social History of Art.* Vol. 1. Trans. Stanley Godman. New York: Vintage Books, 1957.
Havens, Raymond Dexter. *The Influence of Milton on English Poetry.* New York: Russell and Russell, 1961 (1922).
Henke, Suzette, and Elaine Unkeless. *Women in Joyce.* Urbana: University of Illinois Press, 1982.
Hermeren, Goran. *Influence in Art and Literature.* Princeton: Princeton University Press, 1975.
Herring, Phillip. *Joyce's Uncertainty Principle.* Princeton: Princeton University Press, 1986.
Hintikka, Jaakko. "Concept as Vision: On the Problem of Representation in Modern Art and in Modern Philosophy." In *The Intentions of Intentionality and Other New Models for Modalities.* Dordrecht, Holland: D. Reidel, 1975.
Hobbs, Jerry R. *Literature and Cognition.* Stanford: Center for the Study of Language and Information, 1990.
Hodgart, Matthew. "Music and the Mime of Mick, Nick, and the Maggies: Book 2, Chapter 1." In Begnal and Senn.
Hogan, Patrick Colm. "Drowning in *Ulysidas*: A 'Subtext' for Stephen's Mourning." In Bonnie Kime Scott, ed., *New Alliances in Joyce Studies.* Newark: University of Delaware Press, 1988.
———."Influxes of Influence: Agonists Hurl Odyssean Mythpuns and Crackquips: Aristotelian Designs Thought Likely." *University of Hartford Studies in Literature* 21, no. 1 (1989): 26–36.
———. "Mo' Better Canons: What's Wrong and What's Right about Mandatory Diversity." *College English* 54, no. 2 (1992): 182–92.
———. "Molly Bloom's Lacanian Firtree: Law, Ambiguity, and the Limits of Paradise." *James Joyce Quarterly* 29, no. 1 (1991): 103–16.
———. *The Politics of Interpretation: Ideology, Professionalism, and the Study of Literature.* New York: Oxford University Press, 1990.
Holland, John, Keith Holyoak, Richard Nisbett, and Paul Thagard. *Induction: Processes of Inference, Learning, and Discovery.* Cambridge: MIT Press, 1986.
Holland, Norman. *The Dynamics of Literary Response.* New York: Oxford University Press, 1968.
Horkheimer, Max, and Theodor Adorno. "The Culture Industry: Enlightenment as Mass Deception." In *Dialectic of Enlightenment.* Trans. John Cumming. New York: Continuum, 1972.
Jacobus, Lee. "'Lycidas' in the 'Nestor' Episode." *James Joyce Quarterly* 19, no. 2 (winter 1982): 189–94.

Janusko, Robert. "Another Anthology for 'Oxen': Barnett and Dale." *James Joyce Quarterly* 27, no. 2 (winter 1990): 257–82.

———. *The Sources and Structures of James Joyce's "Oxen."* Ann Arbor: UMI Research Press, 1983.

———. "Yet Another Anthology for the 'Oxen': Murison's *Selections*." *Joyce Studies Annual* (1990): 117–31.

Jauss, Hans Robert. "Literary History as a Challenge to Literary Theory." In *Toward an Aesthetic of Reception*. Trans. Timothy Bahti. Minneapolis: University of Minnesota, 1982.

Jewish Encyclopedia: A Descriptive Record of the History, Religion, Literature, and Customs of the Jewish People from the Earliest Times to the Present Day. Ed. Cyrus Adler et al. London: Funk and Wagnalls, 1901–6.

Johnson, Samuel. *Lives of the English Poets*. Vol. 1. Ed. George Birkbeck Hill. New York: Octagon Books, 1967.

Johnson-Laird, P. N. *The Computer and the Mind: An Introduction to Cognitive Science*. Cambridge: Harvard University Press, 1988.

Joyce, James. *Chamber Music*. In Harry Levin, ed., *The Portable James Joyce*. New York: Penguin, 1976.

———. *The Critical Writings of James Joyce*. Ed. Ellsworth Mason and Richard Ellmann. Ithaca: Cornell University Press, 1989.

———. *Dubliners*. In Harry Levin, ed., *The Portable James Joyce*. New York: Penguin, 1976.

———. *Exiles*. London: Four Square Books, 1962.

———. *Finnegans Wake*. New York: Viking Press, 1959.

———. *Giacomo Joyce*. Introduction and notes by Richard Ellmann. New York: Viking Press, 1968.

———. *James Joyce in Padua*. Ed. and trans. Louis Berrone. New York: Random House, 1977.

———. *Letters of James Joyce*. Vol. 1, ed. Stuart Gilbert. Vols. 2 and 3, ed. Richard Ellmann. New York: Viking Press, 1966.

———. *Pomes Penyeach*. In Harry Levin, ed. *The Portable James Joyce*. New York: Penguin, 1976.

———. *A Portrait of the Artist as a Young Man*. New York: Penguin, 1976.

———. "A Portrait of the Artist as a Young Man." In Scholes and Kain.

———. *Selected Letters*. Ed. Richard Ellmann. London: Faber and Faber, 1975.

———. *Stephen Hero*. New York: New Directions, 1959.

———. *Ulysses*. Ed. Hans Walter Gabler. New York: Vintage Books, 1986.

———. "Verismo ed idealismo nella letteratura inglese." In Gianfranco Corsini and Giorgio Melchiori, eds., *Scritti Italiani*. Milan: Arnoldo Mondadori Editore, 1979.

Joyce, Stanislaus. *The Complete Dublin Diary of Stanislaus Joyce.* Ed. George Healey. Ithaca: Cornell University Press, 1971.

———. *My Brother's Keeper.* Ed. Richard Ellmann. London: Faber and Faber, 1958.

Kenner, Hugh. "Beaufoy's Masterplaster." *James Joyce Quarterly* 24, no. 1 (fall 1986): 11.

———. *Dublin's Joyce.* New York: Columbia University Press, 1987.

———. *Ulysses.* London: George Allen and Unwin, 1980.

Kershner, R. B. "Joyce and Popular Literature: The Case of Corelli." In Ben-Merre and Murphy, eds.

Kimball, Jean. "'Lui, c'est moi': The Brother Relationship in 'Ulysses.'" *James Joyce Quarterly* 25, no. 2 (1988): 227–36.

Kiparsky, Paul. "The Role of Linguistics in a Theory of Poetry." In Donald C. Freeman, ed., *Essays in Modern Stylistics.* New York: Methuen, 1981.

———. "Roman Jakobson and the Grammar of Poetry." In Morris Halle, ed., *A Tribute to Roman Jakobson, 1896–1982.* New York: Mouton, 1983.

Kittay, Eva Feder. *Metaphor: Its Cognitive Force and Linguistic Structure.* Oxford: Clarendon 1987.

Koltuv, Barbara Black. *The Book of Lilith.* York Beach, Maine: Nicolas-Hays, 1986.

Lakoff, George, and Mark Johnson. *Metaphors We Live By.* Chicago: University of Chicago Press, 1980.

Laplanche, Jean, and J.-B. Pontalis. *The Language of Psycho-analysis.* Trans. Donald Nicholson-Smith. New York: W. W. Norton, 1973.

Larsen, Steen F., and Janos Laszlo. "Cultural-Historical Knowledge and Personal Experience in Appreciation of Literature." *European Journal of Social Psychology* 20 (1990): 425–40.

Larsen, Steen F., Janos Laszlo, and Uffe Seilman. "Across Time and Place: Cultural-Historical Knowledge and Personal Experience in Appreciation of Literature." In E. Ibsch, D. Schram, and G. Steen, eds., *Empirical Studies of Literature.* Amsterdam: Rodopi, 1991.

Larsen, Steen F., and Seilman, Uffe. "Personal Remindings While Reading Literature." *Text* 8 (1988): 411–29.

Lee, Joseph. *The Modernisation of Irish Society: 1848–1918.* Dublin: Gill and Macmillan, 1973.

Levin, Harry. "The Artist." In Chester G. Anderson, ed., *"A Portrait of the Artist as a Young Man": Text, Criticism, and Notes,* 399–415. New York: Viking Press, 1968.

Liu Hsieh. *The Literary Mind and the Carving of Dragons.* Trans. Vincent Yu-chung Shih. New York: Columbia University Press, 1959.

Lu Chi. "Rhymeprose on Literature: The *Wen-Fu* of Lu Chi (A.D. 261–303)." Trans. Achilles Fang. In John Bishop, ed., *Studies in Chinese Literature*. Cambridge: Harvard University Press, 1966.

Lukács, Georg. "Reportage or Portrayal?" In Rodney Livingstone, ed., *Essays on Realism*. Trans. David Fernbach. Cambridge: MIT Press, 1981.

Lyons, F. S. L. *Ireland Since the Famine*. Revised ed. London: Fontana, 1973.

MacNicholas, John. *James Joyce's "Exiles": A Textual Companion*. New York: Garland, 1979.

Magalaner, Marvin. "James Joyce and Marie Corelli." In Porter and Brophy.

———. *Time of Apprenticeship: The Fiction of Young James Joyce*. London: Abelard Schuman, 1959.

Magalaner, Marvin, and Richard Kain. *Joyce: The Man, the Work, the Reputation*. New York: New York University Press, 1956.

Manganiello, Dominic. *Joyce's Politics*. Boston: Routledge and Kegan Paul, 1980.

Markandaya, Kamala. *Nectar in a Sieve*. New York: John Day, 1954.

Martin, Robert Bernard. *Tennyson: The Unquiet Heart*. Oxford: Clarendon Press, 1983.

Martin, Timothy. *Joyce and Wagner: A Study of Influence*. Cambridge: Cambridge University Press, 1991.

Marx, Jenny. "Articles by Jenny Marx on the Irish Question." In Karl Marx and Frederick Engels, *Ireland and the Irish Question*. Moscow: Progress, 1971.

Mathers, S. L. MacGregor. *The Kabbalah Unveiled*. New York: Samuel Weiser, 1974.

McArthur, Murray. *Stolen Writings: Blake's "Milton," Joyce's "Ulysses," and the Nature of Influence*. Ann Arbor: UMI Research Press, 1988.

McHugh, Roland. *Annotations to "Finnegans Wake."* Baltimore: Johns Hopkins University Press, 1980.

McKeon, Michael. *The Origins of the English Novel, 1600–1740*. Baltimore: Johns Hopkins University Press, 1987.

Milano, Paolo, ed. *The Portable Dante*. Revised ed. New York: Penguin, 1975.

Milton, John. *John Milton: Complete Poems and Major Prose*. Ed. Merritt Hughes. Indianapolis: Odyssey Press, 1957.

———. *The Works of John Milton*. Ed. Frank Patterson et al. 18 vols. New York: Columbia University Press, 1932.

Moody, T. W., and F. X. Martin. *The Course of Irish History*. Cork: Mercier Press, 1967.

Moseley, Virginia. *Joyce and the Bible*. De Kalb: Northern Illinois University Press, 1967.

Mumby, Frank Arthur, and Ian Norrie. *Publishing and Bookselling*. London: Jonathan Cape, 1974.

Nadel, Ira. *Joyce and the Jews: Culture and Texts.* London: Macmillan, 1989.
Nash, Walter. *Language in Popular Fiction.* New York: Routledge, 1990.
Ortony, Andrew, Gerald Clore, and Allan Collins. *The Cognitive Structure of Emotions.* Cambridge: Cambridge University Press, 1988.
O'Shea, Michael. *James Joyce and Heraldry.* Albany: State University of New York Press, 1986.
Patai, Raphael. *Gates of the Old City: A Book of Jewish Legends.* Detroit: Wayne State University Press, 1981.
Peacock, W., ed. *English Prose from Mandeville to Ruskin.* London: Oxford University Press, 1912.
Perkins, David, ed. *English Romantic Writers.* New York: Harcourt, Brace and World, 1967.
Pope, Alexander. Preface to *The Iliad of Homer.* Ed. Theodore Alois Buckley. New York: Thomas Y. Crowell, n.d.
———. Postscript to *The Odyssey of Homer.* Vol. 2. Ed. Maynard Mack. London: Methuen, 1967.
Porter, Raymond, and James Brophy. *Modern Irish Literature: Essays in Honor of William York Tindall.* New York: Twayne, 1972.
Power, Arthur. *Conversations with James Joyce.* Ed. Clive Hart. Chicago: University of Chicago Press, 1974.
Quillian, William H. "Shakespeare in Trieste: Joyce's 1912 *Hamlet* Lectures." *James Joyce Quarterly* 12, nos. 1–2 (fall 1974–winter 1975): 7–63.
Rappoport, Angelo. *Myth and Legend of Ancient Israel.* Introduction by Raphael Patai. New York: Ktav, 1966 (1928).
Reynolds, Mary. *Joyce and Dante: The Shaping Imagination.* Princeton: Princeton University Press, 1981.
Roberts, Thomas J. *An Aesthetics of Junk Fiction.* Athens: University of Georgia Press, 1990.
Rose, Danis, and John O'Hanlon. *Understanding Finnegans Wake: A Guide to the Narrative of James Joyce's Masterpiece.* New York: Garland, 1982.
Saintsbury, George. *A History of English Prose Rhythm.* London: Macmillan, 1912.
———. *A Short History of English Literature.* London: Macmillan, 1900.
Samuel, Irene. *Dante and Milton: The "Commedia" and "Paradise Lost."* Ithaca: Cornell University Press, 1966.
Saurat, Denis. "La cabale et la philosophie de Milton." *Revue des etudes juives* (1921): 1–13.
Schlossman, Beryl. *Joyce's Catholic Comedy of Language.* Madison: University of Wisconsin Press, 1985.
Scholem, Gershom. *Kabbalah.* New York: Quadrangle, 1974.

Scholes, Robert, and Richard M. Kain, eds. *The Workshop of Daedalus: James Joyce and the Raw Materials for a Portrait of the Artist as a Young Man.* Evanston, Ill.: Northwestern University Press, 1965.

Schork, R. J. "'Nodebinding Ayes': Milton, Blindness, and Egypt in the *Wake.*" *James Joyce Quarterly* 30 (1992): 69–83.

Schreuder, Robert, and Giovanni B. Flores d'Arcais. "Psycholinguistic Issues in the Lexical Representation of Meaning." In William Marslen-Wilson, ed., *Lexical Representation and Process,* 409–36. Cambridge: MIT Press, 1989.

Schutte, William M. *Joyce and Shakespeare: A Study in the Meaning of "Ulysses."* Hamden, Conn.: Archon Books, 1971.

Schwarz, Daniel. *Reading Joyce's "Ulysses."* New York: St. Martin's Press, 1987.

Seidel, Michael. *Epic Geography: James Joyce's "Ulysses."* Princeton: Princeton University Press, 1976.

Seilman, Uffe, and Steen F. Larsen. "Personal Resonance to Literature: A Study of Remindings While Reading." *Poetics* 18 (1989): 165–77.

Shakespeare, William. *Hamlet. The Riverside Shakespeare.* Ed. G. Blackmore Evans. London: Houghton and Mifflin, 1974.

Shaw, George Bernard. The author's apology in *Mrs. Warren's Profession.* In *Plays by George Bernard Shaw.* New York: Signet, 1960.

Shawcross, John. *John Milton and Influence: Presence in Literature, History, and Culture.* Pittsburgh: Duquesne University Press, 1991.

———. "'They that dwell under his shadow shall return': Joyce's *Chamber Music* and Milton." In Bonnie Kime Scott, *New Alliances in Joyce Studies.* Newark: University of Delaware Press, 1988.

Shechner, Mark. *Joyce in Nighttown.* Berkeley: University of California Press, 1974.

Shelley, Percy Bysshe. "An Address to the Irish People." In Clark, ed.

———. "A Declaration of Rights." In Clark, ed.

———. "A Defense of Poetry." In Perkins, ed.

Spender, Stephen. *The Destructive Element: A Study of Modern Writers and Beliefs.* London: Jonathan Cape, 1935.

Steffan, Truman Guy. *Lord Byron's "Cain": Twelve Essays and a Text with Variants and Annotations.* Austin: University of Texas Press, 1968.

Stephens, James. *The Crock of Gold.* New York: Collier, 1912.

Stoddard, Richard Henry, ed. *The Works of Lord Byron with His Letters and Journals, and His Life by Thomas Moore.* Boston: Francis A. Niccolls, 1900.

Sullivan, Kevin. *Joyce among the Jesuits.* New York: Columbia University Press, 1958.

Symonds, John Aldington. *Shelley.* London: Harper and Bros., 1879.

Theoharis, Theoharis. *Joyce's "Ulysses": An Anatomy of the Soul.* Chapel Hill: University of North Carolina Press, 1988.

Thorslev, Peter. *The Byronic Hero: Types and Prototypes.* Minneapolis: University of Minnesota Press, 1962.

Tysdahl, Bjorn J. *Joyce and Ibsen: A Study in Literary Influence.* New York: Humanities Press, 1968.

Waite, Arthur Edward. *The Doctrine and Literature of the Kabbalah.* London: Theosophical Publishing Society, 1902.

———. *The Secret Doctrine in Israel: A Study of the Zohar and Its Connections.* London: William Rider and Son, 1913.

Watt, Ian. *The Rise of the Novel: Studies in Defoe, Richardson, and Fielding.* Berkeley: University of California Press, 1967.

Weatherhead, A. Kingsley. *Stephen Spender and the Thirties.* Lewisburg, Penn.: Bucknell University Press, 1975.

West, Robert. *Milton and the Angels.* Athens: University of Georgia Press, 1955.

Wittreich, Joseph, ed. *The Romantics on Milton: Formal Essays and Critical Asides.* Cleveland: Case Western Reserve University Press, 1970.

Wordsworth, William. *The Complete Poetical Works of William Wordsworth.* Vol. 3, *The Prelude.* Boston: Houghton Mifflin, 1911.

———. "Second Address [to the Freeholders of Westmorland]." In W. J. B. Owen and Jane Worthington Smyser, eds., *The Prose Works of William Wordsworth,* vol. 3. Oxford: Clarendon Press, 1974.

Index

Abdiel, 137
Abel, 111, 182, 183, 186
Abhinavagupta, 16, 30, 31, 32, 213
Abiding concerns. *See* Interior monologue
Adah (Byron), 111
Adam, 44, 62, 63, 72, 74, 77–81, 89, 91, 94, 101–6, 110–12, 133, 134, 137–40, 142, 145–46, 148–52, 159, 163–70, 174, 180–83, 189, 193–95, 199–201, 203
Adams, Robert Martin, 74, 213
"Address to the Irish People" (Shelley), 69
"Ad Pyrrham" (Horace), 70
Adultery, 110–12, 134, 139–46, 149–50, 152
AE (George Russell), 26, 28
Aesthetical attitude, 15–16, 19, 32, 46
Aesthetical intent, 6, 15–16, 46, 145, 152, 153
Aesthetic distance (Jauss), 39
Aesthetics of Reception (Jauss), 36, 37, 39
Agrat bat Mahlat (or Machlat), 134
Ahaz, 186
Aitchison, Jean, 22, 213
"Alastor" (Shelley), 84, 125, 134–36, 179
Allusion, 33–34
Amaladass, Anand, 32, 213
Amor matris (mother love), 108, 120, 124, 126, 129
Ānandavardhana, xii, 4, 5, 10, 30, 213
Anarchism, 68, 184
Anna Livia Plurabelle (*Finnegans Wake*), 158, 159, 161, 162, 164, 165, 166, 168, 170, 171–80, 182, 183, 188, 194, 196, 197, 199–203
Anselm of Canterbury, 102
Antheil, George, 83

Anxiety of influence (Harold Bloom), 6–9, 51
Apocrypha, 101
"Apology for Smectymnuus" (Milton), 63, 68
"Areopagitica" (Milton), 68, 206–8
Ariosto, 96
Aristotle, 4, 5, 48, 52, 82, 122, 165, 213
Arnall, Father (*A Portrait of the Artist*), 101–4, 107, 129
Arnold, Matthew, 6, 7
Asmoedeus, 133, 183
Astaroth, 186
Astarte, 186
Atherton, James, 115, 133, 154, 210, 213
"At Vallombrosa" (Wordsworth), 58
Auden, W. H., 2
Augustine of Hippo, 149, 157, 193
Augustus Caesar, 157

Baal, 186
Bacchus, 161, 208
Bacharach, Naftali Herz, 151
Bakunin, Michael, 68
Balakian, Anna, 5
Barnacle, Nora, 72, 74, 75, 76, 77, 87, 89, 90, 95, 108, 109, 110, 118, 131
Barnes, Djuna, 54
Barnett, Annie, 114, 205–6, 213
Bate, Walter Jackson, 4–6, 10, 12, 214
Batho, Edith, 106, 214
Beatrice (*Divine Comedy, Vita Nuova*), 44, 45, 74, 76, 78, 87, 89, 90–92, 93, 94, 97–102, 104, 108–9
Beckett, Samuel, 39, 43

226   Index

Beelzebub, 73, 132, 133, 143, 145, 148, 183
Belial, 148, 186, 187
Bellini, Vicenzo, 55, 56
Benstock, Bernard, xiii, 57, 88, 214, 215
Berkeley, George, 174
Bigland, Eileen, 85, 214
Black, Martha, 50, 214
Blake, William, 26, 57, 78, 79, 82, 83, 86, 87, 91, 104, 121, 136, 186, 196, 214
Blamires, Harry, 57, 214
Blavatsky, H. P., 133, 214
Blindness, 60, 172
Bloom, Harold, 6–10, 14, 17, 34, 40, 43, 57, 214
Bloom, Leopold (*Ulysses*), 36, 74, 75, 77, 79, 80, 81, 94, 112, 116–18, 122, 133, 134, 138, 139, 140, 141–52, 159, 166, 169, 170, 176
Bloom, Molly (*Ulysses*), 56, 74, 89, 94, 95, 112, 116–18, 133, 134, 137, 138, 139, 140, 142, 144, 145, 146, 149, 150, 151, 177, 180
"Book of Ahania" (Blake), 83
Book of Enoch, 183
"Book of Urizen" (Blake), 83, 196
Bordwell, David, 20, 214
Bornstein, George, 5, 214
Boss, Valentin, 58, 214
Boylan, Blazes (*Ulysses*), 94, 116, 132, 133, 138, 139, 140, 142, 144, 145, 146, 149, 150, 151, 152
Bradley, Bruce, 58, 59, 108, 214
Brahma, 179
Brivic, Sheldon, xiii, 91, 214
Brontë, Emily, 137
Browning, Robert, 92
Bruni, Francini, 51
Budgen, Frank, 50, 59, 72, 113, 117, 214
Burke, Edmund, 146
Byrne, John Francis, 77
Byron, George Gordon, Lord, 26, 29–31, 35, 69, 70, 73, 78–80, 83, 84, 86, 99, 100, 104, 108, 111, 120, 125, 126, 137, 183, 191, 192, 198, 214

Cain, 182, 183, 186
Cain (Byron), 83, 84, 111, 183, 191–92, 198
Caitilin (James Stephens), 52
Calderón de la Barca, Pedro, 55, 57
Calvinism, 67, 68
Candida (Shaw), 50
Canon formation, 3, 13–17, 46–47
Carlyle, Thomas, 87
Carter, Jimmy, 142
Cary, Joseph, xiii

Castlereagh, Viscount, 70
Chamber Music (Joyce), 53, 56, 71, 90
Chambers, Haddon, 55
Chaos, 81, 98, 103, 135–38, 184, 196
Character. *See* Literary character
Charles I (king of England), 67, 69, 73, 81, 127, 128
Chaucer, Geoffrey, 59, 69, 88
Chemos, 132, 185, 186
Childbirth, 146, 163–65, 171, 174–77, 179–80, 182, 185, 190, 192–203
Childe Harold's Pilgrimage (Byron), 84
Chomsky, Noam, 21, 215
Circe, 161
Clarke, Aidan, 67, 215
Cleary, Mary, 94, 109
Clery, Emma, 52, 74, 94, 100–102, 104–7, 177
Clore, Gerald, 25, 220
Coleridge, Samuel Taylor, 69
Collier, Ada, 92
Collins, Allan, 25, 220
Colonialism, 11, 60–70, 88, 93, 95–97, 107–9, 118–19, 122, 124, 127–31, 148
Colum, Mary, 54
Colum, Padraic, 15
Columbanus, 124
Community-aesthetic cognitive structures, 28–29
Comus (Milton), 147, 158, 160–63
Confessions of Zeno (Svevo), 54
Congdon, Christopher, 52
Conrad, Joseph, 51
Conroy, Gabriel, 59, 72, 74, 93–97, 207
Conroy, Gretta, 72, 74, 94–95, 177
Constitution (phenomenology), 36–37
Cope, Jackson I., 91, 133, 134, 144, 215
Corelli, Marie (Mary Mackay), 26, 79, 84–88, 92, 131, 138, 139, 185, 215
Corneille, Pierre, 55, 57
Cosgrave, Vincent, 26, 77, 87, 95
Costello, Peter, 51, 64, 74, 78, 89, 114, 215
Crabbe, George, 55, 56
Cranly, 25, 100, 108
Crock of Gold (Stephens), 51
Cromwell, Oliver, 65–69, 95, 119, 131, 190, 207
Cross, Richard K., 50, 215
Cubism, 2
Cuchulain of Muirthemne (Gregory), 52
Curtis, L. Perry, 65, 66, 215

Daedalus (Daidalos), 57, 75, 81, 104, 108, 135
Daedalus, Stephen (Joyce's pen name), 57

Dale, Lucy, 114, 205–6, 213
Damon, S. Foster, 134, 215
Dante Alighieri, 44, 48, 49, 57, 69, 79, 87–90, 92, 93, 99, 100, 101, 104, 109, 134, 155, 215
D'Arcais, Giovanni B. Flores, 22, 32, 221
Dark Lady of the Sonnets (Shaw), 50
Dasenbrock, Reed Way, 51, 54, 215
Davenport, Guy, xiii
"Dead, The" (Joyce), 51, 59, 61, 64, 90, 93–97, 107, 119, 193, 207
Death, 2, 8, 83, 90, 91, 99, 102, 103, 105, 111, 115–30, 133, 136–37, 140–42, 150, 152, 158, 163–65, 167, 168, 170–72, 174, 176, 177, 179–80, 182, 183, 185, 186–92, 197–203
Declaration of 1652 (Milton), 68
"Declaration of Rights" (Shelley), 73–74
Dedalus, Dilly (*Ulysses*), 127–28, 199
Dedalus, Simon (*A Portrait of the Artist*, *Ulysses*), 25, 63, 144
Dedalus, Stephen (*A Portrait of the Artist*, *Ulysses*), xii, 1, 2, 14, 18, 19, 25, 30, 50–53, 55, 56, 57, 59, 61–63, 72–75, 78, 79, 81–87, 94, 97–108, 112, 114, 116–29, 131, 132, 134–38, 140–51, 162, 164, 165, 177, 183, 185, 193, 199, 206, 209
"Defense of Poetry" (Shelley), 84, 88
Defense of the People of England (Milton), 66, 68
Defoe, Daniel, 26, 78, 79, 80, 81, 87, 88
De Gourmont, Rémy, 92
De Monarchia (Dante), 88
Derivativeness, 38–40
de Valera, Eamon, 132
Devil, 71, 73, 81, 82, 84, 85, 87, 90, 98, 101, 110, 129, 132–35, 137, 138, 145–49, 151, 152, 167, 171, 175, 177, 179, 183–86, 188, 191, 194, 198
Devorgilla, 145
Dhvani (suggestion), xii, 30, 31, 32, 47, 132, 153, 163
Dhvani attitude (Amaladass), 32
Dhvanyāloka (Ānandavardhana), 4, 213
Dickens, Charles, 53, 105–7, 215
Dimock, Edward, 12, 215
Divine Comedy (Dante), 48, 79, 87, 88, 93
Doctor Faustus (Marlowe), 182
Don Juan (Byron), 70, 84, 104
Dowson, Ernest, 71
"Drama and Life" (Joyce), 1, 3–4
Dryden, John, 78–80, 88, 110, 133, 151, 215
Dubliners (Joyce), xii, 39, 93, 96, 97, 199
Dufrenne, Mikel, 11, 215
Dujardin, Edouard, 49, 54

Duras, Marguerite, 27

Earwicker, Humphrey Chimpden (*Finnegans Wake*), 80, 157–62, 165, 166–74, 176, 180–83, 185, 187, 188–90, 193–95
Eden, 73, 80, 85, 94, 101, 104, 105, 110, 112, 136, 137, 139, 142, 144, 146, 150, 152, 153, 154, 163, 165, 166, 173, 176, 177, 178, 181, 182, 184, 189, 190, 192, 194–96, 198, 199, 202, 203
Edward IV (king of England), 122
Eikonoklastes (Milton), 67, 68, 73
Eliot, T. S., 14, 35, 66, 79, 87, 113, 215
Ellmann, Richard, 4, 15, 16, 48, 50–55, 57, 70–72, 75, 76, 78, 87, 89, 93, 109, 158, 164, 215, 218
Emer (*Cuchulain of Muirthemne*), 52
Encoding and selection principles, 19, 24, 42, 45, 75, 112. *See also* Saliency
Epic, 57–59, 73, 79, 85, 87, 88, 96, 97, 113, 118, 121, 130, 131, 132, 143, 151, 154, 155, 192, 207
"Epiphanies" (Joyce), 50, 76
Epiphany, 2
Esau, 159, 163
Estella (*Great Expectations*), 106–7
Eve, 44, 45, 72, 74, 76–79, 81, 85, 87, 89–92, 94, 97–106, 109, 110, 111, 112, 133, 134, 137, 138, 140, 144–47, 149, 150–52, 159, 163–66, 169, 170–72, 174, 175–80, 182, 183, 188, 189, 193–95, 197, 199, 203
Excursion (Wordsworth), 58
Exemplum, 20–30, 32, 34, 35, 42, 43, 45, 46, 75, 79, 84, 86, 107, 109, 112, 117, 152, 159, 160. *See also* Model; Prototype; Schema
Exiles (Joyce), xii, 29, 50, 87, 90, 94, 109–12, 193, 194

Fall of humankind, 29, 57, 62, 63, 72, 74, 77–79, 81, 82, 87, 89–91, 94, 95, 98, 101, 102, 109–12, 126, 131–34, 137–52, 155, 156, 159–60, 163–82, 186–99, 201–3. *See also* Adultery; Childbirth; Death; Sexuality; War
Fang, Achilles, 90, 219
Faustus (*Doctor Faustus*), 182
Feilbogen, Siegmund, 55
Felix Culpa (St. Augustine), 149, 166, 170, 188, 193, 195, 198
Fenianism, 63, 64, 69, 108
Finn (*Finnegans Wake*), 198
Finnegan (*Finnegans Wake*), 168, 188, 189, 197

Finnegans Wake (Joyce), xi, xii, xiii, 39, 51–53, 57, 60, 68, 73, 79, 85, 91, 99, 108, 132–34, 143, 145, 147, 149, 151, 153, 154–203, 207, 208, 210
Flaubert, Gustave, 49–51, 53, 216
Fleischmann, Marthe, 89, 90
Fletcher, Harris Francis, 91, 216
Fogel, Daniel Mark, 51, 216
Ford, Jane, 51, 216
France, Anatole, 92
Freud, Sigmund, 8, 9, 49, 54, 55, 56
Frye, Northrop, xiii, 130, 216
Fuller, Samuel, 142
Funk, S., 91, 216
Furey, Michael, 94–95, 177
Fuzon ("The Book of Ahania"), 83

Gabriel, 93–94
Gardner, Lieutenant Stanley (*Ulysses*), 118, 177
Garman, Michael, 22, 32, 216
"Gas from a Burner" (Joyce), 52
Giacomo Joyce (Joyce), 99
Gifford, Don, 49, 87, 101, 102, 119, 122, 124, 136, 137, 142, 143, 144, 145, 149, 216
Gilbert, Sandra, 58, 74, 79, 216
Gilbert, Stuart, 134, 147, 152, 161, 216, 218
Gillespie, Michael Patrick, 205, 208, 209, 216
Gladstone, William Ewart, 63
Glasheen, Adaline, 154, 216
Goethe, Johann Wolfgang von, 55
Gogarty, Oliver St. John, 26, 87
Goldsmith, Oliver, 55
Gombrich, E. H., 1, 37, 216
Gordon, John, 216
Graziano, Anne, 50
Great Expectations (Dickens), 106–7
Gregory, Lady Augusta, 52, 216
Gubar, Susan, 58, 74, 79, 216

Haines (*Ulysses*), 118, 119, 121, 126, 132
Halasz, Laszlo, 33, 216
Hamlet (Shakespeare), 12, 117, 124, 125, 131, 181, 189
Hand, Robert, 94, 109–11
Hart, Clive, 154, 216, 217, 221
Hartmann, Heinz, 9
Hauptmann, Gerhart, 18, 19
Hauser, Arnold, 10, 217
Havens, Raymond Dexter, 58, 217
Hazlitt, William, 77, 78
Hell, 65, 82, 86, 90, 129, 133, 136, 137, 139, 141, 147, 148, 150, 165, 171, 185, 186, 188, 190, 193, 198

Hellas (Shelley), 137
Henke, Suzette, 74, 75, 217
Hermeren, Goran, 4, 5, 8, 30, 34, 217
Herodotos, 185
Hintikka, Jaakko, 2, 217
History of the Devil (Defoe), 81
Hobbs, Jerry, 217
Hodgart, Matthew, 60, 217
Hogan, Patrick Colm, Sr., xiii
Holland, John, 19, 21, 32, 217
Holland, Norman, 45, 217
Holyoak, Keith, 217
Homer, 18, 34, 48, 60, 88, 130, 165
Horace, 70, 71
"How soon hath time" (Milton, sonnet 7), 160
Hughes, Merritt, 64, 220
Hugo, Victor, 87
Hunt, Leigh, 58
Husserl, Edmund, 36

Ibsen, Henrik, 5, 17, 18, 40, 48, 55, 56, 59
Ibsenism, 85, 86
Icarus, 82
Ideology, 11, 82, 95, 97, 181
Idiolect, 21, 33, 35, 46
Iliad (Homer), 130
"Il Penseroso" (Milton), 59, 71, 72, 205, 208
Imago, 41, 42, 44, 45, 46, 74, 75, 76, 89, 92, 94, 95, 98, 99
Imitation, 34
Imperialism. *See* Colonialism
India, 186
Inferno (Dante), 93, 99, 143
Influence, xi-xii, 1–47, 48–62, 68, 69, 71, 77, 84–87, 91, 105, 107, 109, 115, 152–56, 163, 197; and cognition, 17–33, 46; conscious and unconscious, 41; and identification or identificatory idealization, 41–46, 59–70; of individuals and of groups, 34–35; positive vs. negative, 29–30; and transference, xii, 6–9, 41–42, 44–46, 74–78. *See also* Allusion; Derivativeness; Exemplum; Imitation; Innovation; Prototype; Model; Schema; Tradition
Innovation (literary), 1–9; and economy, 9–17, 46–47
Interior monologue, 39, 49, 56, 113, 116–17; and abiding concerns, 117ff.; and perception, 116; and semantic or phonetic associations, 116
Intertextuality, 16, 34
"Irlanda, Isola dei Santi e dei Savi" (Joyce), 65

Issy (*Finnegans Wake*), 161, 162, 166, 167, 171, 173, 174, 175, 176, 177, 182, 183, 185, 186, 189
Istahar, 186
Ivors, Miss ("The Dead"), 94, 109

Jacob, 159
Jacobus, Lee, 217
Jaloux, Edmond, 50
Janusko, Robert, 114, 115, 217
Jauss, Hans Robert, 36, 37, 39, 218
Jesus, 26
Jim the Penman (Young), 57
Johnson, Lionel, 71
Johnson, Mark, 21, 219
Johnson, Samuel, 58, 61, 63–64, 86, 130, 131, 156, 218
Johnson-Laird, P. N., 27, 31, 33, 218
Jonson, Ben, 18
Joyce, James: life of (compared with Milton's), 59–62; politics of, 62–65, 68–69, 107–9, 118 (*see also* Colonialism); satanic self-concept of, 72–74. *See also* individual works
Joyce, Stanislaus, 1, 2, 50, 51, 52, 54, 55–58, 61, 62, 64, 68, 71–73, 76–78, 81, 87, 93, 155, 206, 209, 211, 218
Judas, 26
Julius Caesar, 121, 123, 129, 173, 190
Jung, Carl, 54
Justice, Beatrice (*Exiles*), 74, 94, 109

Kabbalah, 77, 79, 89, 91, 92, 101, 132–34, 140, 145, 150, 151, 165–69, 171, 175, 177, 178, 181–83, 186, 194
Kafka, Franz, 5
Kain, Richard, 52, 53, 59, 73, 76, 78, 220, 221
Kant, Immanuel, 2, 196
Keats, John, 6, 7, 58
Kenner, Hugh, 18, 19, 53, 105, 110, 111, 117, 127, 128, 165, 219
Kershner, Brandon, xiii, 86, 219
Kickham, Charles, 108
Kickham, Rody (*A Portrait of the Artist*), 108
Kimball, Jean, 56, 219
King, Edward ("Lycidas"), 124, 179
Kinsella, Lily, 167–68
Kiparsky, Paul, 22, 219
Kittay, Eva Feder, 21, 22, 219
Koltuv, Barbara Black, 92, 219
Kropotkin, Peter, 68
Kurz, Isolde, 92

Lacan, Jacques, 9

Lakoff, George, 21, 219
"L'Allegro" (Milton), 59, 71, 72, 78, 143, 155, 188, 205, 208
Lamb, Charles, 34
Landor, Walter Savage, 207
Language. *See* Idiolect
Laplanche, Jean, 9, 219
Larsen, Steen F., 33, 219, 222
Laszlo, Janos, 33, 219
Lawrence, D. H., 1
Lermontoff, Mikhail, 50, 55, 56
Levin, Harry, 57, 218, 219
Lexicon, 22, 26, 27, 32, 33, 46, 153, 159, 169; cross-indexing, 22–23; priming, 31–33, 45–47, 116, 128, 137; structure, 26–27. *See also* Exemplum; Prototype; Schema
Libertarianism, 119, 128, 207
"Life of Adam and Eve," 151, 199
Lilith, 91, 92, 98, 101, 133, 134, 140, 145, 146, 148, 159, 162, 165–68, 172, 174–83, 186, 188
Literary character: cognitive structure of, 22–23, 25–26
Liu Hsieh, 219
Livius Andronicus, 121
Locana (Abhinavagupta), 30, 31, 213
Los (Blake), 104
Lu Chi, 4, 6, 219
Lucifer. *See* Satan
Lukács, Georg, 2, 219
"Lycidas" (Milton), 59, 62, 71, 72, 115–19, 121–28, 143, 148, 160, 178, 179, 205, 208, 209, 211
Lynch, 77, 78
Lyons, F. S. L., 63, 65, 118, 219

Macaulay, Thomas Babington, 87
Macbeth (Shakespeare), 55, 121
MacDonald, George, 92
MacDowell, Gerty (*Ulysses*), 134, 145–46, 151, 169
MacGrath, 167–68
Mack, Maynard, 221
Mackay, Mary. *See* Corelli
MacNicholas, John, 109, 110, 220
Madame Bovary (Flaubert), 50
Magalaner, Marvin, 53, 220
Mammon, 132, 167, 185, 206
Manfred (Byron), 29, 30, 31, 45, 84, 125, 126, 135, 136, 186
Mangan, James Clarence, 1, 57, 68, 99
Manganiello, Dominic, 68, 220
Mansfield, Katherine, 6
Markandaya, Kamala, 199, 220
Martin, Robert Bernard, 108, 220

Martin, Timothy, 54, 220
Martyn, Edward, 51
Marx, Jenny, 108, 220
Mathers, S. L. MacGregor, 132, 220
McArthur, Murray, 83, 220
McHugh, Roland, 154, 162, 178, 181, 220
McKeon, Michael, 14, 220
Memory traces (Abhinavagupta), 31–33
Mephistopheles, 72
Michael, 93–95, 104, 121, 135, 149, 150, 157, 164, 165, 177–79, 182, 184–86, 190, 193, 202
Milton (Blake), 136, 186
Milton, John: influence and reputation of, 78–87, 130; life of (compared with Joyce's), 59–62; relation of, to Dante, 87–88; religion and politics of, 62–70, 95–97, 118–19, 128 (*see also* Colonialism). *See also* individual works
Misreading (Harold Bloom), 6–9
Model, 20–25, 33, 34, 39, 42, 44, 50, 52, 55, 70, 89, 94, 97, 98, 100, 106, 108, 109, 113, 130, 134, 137, 152, 153, 161, 165, 183. *See also* Exemplum; Prototype; Schema
Modernism, 1, 2, 5, 17, 48, 57, 113
Moloch, 132, 133
Moore, George, 1, 30, 40, 50–51, 54, 143
Moseley, Virginia, 134, 220
Moses, 190
Mother, 61, 73–77, 88, 108, 117–29, 136, 146, 147, 162, 164, 165, 176, 177, 180, 181, 185, 196, 199–202
Mrs. Warren's Profession (Shaw), 50
Mulligan, Malachi (*Ulysses*), 85, 119, 120, 121, 126, 128, 132, 133, 135, 147, 148
Multi-stage cognitive processes, 27
Mumby, Frank Arthur, 11, 220
Murison, A. F., 114, 205, 207
Murphy, Maureen, 149, 214

Naamah (companion of Lilith), 134
Nadel, Ira, 91, 220
Nash, Walter, 13, 220
Nectar in a Sieve (Markandaya), 199
Neoplatonism, 5
Newman, John Henry, 18, 32
Nisbett, Richard, 217
Norrie, Ian, 11, 220
Noumenon, 2

"Observations on the Articles of Peace" (Milton), 66, 67

O'Connell, Daniel, 182
O'Donovan Rossa, Jeremiah, 108
Odysseus, 117
Odyssey (Homer), 121, 130, 131, 134, 147, 152
Oedipal relations, 6, 8, 9, 10, 41, 42
"O fons Bandusiae" (Horace), 70
Ogeret (companion of Lilith), 134
O'Hanlon, John, 168, 194, 202
Original sin, 98, 126, 143, 144, 145, 149, 164, 176, 180, 195
Ortony, Andrew, 25, 220
O'Shea, Michael, 60, 220

Pandemonium (*Paradise Lost*), 71, 135, 147, 148, 150, 184, 186, 193
Pandit, Lalita, xiii
Paradise Lost, 28, 29, 34, 57, 58, 71, 77–79, 81, 82, 84, 85, 87–89, 91, 93, 94, 97, 101–4, 107, 110–12, 121, 125, 127, 130–53, 154–56, 158–60, 163–67, 169, 171, 172, 174, 181, 182, 184–87, 187, 193–97, 199, 203, 207, 209, 210, 211
Paradiso (Dante), 93, 104
Parnell, Charles Stewart, 26, 63, 88, 149, 188
Patai, Raphael, 151, 220, 221
Patterson, Frank, 220
Peacock, W., 114, 205, 208, 221
Perkins, David, 58, 69, 84, 221
Personal-aesthetic cognitive structures, 28–29
Petrarch, 179
Phenomenology, 36
Picasso, Pablo, 2–6
Pinamonti, Giovanni, 103
Pindar, 69
Pip (*Great Expectations*), 106–7
Platonism, 4, 49
Pola Notebook (Joyce), 1, 52, 56, 59, 61, 64, 78
Pomes Penyeach (Joyce), 71
Pontalis, J.-B., 9, 219
Pope, Alexander, 104, 130, 221
Popper, Amalia, 89–90
Popper, Karl, 1
"Portrait of the Artist as a Young Man," 73, 98
Portrait of the Artist as a Young Man, xii, 2, 14, 18–19, 25, 50–52, 60–63, 72, 77, 79, 82, 87, 90, 94, 97–109, 112, 118, 119, 120, 129, 130, 132, 140, 183, 207
Pound, Ezra, 50, 51
Power, Arthur, 2, 221
Prelude (Wordsworth), 105, 106

Prezioso, Roberto, 9, 109
Pride, 12, 72, 73, 74, 89, 95, 102, 104, 106, 184, 191, 210
Priming. *See* Lexicon
Procedural schema, 159
Prometheus Unbound (Shelley), 58, 84, 107, 108, 126, 137, 197
Prototype, 20–30, 32, 35, 42, 43, 45, 46, 72, 75, 78, 97, 104, 107, 109, 112, 117, 146, 152, 159, 160, 175, 186. *See also* Exemplum; Schema; Model
Proudhon, Pierre, 68
Proust, Marcel, 51
Providence, 68, 82, 104, 112, 160, 165, 180, 192, 194–97, 199, 201, 203
Pseudepigrapha, 151, 169, 183, 199
Psychoanalysis, xi, 8, 9, 17, 19, 33, 40, 41, 44, 46, 54, 55, 75
Punning, 156–60
Purdon, Father, 93
Purefoy, Mina, 146
Purgatorio (Dante), 93, 101, 104
Pyrrha, 70
Pyrrhus, 121, 124, 129

Racism, 14, 64–66, 69, 83, 88, 97, 117
Rainbow girls (*Finnegans Wake*), 162, 186
Raphael, 102, 138–40, 158
Rappoport, Angelo, 133, 181, 183, 186, 199, 221
Rasa (sentiment), 15, 31, 33, 47
Rasadhvani (suggestion of sentiment), 30, 31, 33, 45, 46, 137, 152
Rasiel, 181
"Reason of Church Government Urged Against Prelaty" (Milton), 59, 61, 63, 64, 95, 119, 207
Reynolds, Mary, 48, 100, 134, 221
Riders to the Sea (Synge), 52
Rimmon, 186
Roberts, Thomas J., 13, 221
Rossetti, Dante Gabriel, 92, 215
Rowan, Bertha, 94, 95, 109–12
Rowan, Richard, 94, 109–12
Ruskin, John, 87, 205

Sackerson, 161, 162, 168
Sahṛdaya, 12, 31
Saintsbury, George, 61, 71, 114, 221
Saliency, 19, 20, 24, 29, 30, 79, 80, 86. *See also* Encoding and selection principles
Samael, 91, 133, 145, 167, 183, 186

Samuel, Irene, 87, 221
Satan, 5, 26, 29, 30, 44, 45, 52, 61, 65, 72–74, 78–87, 90, 94, 98, 99, 102–4, 107–10, 125, 129, 131–43, 145, 147–50, 152, 155, 157–59, 164, 165, 167, 168, 171, 174, 177, 178, 182–96, 198
Saurat, Denis, 91, 221
Savage, Melanie, 54
Schema, 20–30, 32, 35, 36, 42, 43, 45, 46, 52, 71, 75, 84, 109, 112, 117, 152, 156, 159, 160. *See also* Exemplum; Model; Procedural schema; Prototype
Schmitz, Ettore. *See* Svevo
Schoeck, Othmar, 57
Scholem, Gershom, 133, 145, 167, 168, 186, 221
Scholes, Robert, 52, 59, 73, 76, 78, 221
Schork, R. J., 60, 159, 196, 221
Schreuder, Robert, 22, 32, 221
"Scribbledehobble" notebook (Joyce), 134
"Second Address [to the Freeholders of Westmorland]" (Wordsworth), 106
Seidel, Michael, 81, 222
Seidman, Robert, 119, 122, 124, 137, 142, 143, 144, 145, 149, 216
Seilman, Uffe, 33, 219, 222
Selection principles. *See* Encoding and selection principles; Saliency
Senilita (Svevo), 54
Seraphim, 101, 139, 155, 183
Serpent, 72, 90, 94, 101, 103, 106, 138, 147, 148, 158, 159, 171, 175, 189, 196, 197
Sexism, 3, 14, 180
Sexuality, 44, 52, 62, 63, 74–80, 92, 95, 98, 99, 107, 109, 112, 116, 132, 133, 134, 138–53, 161, 165–98. *See also* Adultery
Shakespeare, William, 55, 56, 58, 59, 87, 88, 114, 143, 144, 156, 207, 208, 222
Shaun (*Finnegans Wake*), 154, 155, 162, 168, 175, 183, 184–87, 192, 194–98
Shaw, George Bernard, 37, 38, 50, 222
Shawcross, John, xiii, 57, 156, 163, 222
Shechner, Mark, 74, 75, 222
Sheehy, Mary, 74
Shelley, Percy Bysshe, 26, 58, 69, 73, 79, 83, 84, 86, 88, 125, 126, 137, 197, 222
Shem, 57, 154, 155, 162, 165, 166, 168, 171, 174, 175, 183, 184, 185, 186, 187, 191, 195, 196, 197
Shemal (Samael), 183
Shemhaza, 183, 186
Śiva, 179

Snake, 158, 167, 168, 171, 176, 189, 190, 193, 196
Socialism, 68
Sorrows of Satan (Corelli), 85–87, 131, 138, 139, 185
Southey, Robert, 70
Southworth, E. D. E. N., 92
Spender, Stephen, 1–4, 222
Spenser, Edmund, 146
Stallone, Sylvester, 27
State of Innocence and the Fall of Man: An Opera (Dryden), 79–80, 151, 156
Stephen Hero, 2, 50, 55, 57, 73–75, 78, 99, 100, 177
Stephens, James, 15, 51–52, 60, 108, 188
Sterling, George, 92
Stravinsky, Igor, 57
Sublimity, 14, 15, 79, 135, 163
Sudermann, Hermann, 55, 57
Sullivan, Kevin, 58, 59, 83, 222
Svevo, Italo (Ettore Schmitz), 54
Swinburne, Algernon Charles, 71
Symonds, John Aldington, 69, 222
Symons, Arthur, 71
Synge, John Millington, 40, 41, 52, 53, 186

Talbot family, 122
Talmud, 91, 133
Talus (nephew of Daedalus), 57
Tennyson, Alfred, 108
Tentation de Saint Antoine (Flaubert), 50
Thagard, Paul, 217
Tradition, 35, 39–40, 46
Transference, xii, 6–9, 41, 42, 44, 45, 46, 59, 74, 75, 78, 92, 101, 107
Trieste notebook (Joyce), 82
Tristan and Isolde, 189
Tristram, Sir, 163
Trois Contes (Flaubert), 50
Turgenev, Ivan, 50, 55, 56
Tysdahl, Bjorn J., 17, 18, 19, 25, 48, 49, 54, 59, 60, 62, 222

Ulysses (Joyce), xi, xii, 2, 4, 12, 16, 30, 36, 39, 48–51, 53–57, 59, 61, 74, 75, 79, 81, 82, 84, 85, 87, 90, 91, 92, 93–153, 155, 159, 160, 161, 164–67, 179, 180, 185, 193, 199, 203, 206, 207, 209
Universals, 2, 22, 25, 29
Urania, 197
Uranus, 148
Urizen ("The Book of Urizen"), 82, 83, 108, 196

Van der Plaas, Pieter, 207
Vergil, 130, 209
"Verismo ed idealismo nella letteratura inglese" (Joyce), 79
Vico, 49, 54, 55, 56
Vinding, Ole, 55
Virgin/whore syndrome, 41, 44–45, 74–78, 86–92, 94, 97ff., 109. *See also* Beatrice; Eve; Lilith
"Vision of Judgement" (Byron), 70, 73, 137
Viṣṇu, 179
Vita Nuova (Dante), 99–101
Voltaire, 87
Vulcan, 104

Wagner, Richard, 54, 55, 56, 129
Waite, Arthur Edward, 91, 92, 101, 133, 134, 140, 145, 150, 151, 167, 169, 171, 175, 177, 183, 222
War, 62, 72, 132, 158, 163, 165, 185–92, 200
Waterbury, 146
Watt, Ian, 14, 223
Weatherhead, A. Kingsley, 223
Weiss, Ottocaro, 158
Wen-Fu (Lu), 4
Wilde, Oscar, 57, 71, 188
Wittreich, Joseph, 69, 77, 91, 223
Woolf, Virginia, 1–6
Wordsworth, William, 26, 58, 91, 105–7, 223
Wuthering Heights (Brontë), 137
Yeats, William Butler, 3, 4, 5, 6, 9, 15, 52–53, 71, 83, 108, 125, 126, 214
Younge, Charles, 57

Ziska (Corelli), 85
Zohar, 145, 150